AND THEY FELT NO SHAME

CHRISTIANS RECLAIM
THEIR SEXUALITY

AND THEY FELT NO SHAME

CHRISTIANS RECLAIM THEIR SEXUALITY

JOAN OHANNESON

WINSTON PRESS

All Scripture texts in this work are taken from *The New American Bible*, copyright © 1970 by the Confraternity of Christian Doctrine, Washington, D.C. Used by permission of the copyright owner. All rights reserved.

Permission to quote material from the following sources is gratefully acknowledged: "Time of Waiting in Amsterdam" from *Selected Poems* by Ingrid Jonker, trans. Jack Cope and William Plomer, from the Afrikaans, in *The Other Voice*, ed. Joanna Bankier, et al, New York: W.W. Norton, 1976. "Four Auguries" from *Selected Poems* by Margaret Atwood, New York: Simon & Schuster, 1976. "Return to Frankfurt" from *Uberallnie* by Marie Luise Kaschnitz, Dusseldorf: claassen Verlag BmbH, 1965. "Eucharist" by Patricia Harrington, in *St. Anthony's Messenger*, July 1980, Cincinnati, Ohio. "crossed hearts" by kim ohanneson, unpublished. "Slumbersong" from *Translations from the Poetry of Rainer Maria Rilke* by M.D. Herter Norton, New York: W.W. Norton & Co., Inc. 1938, 1966. "Saturday's Chastity" by Albert Haase, OFM, in *St. Anthony's Messenger*, May 1978, Cincinnati, Ohio. "After Dusk" from *Listen to Light* by Raymond Roseliep, Ithaca, N.Y.: The Alembic Press, 1980. "Lovesong" from *Translations from the Poetry of Rainer Maria Rilke* by M.D. Herter Norton, New York: W.W. Norton & Co., Inc., 1938, 1966. "Did the Woman Say . . . " by Frances Croake Frank, in the *National Catholic Reporter*, 21 December 1979. "5 Riders in Cardinal Red" from *The Western Edge 33 Poets: An Anthology of Poetry from Mendocino County*, by William Bradd, Mendocino, CA: Ten Mile River Press, 1979. "The Good" from *Selected Poems of Brendan Kennelly* by Brendan Kennelly, Dublin: Allen Figgis & Co., Ltd., 1969. "Mensch" by Jean Houston, in *Dromenon*, Spring/Summer 1980, New York, N.Y. "Yes" by Carole Coleman Michaelson, delivered at Southern California Congress of Religious Education, Anaheim, Cal., February 14, 1981. "Sexuality—God's Gift," A Pastoral Letter by Bishop Francis J. Mugavero, Roman Catholic Diocese of Brooklyn, N.Y., 1976. "Valuing Your Sexuality" Office of Religious Education, Archdiocese of Milwaukee, Milwaukee, Wisc., 1980. "Guidelines for Workshop on Sexuality and Spirituality," Office of Young Adult Ministry, United States Catholic Conference, 1312 Massachusetts Avenue NW, Washington, D.C. 20005. "Education in Human Sexuality," National Committee on Human Sexuality, Department of Education, United States Catholic Conference, 1981.

Cover design: Studio One

Cover illustration: Kathryn E. Shoemaker

Library of Congress Catalog Card Number: 82-70488
ISBN: 0-86683-676-4
Printed in the United States of America
5 4 3 2

Winston Press
430 Oak Grove
Minneapolis, MN 55403

For Greg,
whose love urged me on.

Our sexuality is not frightening or uncontrollable; it is not an idol or a slave. It is a mystery at the heart of our familiar selves; it is ourselves as we live with other people we love—parents, friends, children, lovers, husbands, wives—in individual relationships and in groups and communities.

- How does it develop?
- What does it mean to grow up as a sexual being, to unfold to individuality with other people?[1]

Rosemary Haughton

CONTENTS

FOREWORD

The history of a conscious and concerted ministry to young adults in and through the American Catholic Church is of fairly recent origin. The impetus to begin the ministry came from the bishops themselves through the creation of a national office in 1974. I held the position of Representative for Campus and Young Adult Ministry for the United States Catholic Conference from its inception to my appointment as President of Biscayne College in 1980. In those few years ministry with young adults became a significant concern of church personnel at all levels.

In 1981, after elaborate consultation with a broad diversity of young adults, a *Plan of Pastoral Action for Single Young Adult Ministry* was published under the auspices of the USCC and the NCCB. Many dioceses and parishes have developed offices and devoted personnel to fostering this ministry.

In most cases, ministries organized at the local level have been initiated and directed by the young adults themselves; the character and focus of the ministry has taken its particular quality from the concerns of the young adults involved. These concerns and interests are so various that it is more proper to speak of young adult *ministries* in the plural. The results are often highly innovative and imaginative. And it is only proper that young adults should be the primary ministers to their peers; Vatican II expressly called for the ministry of "like to like." That the ministry should have taken so vital a form in so short a time is sure evidence of the gracious activity of the Holy Spirit.

In his address delivered on Boston Common in 1979, Pope John Paul II underscored his faith in the energy and direction of young adults: "Young people are asking important questions. . . . This questioning tells the world that you, young people, carry within yourselves a special openness with regard to what is good and what is true. This openness is in a sense a 'revelation of the human spirit.' " This "spiritual authenticity" to which John Paul referred is what young adults long to have recognized and affirmed in their local church communities.

For everyone who has found mentors and guides among the local faith community, many more have encountered the "wasteland" described in Chapter One of this book. At the heart of the separation of Church from young adults is a failure to communicate: The Church has failed to listen with care and sympathy to the struggles and questions that compose the spiritual journeys of young adults, and young adults have failed to appreciate that the Church has a story of its own to tell and that listening to it involves journeying with the Church for awhile in a spirit of openness.

The separation of Church from young adults is all the more tragic because each has so much to offer the other. Young adults have an almost intuitive appreciation of the "bodiliness" that has to be at the center of all spiritual realities for them to be authentically human. That is something the Church affirms in its theology but becomes wary of when it is translated into specific relationships.

The *Pastoral Plan for Single Young Adult Ministry* describes a process of ministry with young adults. Modeled on the ministry of Jesus, it begins with presence and listening and moves on through healing to integration: "The ministry of Jesus began with *presence*, which enabled those he encountered to learn more about themselves and to discover the reality of God's life in their midst. He actively *listened* to the stories of the oppressed and those searching for good news. People found themselves in the presence of one who cared deeply about them and their life stories. *Healing* emerged from compassionate listening. . . . Accepting the mission of Jesus is being called into the community of those whose lives have been joined together by their common belief in Christ. *Integration*, as a call to partake in his mission, was an essential aspect of Jesus' ministry." The process so described is a ministry to which all Christians are invited.

Joan Ohanneson has taken seriouly the challenge to *be with* and *listen to* young adults, and so has, in writing this book, undertaken a ministry to and with young adults. When we invited Joan to be present at the Fourth Annual Young Adult Ministry Conference on *Spirituality and Sexuality of Young Adults*, held in Los Angeles in May of 1979, it was with the intention of extending the scope of the Conference beyond the four days planned. So important a topic seemed to necessitate being transformed into print so that its content and impact could be more broadly disseminated.

In writing *And They Felt No Shame*, Joan has drawn not only on the original Los Angeles Conference and other workshops sponsored by the USCC Department of Young Adult Ministry, but countless other encounters with young adults as well. She has been present to a great many young adults and listened well while they told their stories. Her book has become a forum for many young adult voices, both those quoted directly and those unacknowledged whóse words nonetheless echo in these pages.

I continue to be impressed and even awed by the depth of the spiritual quest they describe. These are not young adults looking for easy pleasures and quick answers. They are people searching for the best that life has to offer and are prepared to endure the pain and uncertainty of that quest. What they ask for so eloquently is a Church—and church people—to share that search with them.

I know *And They Felt No Shame* will serve to introduce the world of young adults—with its quest for the integration of spiritual and sexual values in individual Christian lives—to people who may not have heard this quest expressed in quite these terms before. Through these pages young adults have spoken with agonizing honesty and integrity. Let us pray that the Spirit will move the hearts of good men and women everywhere so that these voices may not be merely listened to but genuinely heard.

Patrick H. O'Neill, OSA

PREFACE

In *And They Felt No Shame,* Joan Ohanneson has written a poignant, painful, probing but ultimately celebrational account of the coming end of the dark ages of the body in the doctrines and practices of the Roman Catholic Church. In these pages of interviews and compassionate inquiries she has harvested the heartache and woundings of Catholics from every walk of life. Their responses let loose a fury that is at once a catharsis and a redemption, a heroic journey that leads from body apocalypse to the resurrection of the body.

Whether you chalk it up to Aquarius or necessity, we are apparently at the end of an age. Millennia-old constructs of belief and behavior are eroding under the unparalleled pressures of modern life. The age in which we live is quaking amidst the tremors of systemic breakdown. The moral mandates, the structural givens, the standard-brand governments, religions, economics, the very consensual reality is breaking down, the underlying fabric of life and process by which we organized our reality and thought we knew who and why and where we are. The world by which we understood ourselves is a world that no longer works and that no longer provides us with the means and reference points by which we understand ourselves.

So much of the anguish expressed in these pages is the natural outcome of what inevitably occurs when a traditional institution demands that its followers adhere to the principles formulated in the psychological and social reality of a much simpler time. There is no question but that we are gravely threatened by problems due to a lack of depth, complexity, and vision in an age of radical and frenetic change. These problems include failure to make use of the range of human capacities so necessary if we are to survive as well as extend the domain of human and social possibilities.

And yet while political and religious organizations cling to the atavisms of earlier ages, the wasteland continues to spread. We have only to look about us and see a growing wasteland with its hazards of mass destruction through nuclear and biological weapons; its threats to privacy and freedoms; its growing overpopulation and exacerbated under-employment; its increasing air, noise, and land pollution and depletion of the earth's resources; its information overload and vulnerability to collapse and breakdown; its dehumanization of ordinary work; its exploitation of conflict and of adversarial modes as the daily way of life among people and institutions. The proliferation of institutional megastructures have left us with a vast chasm between public and private life because political and religious orders have become detached from the values and realities of individual life, and the individual is giving less and less moral sanction and legitimacy to the political and religious orders.

Beyond the wasteland the good news is coming closer. Because of the technological cords that link us to all other nations, because of our need to join with these nations to preserve the earth's remaining resources, we are on the brink of opportunities for human and cultural potentiation on a scale never before known.

As *And They Felt No Shame* shows so graphically, answers lie not in restricting and inhibiting, as too often happens in times of social difficulty, but in opening up to new alternatives and possibilities, new options and avenues, for the creative use of hitherto untapped human capacities that are far less dependent on material resources.

It is an irony that at a time when we are experiencing a loss of hope in the social domain, the vision of what human beings can be has never been more remarkable. We are living at the beginnings of what promises to be a golden age of brain, mind, and body research. We may well be standing with regard to these where Einstein stood in the year 1904 when he discovered the special theory of relativity that helped accomplish the great revolution in physics. The new advances in brain, mind, and body research increasingly allow us to view and probe the capacities of the human being and gradually to learn how to use these capacities much more productively.

What all of this seems to suggest is that for the first time in human history people may become what they are—fully human. We may be in the time of the opening up of the ecology of inner space to humanity at large because the problem of human survival, when you come right down to it, may no longer be that of discovering new economic or political solutions but rather one of a growth of the qualities of mind, body, and spirit of the human race.

Everything about us is equally human and has its own genius and sacramental character. We are reason and imagination and all the states between, and that which we do not see is but the other side of the moon of ourselves which remains to be explored and inhabited. We are also the dream plays and visions, the autonomous life of the deep psyche which shades into the collective life of the One.

The diverse urgencies of our time create an atmosphere in which remarkable growth is possible. It is the hothouse effect—things are rushing to life within ourselves. These are times that are being quickened. We are trying to discover a conscious balance between all the forces that we are and of which we partake. The full dimensions of human freedom and possibility are coming to term.

In this area the Church can begin to explore and design new structures for education, health, labor, welfare, and religious life. It can help uncover the potentials lying dormant in ourselves which may prove so necessary to our continuance as a species and so critical for the needed transformation of our social forms. In raising deep questions concerning the natural continuum between sexuality and the sacred, and perceiving the body as a whole and holy vehicle of spiritual transformation, Joan Ohanneson is challenging the Church to extend the horizon of human freedom and of human possibility.

Jean Houston
Pomona, New York
April, 1982

ACKNOWLEDGMENTS

No author writes a book alone. I am especially indebted
• to the countless numbers of young adults who have trusted
me with their stories during the past three years. As a
continuing source of inspiration, hope, and challenge, they are
a *gift* to the Church.
• to Rev. Patrick H. O'Neill, OSA, who first called young
adults in the Church into a welcoming faith community. His
belief in and empowerment of these young adults is a
reflection of his generous heart and spirit. Young Adult
Ministry will be his continuing legacy in the Church.
• to the many, many spirit-filled people who minister to
young adults throughout the United States, especially Nancy
Hennessey Cooney, Dr. Dan DiDomizio, Grace McGinnis
Lamm, Professor Scott Hope, Cynthia Hicks Halloran, Rick
Haraway, Rev. Bob Lotz, Michael Myszka, Kathy Szaj,
Rev. Joseph Kenna, Representative for Young Adult Ministry
at the United States Catholic Conference, and Rev. Angelo
Fazio, Director of the National Center for Young Adult
Ministry at Merrimack College, North Andover,
Massachusetts.
• to the many resource people who graciously assisted me
with both encouragement and expertise, especially
Rev. John F. Mattingly, SS, and Pam Nurse of St. Patrick's
Seminary Library, Menlo Park, California; Patricia Helin, for
scriptural and historical research; Rev. William T. O'Keeffe,
SS, and Margot Forcier-Call for German and French
translations; Dr. Marshall Joseph, Thom McCarthy, Rev. John
Jordan in the area of the Vietnam veteran; media research
provided by Christine Kress in Germany and Rev. Harry
Schlitt and Marty Axelrod in the United States. And to my
typist and soul-mate Betty Van Arsdale for her special
presence throughout.

• to those who walked with me in prayer, especially the Carmelite Community at Carmel of Reno, Lelia Setti, Connie Popp, George Kohles, FSC, Marion Call, Eileen Ereneta, Michael Cummins, my colleagues on the Young Adult Ministry Board and the Directions Staff of the Archdiocese of San Francisco and San Jose. And a special thanks to the staff and participants of Aura IV at Grailville, Ohio.

• to my four young adult daughters Kim, Beth, Jill, and Erin for their belief in the importance of this book and their invaluable input throughout, but especially to Kim for her careful editorial attention to the integrity of the questions, ideas, and challenges presented in these pages. And most of all, to my husband Greg who holds me and shares my dream.

Joan Ohanneson

INTRODUCTION

This is the story of The Body Generation.

These are your sisters and brothers, your sons and your daughters, the man down the hall, the woman next door, your young adult friends and neighbors and co-workers, some who still go to church but many who do not.

They are, however, a generation committed to Jesus as The Believable One. They believe him to be a man who keeps his promises. One of those promises is his word that he came to bring them *life* . . . "life in all its fullness." They believe he embraced their own humanity to assure them that they could be, should be, *more*!

They speak of this promise as Jesus' call to integration and wholeness. They look at the fragmentation within their own lives and see that wholeness must begin within themselves as body-persons.

This book is about that search. It contains their questions and some of their answers. It is a search that centers on and contrasts the body experience in both the Church and the culture. It examines the language and symbols and metaphors with which the Church describes itself as the Body of Christ. It circles the Church's teaching about the human body and its attitudes about sexuality. It looks at the life-styles of the members of its Body. It analyzes and tests its politics in terms of its teachings. It assesses its wars and inspects its battlefields. It reflects on the ways it binds the wounds of its brokenhearted: the Vietnam veteran, the hustler who sells his young body on Hollywood Boulevard, the victim of rape or battering, the young adult churchwoman who has been forced to abort her dreams.

These pages also include answers which were uncovered in the search, answers provided by those who listened with love to the questions and trusted the answers deep within their hearts. As ministers to young adults, they see the integration of sexuality and spirituality as the primary need.

As Church, we have much to learn from the young adults who shared their needs and fears and dreams on these pages. We must ask, too, if indeed their questions are not our own.

They are a generation who have come to define sexuality as their total approach to life as a male or female person. "Sexual intercourse may be something one 'does,' " they say, "but one's sexuality is beyond genitality. Genital expression is only one aspect of our human self-expression. Sexuality is our *total* self-definition; it is who we *are*."

They believe that the fullness of sexuality is experienced in relationships, but the search for meaning in those relationships is a search for God. Because of this, they believe that our bodies and souls are inseparable, and that we do violence to both God and ourselves when we see them as being in opposition to each other. Rather, they believe, our experiences as sexual beings should inform and enlighten our spiritual reflections. Together, our spirituality and sexuality remind us of the great hope to which we have been called. (See Eph 1:18)

This is a generation that believes in the goodness of creation, a goodness which Jesus enfleshed in his Incarnation. Because of this, these young adults believe the most important name this Jesus deserves to be called is Lover.

TIME OF WAITING IN AMSTERDAM

I can only say I have waited for you
through western nights
at bus stops
in lanes
by canals
on airfields
and the gallows of tears

And then you came
through the forlorn cities of Europe
I recognized you
I set out the table for you
with wine with bread with mercy
but imperturbably you turned your back
you detached your sex laid it down on the table
and without speaking a word
with your own smile
abandoned the world

Ingrid Jonker

CHAPTER ONE

WASTELAND

"The worst sin against our fellow creatures is not to hate them, but to be indifferent to them; that's the essence of inhumanity." [1]
George Bernard Shaw

"I was away from home and you gave me no welcome, naked and you gave me no clothing. I was ill and in prison and you did not come to comfort me."
Matthew 25:43

There is a wasteland in the Church.

This wasteland is caused by the absence of young adults—of their energy, vitality, and creativity. The wasteland exists among spires and empires of stained-glass windows, and silver chalices. No gold-embroidered scarlet vestments can hide the signs of its barrenness; no exotic incense can dispel its film of dry dust in the air.

Footprints are in this wasteland—the footprints of seekers, dreamers, prophets. These footprints reveal different journeys. Sometimes the footprints show strong and determined strides. Sometimes they show circles and stops . . . hesitation. In this wasteland are many, many abandoned campfires. Clearly, in time, each of the travelers must have grown cold and journeyed on.

This is the wasteland where young adults in the Church wander. Young adults ranging in age from eighteen to thirty-five comprise approximately one-third of this country's population. They come to church hopeful, enthusiastic, full of ideas. They are eager to share their perceptions of sexuality and spirituality with the church community. They feel they have something to share out of their unique life experiences.

"Surely," they say, "we can help turn this desert into a lush, blooming Garden of Eden." And day after day, they search the parched earth, looking for fertile ground, scratching for green sprouts and wellsprings.

"Are there no signs of life here?" they say. "Are there no pipelines?" they ask one another. "Where is the living water we were promised? How can we work alone?"

The wind carries their questions. . . .

"Can you hear us?" they call out to the Church. "We are hungry, we are thirsting! Have you forgotten we are here?"

The wind answers them in sighs.

In time, the sun sets on their disappointment. They sit and sift the dusty soil through their fingers. "We tried!" they cry. "But we need support. We will plough and furrow the earth, plant the seeds and pull the weeds, but we cannot bear the heat of the day alone. Without living water, we cannot survive."

They walk toward the horizon, their silhouettes growing smaller and smaller. Their voices trail in the wind like wisps of smoke. "There is no understanding, no hope, no shelter here." In time, they disappear.

Will we see them again, or will they join the youthful army of former believers who have preceded them . . . those whose footprints the winds of time have blown far away?

The wind mourns them . . . "Might have been . . . would have been . . . could have been. . . ." One wonders whether the sight of a single blossom here might have fed their souls and saved their lives.

The Body of Christ is on its knees in the wasteland. It is a young body . . . full of reaching, stretching, giving. It is the

Church's present strength and hope for tomorrow. Its future hangs in the balance, lies in the limbs and wombs of its young adult wanderers.

The echoes of their voices haunt us. . . . "My heart and my flesh cry out for the living God. Even the sparrow finds a home, and the swallow a nest in which she puts her young" (Psalm 84:3-4).

"Young adults? But where are we going to find the time, the money, the resources?" say the Appraisers of the Church. On the sidelines the Surveyors shake their heads and shuffle their feet and finally sigh and shrug.

"Priorities . . . it's a matter of priorities. There are schools to run and churches to heat and kids and old folks to take care of. Besides," they say, looking out at the vast expanse of real estate, "we know the territory. They'll be back. You can count on it. Never fear!"

They listen, but they do not hear.

Today's young adults are trying to call the Church to its senses. They are saying to the institution: "You are overwhelmed with a *fear of sexuality*. As the Body of Christ, you have blocked your ears and shut your eyes and turned your face away from the future. You are suffering from a loss of heart!

"As the Body of Christ, you have been holding your breath for centuries. You gasp and pant and dare not fill your lungs with fresh air and breathe.

"Look at your hands. Are they pressed together in prayer or in fear and trembling? Are your fists clenched tightly in anger? Open them . . . hold your palms upward. Allow yourself to be vulnerable. Only then can they be the hands of Jesus: hands as free to give as to receive.

"As Church, how do you touch the Body of Christ—with love or indifference? When you risk and reach out to young

adults, what do you fear? When you withhold your touch, do
you do violence by your absence?

"As ordained ministers, name the wasteland in your own
life. Claim it! Is it a memory of your own young adulthood?
Does the barrenness you see before you remind you of your
own body's broken promises?"

You are not alone. . . .

Listen. . . .

Listen to their voices in the winds of the wasteland.

Are not all of our dreams contained in the following statements by young adults of their human needs? . . .

I struggle with fear. . . .

"I struggle with being free enough to touch, to
embrace. . . . I fear where it might take me. I fear
losing control. Does losing control have any relation to
my fear of surrendering my life to God? And how can I
interact with a God who is not sexual?"

I am afraid of intimacy. . . .

"By not exposing myself, I can't be rejected. But sooner
or later, when my mask slips off, I'll be revealed. I must
beware of substituting sex for responsible intimacy."

I want to be a sexual Christian. . . .

"We cannot love God with our whole hearts and minds
and bodies without being sexual Christians. My eyes,
my gestures, my touch, my embraces must reflect the
Christ who was trusting and vulnerable. I need to hear
the Church proclaim from the pulpit that my sexuality
brings me closer to God."

I have been hurt by the Church. . . .

"My struggle with my sexuality is my struggle with
being me. Because of my past painful relationship with
the Church, my tendency has been to withdraw, to not

get involved. I can only afford to let little bits of me out; I keep holding back. I'm afraid. I don't want to be hurt by the Church again."
I am gay and struggle with self-hatred. . . .
"I struggle with trying to work through my own theology. I cannot go through the rest of my life feeling that I am a sin."
We need to bind each other's wounds. . . .
"We are all 'wounded in our sex' and only recently have stopped to sign a treaty with our bodies. Maybe we all need to help bind each other's wounds. The wounds to soul, to psyche, reveal needs never imagined in our innocence, the need of the other, the insufficiency of self. Sometimes pain clarifies."
The Incarnation gives me courage. . . .
"I believe the Incarnation is God's motherly and fatherly quest to seek intimacy with persons. Our willingness to succeed in sexual intimacy would outweigh the fears of failure and fear of one another. This is the gospel message, the courage from which all blessings flow."
My earthiness makes me aware of God. . . .
"How can I best become a Christian woman of hope, not just in mind and heart, but in mind and heart *and body*? I love being a sexual person! I love the union it causes with the world around me. It forces me to be part of the earth. I can no longer stand detached. I must be involved in loving, life-giving relationships. There is an earthiness to such love, a grounding that I find quietly exciting. Never before have I been so aware of God."
My sexuality is a gift. . . .
"When I think of a morality centered on the person rather than the act, I begin to see sexuality as a gift we have been given to build community through ministry.

It is my sexuality, my embodiment, my sensitivity that is
my charism for ministry."
As a man, I cannot be free unless women are free. . . .
"As a single male layperson, I have begun to realize that
there are some definite issues in the Church for me about
my sexuality. But I have also come to realize that these
issues are nowhere near as restricting as they would be
for a woman in my position, no matter how prophetic
she may be."
Single young adults must ask the sexual questions. . . .
"Young adults have an opportunity to uncover the tensions and risks of being a single layperson in ministry
and open them up for discussion. The tensions and risks
would not be as hidden for laypersons as they would be
for those who choose celibacy.

"In person-centered morality, sin is far more subtle
and insidious than our 'old' morality allowed us to envision and articulate. This new morality challenges us to
reject exploitation, indulgence, non-communication; to
be prophetic by speaking out and confronting, daring to
rock the boat."
I need to confront rape and sexism. . . .
"As a man, I see a need to confront rape and sexism,
their subtleties and ramifications. I need to confront the
mass, truncated male ego in all its macho forms. I speak
here of war, competition, force, and power."
Sexually, the Church is often antisocial. . . .
"It occurs to me that the Church's 'stand' on sexuality is
inherently antisingle, but ultimately, antisocial. While
single young adults are aware of many sexual prohibitions, the Church actually says little about how to live
positively as a sexual being within marriage. In both
life-styles, it seldom addresses for either life-style the

negative aspects of sexuality, such as exploitation, lack of communication, need for affirmation and intimacy. As sexual beings in the Church, single people face alienation, and married people face normlessness."

Father Pat O'Neill, OSA, who has been called the mentor of young adult ministers in the United States, calls young adults "the poor of the gospel."

"To be poor in the biblical reality is to be without power, without understanding, without hearing," he says. "Single young adults are not asking the Church to do something for them but rather *to be with them.* They are not so much interested in dogmatic truths as in personal stories. . . . They seek one another out, asking 'Why do *you* believe?' 'Why do *you* still bother with organized religion?' 'What does Mass mean to *you?*' " [2]

It is not that young adults are not interested in religion. If anything, they are consumed with the spiritual quest. But the same spiritual energy that their parents poured into national church groups and parish programs, young adults are channeling into areas of sexuality and morality dealing with not only the quality but also the very meaning of life. They may not be at Sunday Mass, but they are working for nuclear disarmament, the equal rights amendment, and the environment. A decade ago, it was the Peace Corps and Vista.

As the drumbeat of our technological society grows louder, young adults continue to turn inward. Transcendental meditation, yoga, charismatic prayer groups flourish. Dolores Lecky points out that those young adults who might have chosen religious communities a few years ago are now choosing theology and ministry training as a professional and vocational choice *at their own expense and without any guarantees.*[3]

Who are these young adults and where do they come

from? What are they looking for in terms of their everyday
lives and needs? How can they energize and renew the
Church with their gifts and energies?

They are mainstream professionals from industry, business,
law, medicine. They are educators, students, social scientists.
They are marginal people . . . gay, divorced and separated,
disabled veterans, ex-convicts, the unskilled, the unemployed,
the underemployed. They are the dream-speakers: the artists,
the poets, the ministers. They are the greatest source of
untapped richness in the Church.

These are the spiritually homeless. Their lives have been
uprooted emotionally, politically, geographically. They are
the children of divorce, the peace movement, the sexual
revolution. They look around and wonder whom they can
trust.

For the children of the sixties, all institutions are suspect.
The Church, as institution, must also pass the test.

How will the Church listen to questions from the children
of a New Age, technological society? How will it instruct
them to maintain their integrity in the political process? How
will it help them meet the challenge of integrating their
sexuality and spirituality, their bodies and souls?

As institution, what does the Church offer to the four
particular adults described below? How does it help them in
their struggle with matters of human dignity, shared decision-making, and freedom of conscience?

. . .

"Why did a nice Catholic lawyer from Philadelphia decide
to work with teenage gangs in the inner city . . . is that
what you're asking?" said Ellen, smiling as she brushed back
the blond bangs from her forehead.

She raised her eyebrows, took a deep breath, and sat back in her chair.

"It probably wouldn't have happened if I hadn't spent a night in jail in the sixties and watched other young people like myself being pushed around.

"I was working as a researcher at *Time* magazine then, and one day on my lunch hour I noticed a demonstration which looked pretty lively in front of the UN building. I wandered over and before I knew it, I was swept into the crowd. There was a lot of shouting and chanting, and all of a sudden the police pulled up and started coming at us from every direction. Suddenly, someone behind me yanked me by the hair. Instinctively, I kicked my leg back hard in an attempt to free myself. When I turned around, that 'someone' turned out to be a cop.

"The experience in jail changed my life," said Ellen. "In twenty-four hours, I learned more about evil than I cared to know. More than anything, it taught me about powerlessness. It also taught me that there are many different ways to pray. That's when I decided to study law.

"The political climate was also a big factor. So many things happened so fast that even now, from a distance, they seem hard to assimilate.

"Think of it: the Kennedy and King assassinations, Vietnam, Kent State, the madness in Chicago with Mayor Daley and Gene McCarthy. I kept trying to find a way to make some sense out of it, to get control of my life, to *not be powerless!* And it wasn't just me. Most of my friends felt the same way. But when we tried to explain that feeling of powerlessness to people, they didn't know what to say to us or do with us. And that includes people in the Church."

She shrugged in a gesture of impatience. "Looking back, I

don't really know what we expected from the Church. Maybe it was just to tell us that we weren't crazy. Or maybe to keep reminding us that Jesus went through most of his life feeling powerless and to keep on pushing and stick to our ideals. A few did. But so many of my friends who were priests and nuns in the sixties were trying to work out their own identities in the Church that in many ways it was like the blind leading the blind.

"All I know is that somehow Sunday Mass seemed to recede from our lives gradually until one day many of us realized that we had just stopped going. Now I only go to church when I go home or when my Mom visits me, and then only because I know it makes her happy. It just isn't part of my life anymore." Again she shrugged, but this time she smiled.

"My work with these kids has become my 'church,' and yes, I guess you could call it my ministry. I try to challenge them to develop effective skills to improve their communications. I try to make them aware of what their responsibilities are if they want healthy minds and bodies. I try to spend a lot of time listening to them, asking questions, learning from them, celebrating their small successes and helping them to move to bigger ones. I do everything I can to encourage them to examine their options, to see alternatives to their own feelings of powerlessness.

"Most of all, I want to affirm them in the midst of their struggles. I want them to know that they have a *right* to their questions. Unless they believe that, they'll never have the courage to look for the kinds of answers that will help them leave the streets and move beyond the neighborhood. They have a right to believe they have a chance!"

. . .

Dennis is both surprised and delighted that the band has so many bookings. If anyone had told him ten years ago, when he was a student in a Jesuit prep school, that he'd be a hot musician surrounded by a flock of "groupies," he would have laughed them away. Dennis is twenty-three.

In the smooth, blond, suntanned mix of Hollywood hype and illusion, Dennis's freckle-faced, red-headed, Tom Sawyer look is also a surprise. While he describes his relationship with the Church as "indirect"—"What I took from the Church is in my head and not my heart"—he nevertheless values his Jesuit training. "It taught me to think logically," he says.

For Dennis, that "logic" does not extend to sexuality. He finds the Church's understanding of sexuality "incredible." "It seems to me, at least from my life, to project a joyless misunderstanding of God.

"I can't believe in a God who is out to get me," says Dennis. "A God who is just waiting for me to make a wrong move before he wipes me away. How can you love a God who scares you to death?" he asks, shaking his head.

"When I look back to my senior year in high school, I was horny the whole year long. I can't believe that what was happening in my body was wrong or abnormal, that God was punishing me. But the word that came down was that birth control and abortion were both wrong. They got you before and after the fact," says Dennis. "God as a straitjacket doesn't make sense to me."

But the Jesuit influence lingers, even in ambivalence. "If I have kids, I'll probably send them to Catholic schools," says Dennis. "I think the basic bones of the Church . . . marriage and family values . . . are valuable. But I would sure like the Church to be more ecumenical in spirit . . . both in house and in the larger church community."

He grins. "I feel closest to God when I'm skiing or playing
my drums," says Dennis. "When I'm freest and happiest,
that's when I'm sure he's there.

"I wish the Church felt that way," he said. "I think God's
got a bigger heart than they give him credit for."

. . .

"It takes guts for the kids to walk into the clinic," says
Barbara, a twenty-five-year-old Hispanic woman who is a
health counselor. "It's saying, 'I'm sexually active and I'm
either afraid or in need.'"

The clinic is funded by the State Office of Family Planning.
It provides low-cost, confidential health services to the work-
ing poor, who don't qualify for health services elsewhere.
Seventy percent of the clinic's patients have Spanish surnames.
They range from twelve to thirty years of age.

"There are two types of people whom we see," says Barbara. "The fourteen- to sixteen-year-olds who are sexually
active and who want birth control help and women who come
in for pregnancy tests but who are still into sexual denial.
Those women walk into the clinic out of fear of pregnancy,
but they walk out without contraceptives. In that way, thay
don't have to take responsibility for the choices they have
made which brought them here.

"We provide education and advocacy," says Barbara, who
is a bilingual graduate student with a degree in biology. "We
try to help people understand that they have both choices and
medical rights," she explains. "We also try to help them to
understand their bodies and the mystery of their internal
organs. We provide services to 5,000 teenagers and young
adults each year.

"The contraceptive burden is on women," says Barbara.

"Men won't take responsibility. 'My girlfriend's using some-thing,' they say. Sometimes I have to tell them that a condom is cheaper than a coke at McDonald's," says Barbara, "and they laugh, but they can relate to that.

"For pregnant women, there are three alternatives: abor-tion, keeping the child, or putting it up for adoption. Women who decide to keep the baby have very little going for them except emotional rewards. To be pregnant or to be a mother means that at least you won't be on the streets.

"I feel so much sadness and anger when kids come into the clinic and I see their fear. If they're gay, they're afraid of hepatitis. They tell me, 'I live in my car,' or 'My parents threw me out,' or 'I been on the street.' If they're young girls, they come in with their mothers for their pregnancy tests. Then there's the drug scene—grass, PCP, cocaine—and, of course, VD. We're dealing with epidemic gonorrhea now," Barbara says.

Where does the Church come in?

Barbara feels there's so much it could do.

"There's no reason for them to feel that to be a Catholic is to be sexually paralyzed," she said. "The Church could pro-vide so much professional help, so much information if it would only open its eyes. In sexual matters, it's got to get out of the 'gray area.' It's got to help women, especially, to see their bodies as gifts, not punishment.

"We have women come into the clinic who have been taught that touching their bodies is sinful and they are terri-fied. They won't use a diaphragm and can't bear the thought of even breast self-examination, even though they have had babies and nursed children. They allow husbands or men or children to touch their bodies or use them, but they them-selves cannot.

"I think all wholesome sexuality begins with a sense of self-acceptance," says Barbara. "The Church has a responsibility to provide that. For the 'chola' in the streets, for the street gang, the Church can fill this identity crisis. If it says to the kids, you can find friendship, peace of mind, identity here, then they'll be at home there and want to come back.

"For so long, you could only be a kid or a grown-up in the church; there was no place for you from fourteen to marriage," she says.

"If parishes would only have family planning clinics where they teach the Billings method to teenagers, they'd be providing a tremendous service," said Barbara. "For some, it might provide the only hope that there's life beyond the end of the street."

. . .

At twenty-four he "stands tall." It has as much to do with the way he carries himself with a combination of pride and self-acceptance as it does with his six-foot stature. Yet, even with the punk-rock haircut, garnet earring and new name ("Call me K"), one can easily imagine him in a West Point uniform, standing at attention. His clean-cut good looks qualify him as a natural for an Army recruiting ad.

Four years ago, K was a "plebe" at West Point, an experience which gave him invaluable insights into his developing value system.

"They kept saying we were the cream of the crop, but they kept kicking the hell out of us. Everything was the 'whole man' concept: Be athletic, intellectual, an individual, strong. It's a necessity. You go to West Point to be a combat officer. Even though I knew after nine months that it wasn't for me, I stayed because I wanted to prove to myself that I could do it.

That I could take the first year with all the discipline and then make it through the next year as well. "And I did it. I did it all. I played sports; I was personable. I did what I was told. When I left, I was in the top ten percent of my class.

"But what I came to realize," says K with a wry smile, "is that there is no way to be a 'whole man' at West Point. It's a contradiction in terms. In order to be a 'whole man,' you have to be an androgynous person, a person who has fully integrated both the masculine and feminine parts of himself. A whole man must not only be rational and aggressive and cool and invincible, but he must also be sensitive and nurturing and emotional and gentle. West Point cannot allow that side of a man to be developed because its job is to train warriors. Maybe that's why the attrition rate is forty percent; the key word in that life-style is maintaining perfect control at all times.

"It doesn't have anything to do with having women around," K continues. "As a matter of fact, the first class of females came in while I was there. But they were males by the time I left, even though they couldn't be combat officers," he notes. "I have a lot of respect not only for the women who graduated from there but for those who even went there," he says. "I hope in years to come they can put the experience into perspective in terms of their lives."

Since leaving the Academy, what has K been able to put into perspective?

"I'm trying to put together a belief system that has integrity," says K, leaning forward in his chair. "The Church doesn't do it for me," he adds. Then, for a long time, he is silent. Finally, he looks up and smiles. "It's tough," he says.

As an engineering student, K is currently involved in a project which analyzes safety systems for nuclear reactors. He looks forward to playing music at the end of the day; he values his artistic side and speaks often and with reverence of creativity. But responsibility is a word which also surfaces over and over in the conversation.

"I can't see how we can separate individual responsibility from responsibility for the environment," he says. "As individuals, we have to do a lot of deep thinking about the ways in which freedom and truth and compassion intersect.

"Unless you open yourself to the possibility of nurturing on every level, you can't talk about human wholeness," says K. "I guess it's a longing for union with another at the deepest level," he said.

Has he ever had an experience of "wholeness"? His face lights up instantly. "Once," he said, "but it was an experience I had within my own being. It had nothing to do with anyone else. It happened in the midst of nature. I had a sense of total union between my body and soul.

"I had been hiking in the High Sierra," he says, "and I found myself standing in the midst of a grove of trees, with the sun filtering through. Suddenly, I found myself in a state of 'trans'—I felt totally at one with the trees and the environment. My whole being felt completely open and transparent. I was totally aware of my body, but my spirit was in ecstasy. It was sensual but not erotic. I only remember that I felt totally and completely alive in my whole being.

"I guess my search at this stage is for union," says K. "What does that really mean?" He leans back in his chair and is silent again. "Right now," he explains, "I'm celibate because I'm not into gameplaying or ego gratification. I sleep with people but I don't think you can have sex with everyone. You have to keep a balance between sex as tension release and spiritual self-respect.

"All celibacy means to me is that I haven't found the person I want to have a child with. When that happens, the search for that kind of union will have ended." He smiles, adding, "And another one will have begun."

• • •

In each of these young adults' stories, there is a common spiritual denominator. *Each of them is in touch with a dream.* Whether that dream is for themselves or for others, it calls them to be kinder, stronger, full of life-giving energy. It calls them from every corner of their lives to be *more!*

Each of them is struggling with some aspect of spirituality and sexuality. Each of them is seeking ways to integrate soul and body.

"The Church has everything to gain by reaching out to them," says Dr. Michael Warren, who has worked extensively with young adults at New York's St. John's University. He believes that an evangelizing ministry to young adults will be a liberating ministry to the Church. "The reason," he says, "is that young adults will not allow themselves to be marched through assemblyline programs like elementary school children. Older teens and young adults reject systems.

"But the Church, which is structured on a conformist mentality, sees them only as 'system misfits,' " says Warren, "rather than trying to reach out and minister to them in imaginative and innovative ways. The old task of ministry was to serve the assembled. The new task of ministry is to assemble those to be served."

He calls for the kind of transformation called conversion, an approach that is not open to mechanization or easy manipulation. Instead, this approach calls persons in ministry to stand in awe and reverence before the mystery of human freedom and the comparatively slow process of human development.

"Young adults are not going to respond to the superficial bandwagon initiatives of spiritual hucksters," says Warren. "They want something better; they deserve something more. They are looking for the signs of transformation in the very persons and communities that would call them to transformation. Young adults, just like so many middle adults and older adults, are looking for trustworthy guides and for communities which will keep faith with them." [4]

Who will transform the wasteland?

Who will decide if the Church is worth it?

Will it be the ministers who stand in the pulpits and face the prospect of a future filled with empty pews or the young adults who have no choice but to trust the stirrings of the Spirit within their own bodies and souls . . . the whispering dreams which tell them that God is with them, that they do not walk alone?

Together, the People of God have promises to keep to one another. They have seeds to sow and harvests to gather side by side. Those who live in God's love embrace the wasteland and the young who wander in it, remembering that nothing, including budgets, is impossible when one has faith in a Good Shepherd whom they call God.

Too much is at stake for the Church to continue to ignore the needs of young adults. Their absence impoverishes and scandalizes the People of God.

We must walk into the midst of the wasteland to welcome them. We must bring them the blessings of their heritage and assure them that they are the Church's harvest of hope. We must tell them, "You are the children of prophets, the heirs of the covenant. . . ."

Because of you . . .

The desert and the parched land will exult;
the steppe will rejoice and bloom. . . .
Streams will burst forth in the desert,
and rivers in the steppe.
The burning sands will become pools,
and the thirsty ground, springs of water. . . .

And we will walk with you. . . .

It is for those with a journey to make,
And on it the redeemed will walk.
Those whom the Lord has ransomed will return
and enter Zion singing. . . . (Is 35:1, 6-7, 9-10)

FOUR AUGURIES

ii

Though your body stowed in its heavy coat
is still a body: the sleeves promise me

arms, the pockets let loose their hands,
the lines on this hand hide a future

I decode only by the sense
of touch, light and urgent

the blind must rely on

Margaret Atwood

CHAPTER TWO

THE CHURCH AS BODY LANGUAGE

"In the faces of men and women, I see God, and in my own face in the glass. . . ." [1]

Walt Whitman

The Church exists, we teach our young, to help save our souls but, in fact, never lets us forget our bodies.

It informs us, controls us, inspires and instructs us through our bodies.

It speaks in body language. It surrounds us with body imagery.

The body is one and has many members, but all the members, many though they are, are one body; and so it is with Christ. . . . God has set each member of the body in the place he wanted it to be. If all the members were alike, where would the body be? . . . The eye cannot say to the hand, "I do not need you," any more than the head can say to the feet, "I do not need you." . . . If one member suffers, all the members suffer with it; if one member is honored, all the members share in its joy. You, then, are the body of Christ. Every one of you is a member of it. (1 Cor 12:12-27)

Its central figure is Jesus, God-made-human.

Its central truth is his entering-into-flesh in the Incarnation.

Its central symbol is the Eucharist, which is his body and blood.

Its central event is the Resurrection, the raising of his body.
Christmas, the day of his birth, has become a universal
celebration.

For centuries the circumcision of his body was celebrated
as a feast day.

The most solemn day in the church calendar honors and
remembers the death of that body on Good Friday.

The sacramental rituals of the Church focus on the body
and follow it through a lifetime—from baptism, which
welcomes the body and celebrates its "rebirth" as a new
creation in Christ, to anointing of the sick, which blesses the
body in time of illness or danger and prepares it, in its final
hours, for death.

Its feast days focus on the events of Christ's body: the feast
of Corpus Christi, the triumph of Christ's body's Transfigura-
tion, the ascension of Christ's body into heaven.

The symbol of the "laying on of hands" by its ministers
expresses the Spirit's presence in its sacramental rituals.

Its "kiss of peace" calls us to touch one another in greeting
during the Mass as a symbol of our reconciliation with God
and with one another.

Day by day, year by year, the body is used in image and
metaphor. We grow up learning about our human condition
as it's presented in Scripture. We learn about good and evil
through body imagery.

If your right eye is your trouble, gouge it out and throw
it away! Better to lose part of your body than to have it
all cast into Gehenna. (Mt 5:29)

The eye is the body's lamp. If your eyes are good, your
body will be filled with light; if your eyes are bad, your

body will be filled with darkness. And if your light is darkness, how deep will the darkness be! (Mt 6:22-23)

Even beyond death, we are called through our bodies. "Eye has not seen, ear has not heard, nor has it so much as dawned on man what God has prepared for those who love him" (1 Cor 2:9).

The miracles of Jesus center on the body. His healing is one of the hallmarks of his ministry. His approach to healing centers on social outcasts, those who are wounded in their bodies and in their spirits; thus Jesus' healing is a call to human wholeness; it embraces both body and soul.

Knowing the body's physical needs, Jesus never fails to nurture people's bodies, whether it be in the feeding of the multitude of 5,000 in the miracle of the loaves and the fishes or the healing of individuals such as Jairus's daughter, who was believed to be dead. "He took her by the hand and spoke these words: 'Get up, child.' The breath of life returned to her immediately; whereupon, he told them to give her something to eat" (Lk 9:54-55).

The Church's devotions center on the body of Jesus: The Sacred Heart . . . encircled by a crown of thorns, drops of blood falling, wounded . . . Adoration of the Blessed Sacrament . . . the consecrated Eucharist, the body and soul of Jesus . . . before which "every knee must bend" (Phl 2:10). The Passion of Christ . . . the profound bodily suffering reenacted in the stations of the cross during the Lenten season. And the readings of Holy Week which chronicle, in unforgettable language, the Agony in the Garden, where we can almost feel his pain. . . . "In his anguish, he prayed . . . and his sweat became like drops of blood falling to the ground" (Lk 22:44).

Hundreds of thousands of men and women remind us of that Body's suffering through the names of their religious congregations . . . the Passionists, the Precious Blood Fathers, the Sisters of the Adorers of the Sacred Heart. Churches . . . are called by names such as Five Wounds Church and Corpus Christi.

The names of prayers often expess natural functions of the human body: One is called an ejaculation. Webster's diction-ary definition: 1 to eject from a living body; specifically: to eject semen in orgasm 2 to utter suddenly and vehemently. A Catholic dictionary definition: *ejaculation*: a prayer consisting of a few words which can be repeated often or at any time (e.g., "Jesus, mercy!" or "Mary, help.") Many ejaculations have indulgences attached to them. [2]

Another prayer is called an aspiration, literally, a prayer said in one breath. In religious life, an "aspirant" is one who seeks entry into religious life, literally "panting" for entry.

Jesus transmitted stunning messages through the body: the image of himself as servant when he washed the feet of the disciples at the last supper and, conversely, his reaction when his feet were washed with a woman's tears at the house of Simon. Because of the outpouring of love which prompted her ministry to his body, he gave her the highest praise ever accorded to a person in Scripture. "I assure you, wherever the good news is proclaimed throughout the world, what she did will be spoken of as her memorial" (Mt 26:13).

Body language also surrounds Mary, the mother of Jesus, whose very identity centers on her bodily "history." Feasts like the Immaculate Conception and the Assumption of her body into heaven have been elevated to the status of revealed truth. Such bodily events as her Maternity, her Nativity, her Purification at the Temple forty days after the birth of Jesus, and her Immaculate Heart have all been designated as feast

days by the Church. The "mystery" of her status as both
Virgin and Mother focuses on her body. .
The two physical manifestations of Mary's body which
have been celebrated are suckling and weeping. .
In the case of the former, an actual cult of the Madonna's
milk developed, and the association of Mary's milk with her
powers of intercession and healing inspired an extraordinary
quantity of relics in Europe. From the thirteenth century,
phials in which allegedly her milk was preserved were vener-
ated all over Christendom in shrines that attracted pilgrims by
the thousands. Sometimes the relic purported to be a piece of
ground at the grotto in Bethlehem where a few drops had spilt
where Mary was nursing. At other times, the Virgin's milk
had appeared miraculously, transcendental milk from heaven.
It sometimes liquified on feast days as if it were fresh. And it
had the advantage, unlike a saint's milk, of being almost
indefinitely divisible. [4]

As for Mary's tears, they became institutionalized in her
title Our Lady of Sorrow, the image of the Mater Dolorosa.
Indeed, Marina Warner chronicles the fact that all over the
Christian world statues and images of the Virgin weep. In
1953 in Syracuse, Sicily, a plaque of the Virgin cried from
August 29 to September 1 on the wall above the marital bed
of a Communist worker and his wife. Soon crowds were
flocking to the tiny house, miracles were acclaimed, the tears
examined by scientists and pronounced human. In 1972, a
priest was touring America with a weeping statue of the
Virgin, carved, he claimed, on the instructions of Lucia, the
last survivor of the three children who saw Mary at Fatima in
Portugal in 1917. In 1975, when the Vietcong took Saigon,
some Catholics in the city insisted that the Virgin's statue
outside the Cathedral wept. [5]

And finally . . . the concept of the Church as Body of

Christ is one grounded in the union that exists between the Christian and the *risen* Body of Christ.

As Christians, we are surrounded on every side by these messages, symbols, and images of the body.

Young adults ask what has been the effect of these symbols on our lives as children, adolescents, Christians seeking wholeness and integration. Have they helped us to grow in strength, walk in dignity, stand in spiritual splendor? Have they helped us to feel good about our bodies . . . indeed, to glow with the bodily self-esteem that is both our birthright and destiny?

In our human existence, we begin and end with our body. That body, we are taught, is the dwelling place of the Holy Spirit. It is the place where spirit and matter meet.

"There is but one body and one Spirit, just as there is but one hope given all of you by your call" (Eph 4:4).

In each of our lives, how do we respond to that call from the echo chambers of our own consciousness? . . . a call which began as a spark of love in the heart of God. . . .

Before I formed you in the womb I knew you,
before you were born I dedicated you,
a prophet to the nations I appointed you. (Jer 1:5)

FROM *RETURN TO FRANKFURT*

The girl thinks if I can only manage
   not to step on any of these
   delicate hands of shadow
   cast on the sidewalk by the chestnut trees

The boy thinks if I reach the trolley
   in time and if it doesn't have to wait
   at the switch and the traffic policeman really
   does his job and tries to clear the street

If thinks the girl before I reach that tree
   the third on the left no nun comes out at me
   and if not more than twice I pass small boys
   crossing the street in groups, carrying toys
   oh then it's certain that we'll meet

Unless the boy thinks there's a power failure
   unless forked lightning strikes the driver
   unless the trolley-car gets smashed to bits
   surely we'll meet yes I can count on it

And many times the girl must shiver
   And the boy thinks will this last forever
   until under the chestnut trees they meet,
   wordless and smiling, in some quiet street.

Marie Luise Kaschnitz

CHAPTER THREE

LEGACY

A Body and Soul in Search of a Heart

"Everything is the sum of the past and nothing is comprehensible except through its history." [1]

Teilhard de Chardin

It has been slung across their young shoulders almost from the beginning . . . a heavy rope, rough to the touch, with bristles that cut deeply into their shoulders, a rope which, in time, bent their backs.

It has chafed them from childhood, and as they grew, the healed-over hurts became scar tissue, and it pockmarked their psyches as well as their skin.

The rope is both the lifeline and legacy of the Catholic Church's traditional teaching on sexuality. It has been passed down from generation to generation as columns of Christians moved through the mists of history. For some, the rope was a guideline which led them and offered them something to hang onto. For others, it was a jumprope. For still others, a noose. Over the centuries, the rope shifted from shoulder to shoulder. At times it was dropped by many and discarded altogether. Often it slipped off shoulders, only to be picked up again along the journey. Many of today's young adults have simply shrugged it away.

Of what fibers is that rope fashioned?

Where did it come from?

How has it changed?

The rope began as a luminous thread of love which Jesus unfolded as he traveled among us. A love that assured us that he had come to bring us life, "life to the fullness," a fullness of being in a body wedded inseparably to its soul. It was an unimaginable love out of whose womb we were created, and a heart who looked on its creation and saw that it was good.

In time and through a thousand anxieties, the shimmering thread of love that Jesus had revealed became enclosed in what were intended and perceived to be protective coverings. In the process, the strands of his thread of love were subjected to tremendous tension. In time, they were reinforced by new threads meant to strengthen Jesus' thread. But more often than not, the strands of the new threads were dark ones. Increasingly, one had to strain to find the thread of light with which Jesus began.

As the fledgling Christian community struggled with self-definition, it turned to Paul for answers. To understand the answers Paul gave, we must place them against the backdrop of events which were then occurring within that Christian community.

As Paul traveled from place to place, he responded to here-and-now questions of everyday living with which those early Christians struggled. This included crisis situations, such as that in which the Corinthian Christians found themselves. The Corinthians had become infamous due to their rampant sexual abuses.

When Paul pleaded with them and called them to abandon their sinfulness, he was restating with great urgency his basic call to repentance and conversion . . . the dominant theme of all his communications with the Christian community.

In light of the Corinthians' conversion, how then should they deal with marriage and sexuality? Paul faced a dilemma when it came to providing simple answers. On the one hand, Paul's attitudes toward sexuality reflected his Jewish culture; because he viewed sex as part of creation, he saw it as good. Further, he saw marriage as the symbol of Christ's union with his Church (Eph 5:21-33). Indeed, when husbands love their wives as their own flesh, they become reflecting mirrors for Christ's love for the Church.

On the other hand, Paul's attitudes towards sexuality were preempted by his all-consuming conviction that the Second Coming of Christ was imminent. He told the Corinthians that "time is short" (1 Cor 7:29) and that "the world as we know it is passing away" (1 Cor 7:31).

Given Paul's position as shepherd of the Christian community, one can easily understand Paul's concern and urgency that members of that community be ready. He did not hesitate to call them to turn away from anything or anyone that might be an encumbrance or distraction. This included one's spouse! In essence, he was saying, "The simpler you make life, the better!" With this in mind, also, Paul not only stated his preference for the single life but glorified it. He encouraged both virgins and widows to remain single.

But Paul was also realistic. In charity, he knew that such a decision would not always be practical or humanly possible for everyone. Thus he instructed those who were so inclined to marry to do so, rather than to "burn" with passion.

Unfortunately, Paul's negative messages about sexuality (including those concerning women) have far overshadowed his positive ones. He is quoted far more often for his warnings on sexual abuse and his preference for the single state than he is on his messages about the spiritual equality of the sexes—("There does not exist among you, Jew nor Greek, slave nor freedman, male or female. All are one in Christ

Jesus" (Gal 3:28)—or his statements that the love of husband
and wife is analagous to Christ's love for the Church
(Eph 5:28-30).

Yet both kinds of messages are critical to a balanced understanding of Paul's legacy.

Undeniably, the complexity of Paul's message regarding
sexuality has led to confusion and ambivalence. Historically,
however, the Church has chosen to echo his negative warnings about sexuality and the exaltation of virginity as the ideal.

Thus, Paul's messages were wound around Jesus' message
in order to preserve and protect it. . . . They were threads
that were intended to develop Jesus' message of integration
and wholeness. . . . They became, instead, intertwined with
Paul's own taut threads of asceticism and virginity.

Ironically, Paul's belief in the immediacy of the Second
Coming, which inspired his asceticism, is only now being
reinterpreted in the light of history. The impact of his
message, however, continues to influence our attitudes
toward sexuality.

The Church Fathers who followed Paul continued to reinforce that tradition of ambivalence, in one form or another,
over the centuries. Despite the brilliance, scholarship, and
spirituality of their writings and teachings in other areas, their
practical understanding of human sexuality was sadly and
seriously incomplete. When it came to questions of spirit and
matter, these men were caught up in personal cobwebs of
conflict and struggle. The ramifications of that confusion
have had a profound effect on Christians' lives throughout
church history.

The Church Fathers chose to deal with their minds and
bodies by separating them. Thus, a dualism developed—or,
through Greek influence, was perpetuated—and cast a dark

shadow over human sexuality that reaches into the lives of Christians to this day.

While the Church Fathers never went so far as to deny the basic value and sanctity of marriage, most insisted that the purpose of marriage clearly was the begetting of children. Sexual desires came to be seen as nothing more than the unfortunate effects of Original Sin. All children were seen to be born of their parents' "sin" because procreation was possible only with the seductive aid of physical lust. But it was considered a tolerable sin because God wills that we should be fruitful and multiply, and it provides a legitimate way of keeping "perverse desire within its proper bounds." [2]

The body was seen as the soul's prison, an encumbrance identified not so much with evil as inferiority. It is one of the ironies of history, however, that the Christian tradition is closer to the Greeks in Athens than to the Jews in Jerusalem. The tradition which was to profoundly affect the sexual outlook of Western civilization was not based on Jewish culture, which celebrated sexuality as a gift from God. Rather, Christian tradition drew heavily on Greek culture, which celebrated asceticism, self-denial, and triumph over the flesh.

William Phipps notes that initially the Church was nurtured under the wing of the ancient Jewish culture, but before the young community had come of age, the destruction of the Jewish state forced it to center itself away from Jerusalem. As it moved westward, and became predominantly gentile, the Church began to assimilate radically different Hellenic (Greek) ideas about the body and the nature of ideal personhood.

By the time the Church was several centuries old, it was permanently scarred by the stance of several Mediterranean cults and philosophies. The assumption that sexual

abstinence is requisite to sublime purity was a pagan outlook
shared by many common people and intellectuals of the
Graeco-Roman world. That viewpoint was adopted by earliest Christianity. [3]

And so the thread of the Church Fathers became intertwined with that of the Greek philosophers, the most prominent of whom were Plato and Aristotle. Plato wrote that the
true philosopher is not concerned with sexual pleasure. . . .
Sexual desire is a diseased aspect of the personality. . . . The
well-balanced personality is one who sublimates his sexual
energies in intellectual pursuits.

Aristotle was at least as negative. A woman, he noted, is "a
mutilated male." The male is by nature superior. He com-
mands; the female obeys. [4]

When it came to women, the Greek philosophers' ethic of
moderation and balance ("nothing in excess") did not seem to
apply.

In the minds of these writers, asceticism and self-denial
were the only forms of true perfection, or "holiness." The
supreme reality on which they focused was the soul rather
than the body in which they lived. They viewed their bodies as
inescapable burdens, if not outright enemies.

Marriage was grimly tolerated (for procreation only) and
often rejected outright. In that rejection was a clearly articulated contempt for women.

Thus the borrowed threads of sexism became inextricably
interwoven with the threads of love in a tradition which
claimed to "protect" the message of Jesus but which, in fact,
distorted it. Jesus not only showed no anger toward women
or denial of them but in fact provided a stunning countersign
in the Jewish culture by treating women with respect, affirmation, and equality. Yet these sexist threads managed to
become deeply embedded in Christian tradition and have, in

many ways, strangled the lives of both men and women ever
since.

New threads were created by the teachings of the Church
Fathers. Origen (A.D. 185-254), described by Leonard Swidler
as an extraordinary intellectual who was also endowed with a
certain impetuosity, at one point was prevented from seeking
martyrdom only by his mother's hiding of his clothes. At
another point, in a literal application of Matthew 19:12
("There are eunuchs who have made themselves that way for
the sake of the reign of heaven. Let anyone accept this who
can."), he castrated himself. [5]

Tertullian (160-225), whose pervasive influence has led him
to be called the Father of Latin Theology, saw "materialism"
as the basic evil in the world, sex as the most central dimension of the basically evil "matter," and woman as the personi-
fication of fundamentally evil sex. He not only blamed
women for bringing sin into the world but added to that guilt
the responsibility for the death of the Son of God. Of women
he said, "You are the devil's gateway! . . . What is seen with
the eyes of the creator is masculine and not feminine, for God
does not stoop to look on what is feminine and of the flesh." [6]
One wonders how he reconciled such a statement with the
fact that Jesus appeared first to a woman, Mary Magdalene,
after his Resurrection.

Epiphanius (315-403), who became the Bishop of Cyprus
and later Bishop of Salamis, revealed clearly his male supremacist attitude: "For the female sex is easily seduced, weak, and
without much understanding. The devil seeks to vomit out
this disorder through women." [7]

John Chrysostom (347-407) was an extraordinary preacher
and was made Patriarch of Constantinople in A.D. 398. He
wrote to a monk who was contemplating marriage, "Should
you reflect about what is contained in beautiful eyes, in a

straight nose, in a mouth, in cheeks, you will see that bodily beauty is only a white-washed tombstone, for inside it is full of filth." He denigrated marriage as good only to keep men from "becoming members of a prostitute." [8] Chrysostom believed the primary purpose of marriage to be not procreation but to extinguish the fires of lust. In his writings he repeats this more than twenty times. [9]

Jerome (342-420), an ascetic and a giant Sacred Scripture scholar, had a number of women disciples. But they had to adopt a life of extreme asceticism, so as to "become a man." [10]

Jerome could accept marriage, reluctantly, only because from marriages virgins were born: "I praise marriage and wedlock, but only because they beget celibates; I gather roses from thorns, gold from the earth, pearls from shells." [11] Further, he warned, "A man who makes love to his wife too passionately is an adulterer." [12]

On a deeper level, Jerome struggled with his own sexuality; while living the most extreme ascetic life in the desert Jerome was filled with wild sexual fantasies:

Although in my fear of hell I had consigned myself to this prison where I had no companions but scorpions and wild beasts, I often found myself amid bevies of girls. My face was pale and my frame chilled with fasting, yet my mind was burning with desire and the fires of lust kept bubbling up before me when my flesh was as good as dead. [13]

But the greatest influence on Christian sexual tradition was that of Augustine (354-430), who is considered, without question, to be the greatest of the Latin Fathers and the most powerful of the Doctors of the Church. Born in North Africa, Augustine eventually became a Christian and the Bishop of

Hippo in North Africa. Before he was converted to Christianity, Augustine had been a devotee of Manicheism, an explicitly dualistic philosophy-religion that greatly stressed the essential evil of matter. This notion Augustine largely carried over with him into Christianity, and through his massive influence the idea entered the rest of Western Christianity. [14]

His writings were unparalleled in terms of their impact on the sexual outlook of Western civilization. They grew out of an intense struggle with his own sexuality, a struggle of memories in which he was caught in the cross fire between a love-hate relationship with a pious but dominating mother and a fifteen-year common-law marriage in which he fathered a son by a woman he loved deeply but whom he eventually abandoned for a concubine.

Like his predecessors, Augustine "condoned" marriage as a necessary evil. While admitting that sexual consummation produces "the greatest of all bodily pleasures," Augustine believed it was dishonorable for Christians to seek sexual pleasure even within marriage. Marital coitus can be engaged in without committing a "venial sin" only if spouses are exclusively motivated by a grim determination to propagate. "Since you cannot reproduce in any other way," he laments, "you must *descend against your will* [italics mine] to this punishment of Adam." Thus the Bishop of Hippo advises a man to love his wife as he loves his enemy . . . he should accept both as creatures of God but hate what makes them corrupt. With respect to the latter, a husband should hate his spouse's desire for sexual pleasure. According to Augustine, to renounce sexual intercourse entirely was to hasten the coming of the perfected City of God. [15]

In short, if sexual intercourse was something you were forced to engage in, it was certainly not something you were supposed to enjoy

Augustine was particularly obsessed with his powerlessness
to control the activity of his penis. He saw the inability of the
will to directly regulate erections as the result of man's disobedience to God. For Augustine, unruly passions were a constant reminder of Adam's original disobedience, which was
passed on to posterity through the instrumentality of sexual
intercourse. [16]

The fullest and most important discussion of sexual sins
was undertaken in the Middle Ages by Thomas Aquinas
(1225-1274), who was declared a Doctor of the Church in 1567
by Pope Pius V. Aquinas is considered to be the single most
influential theologian in the shaping of Catholic tradition.

Michael Valente notes that Aquinas's radical insistence on
the absolute infallibility of scientific knowledge, his dedication to reason, and his focus on the primacy of charity in
theology could have brought him to a serious modification of
Augustine's view. It did not, however. Aquinas says that only
the offsetting good of procreation is sufficient justification for
escape from the heat of passion into the sacrament of
matrimony. [17]

Augustine was a great theological influence on Aquinas in
matters of sexuality. Like Augustine, Thomas Aquinas saw
virginity as the ideal. Though Aquinas is credited with being
instrumental in bringing marriage to the status of a full sacrament, he was not unaffected by the long dispute surrounding
marriage and the question of its being an effective sign of
grace precisely because of its carnal nature. [18]   Although
Aquinas spent a good deal of time considering the sins of
lechery, he nevertheless found prostitution tolerable as the
lesser of two evils for men. The prostitute was like "the sewer
in the palace. Take away the sewer and you will fill the palace
with pollution. . . . Take away prostitutes and you will fill it

with sodomy." The "use of harlots, therefore, became a lawful immorality." [19]

And since offspring were the only legitimation for genital expression, Aquinas taught that masturbation or homosexual acts were graver sins than rape or incest. The former were classified as unnatural because procreation was impossible. With rape and incest, however, conception could result, and so they are natural sins. [20]

Thread after thread, century after century, the rope thickened, tightened . . . knotted like angry fists in places, curiously twisted in others. . . .

They bind up heavy loads, hard to carry, to lay on other men's shoulders, while they themselves will not lift a finger to budge them. (Mt 23:4)

And in the intervening centuries, has the message changed? Has the burden of that rope grown lighter?

As late as in 1963, the eighteenth edition of a work titled *Moral Theology* authored by Heribert Jone was issued and used in seminaries as a handy, popular reference text. In it, the emission of semen was still referred to as "pollution."

Sodomy (rectal intercourse) is defined as unnatural copulation with either a person of the same sex . . . in which it is called perfect sodomy, or with a person of the opposite sex . . . in which it is called imperfect sodomy.

If there is a reasonable cause for doing so, one may look at the private parts of one's own body, but to do so out of curiosity would be gravely sinful.

One may observe animals mating only if it does not

provide sexual pleasure. One would be committing a venial sin, however, if one looked out of curiosity or amusement.

"Going steady" may be looked upon as an occasion of sin. [21]

Indeed, the search for sin, with all its theological hair-splitting and handwringing, continued to be a full-time occupation, consuming the entire lifetimes of writers and theologians. Most of them continued to conclude that sexual pleasure was probably suspect, if not inherently evil.

It was not until 1965 and the advent of the Second Vatican Council that any major breakthrough in the Church's traditional understanding of and approach to sexuality appeared on the horizon.

In its Constitution on the Church in the Modern World, the Church for the first time clearly rejected procreation as the primary purpose of marriage. Instead, it recommended as the focus the "*nature* [italics mine] of the human person and his acts. In marriage, the human quality of expressions of sexuality must contribute to the growth and development of oneself and one's partner. Thus, the unifying aspects of sexual expression . . . the life-giving sharing and intimacy . . . experienced in the relationship is acknowledged to be of importance equal to the bearing of children. Only by integrating and harmonizing these two areas . . . the unitive and the procreative . . . can marriage hope to achieve the 'fullness of life' it was meant to have." [22]

The Christian as Sexual Person had come of age at last. Now the message was, in effect, that in marriage, "making love"—and enjoying it—was as important as "making babies."

The fact that this message was introduced in the mid-sixties is not without significance. During that period, today's population of young adults was also "coming of age."

In the last twenty years, that generation has tested its own theories of "making love and/or making babies." In addition to the home and the culture, one of their testing grounds has been the Church.

In their travels, today's young adults have heard the Good News about the Mystical body. Further, they want to believe that Jesus was also part of a Body Generation.

Observe that no one ever hates his own flesh; no, he nourishes it and takes care of it as Christ cares for the church—for we are members of his body. (Eph 5:29-30)

They ask . . . "If this is true and if the Church really believes it, then why wasn't it preached from the pulpits with confidence? Why wasn't it whispered to us, in love, as we knelt in our adolescent shame in the confessional?"

They want to unravel the rope and reclaim the thread of light that Jesus revealed when he healed their first sisters and brothers. They want that thread to become a beacon of light that beckons to their generation, calling them to believe in the goodness and wonder of their bodies. They want to reclaim a "fullness of'life" which embraces their bodies and souls and sees them as inseparable.

In that context and out of their life experience, they believe they have something to give to the Church. Indeed, they feel it is their responsibility to do so. Like every generation, they believe they have a contribution to make to the tradition. They know, also, that in the process they need to listen and continue to learn.

They long for the Light of the World to illumine their lives and dispel the fear and uncertainty that often surrounds them in their New Age technological loneliness.

Alongside the poet, they pray and protest against a spiritual darkness. . . .

A new generation of the Beloved cries . . .

"Rage, rage against the dying of the light." [23]

EUCHARIST

In a heavy summer of walking alone
I seek the cool purity of solitude
in vain.
The arm-locked warmth of lovers
burns
and in my dreams, I still remain
entangled in his claiming arms
and wake to cry in empty rooms.

Death comes punctually—
on Saturdays the world is coupled
but my voice
runs into walls, stopped
by unanswered telephone calls.
My own scorn is judge enough.

Sunday morning prods
my broken body to kneel
with barely open hands
taking in darkness
the offered bread—
ludicrous
that to my cavernous hunger
hands give only crumbs.

But as I leave the sunlight plays
on wheat-like weeds.
I sway, my slim form
glows to the sun, toes

draw dirt around them
and my eyes let out my soul
to widen bluely as the sky
and then return, singing,
to myself,
the words he said:
the words he said:
"*This* is my body!"
and I'm alive again.

Patricia Harrington

CHAPTER FOUR

HALL OF MIRRORS

The Media Generation

"It's easy to find someone to sleep with at Oakwood," he commented, "but it isn't easy to find a friend. Sex is in great supply in the Western world but friendship is not." [1]

Suzanne Gordon

NEWSPAPER CLASSIFIED ADS—PERSONALS COLUMN

- *Successful & good-looking businessman would like to meet exceptionally attractive lady 18-34 for a lasting and quality relationship. Reply only if your looks make you stand out in a crowd. If you are tired of working and would like to enjoy the good life with a nice guy, please phone without any pressure. Call Jim.*
- *Attractive professional female, 27, new to area, have seen California splendor alone. Looking for someone to share a sunset and a storm.*
- *Man wants to meet same. Handsome white male with beach house and new 911SC seeks slim bi-guy over 19 for good times.*
- *Is there a virgin left? I'd like to know and marry one. Write P.O. Box 114.*

It has been said that a society's organization and values system are reflected in its perception of the human body. [2]

What messages have today's young adults received about their bodies while growing up in the last few decades? What have been the major influences that determined the bodily self-definition and self-image which they, in turn, bring to the culture today? To be a young adult in today's society is to have grown up in a hall of mirrors known as the media, where one experiences instant response and gratification on demand. Within hours and sometimes minutes, every news event, celebration, catastrophe, or celebrity flashes across the mirror of their television screen. They have grown up expecting to be informed, alerted, educated, distracted, and amused.

Sex is always news, and television producers are quick to capitalize on it. They make sure that their viewers are supplied with a steady stream of information about the latest developments in sexuality in medical research, psycho-sexual studies, and the impact of legislation on alternative sexual life-styles in the community. Sex is on the television reflecting-mirror from morning until night. Every local or national talk show, news broadcast, or public affairs program discusses sexual issues whenever possible. The *Donahue Show*, currently one of the highest-rated daytime information-talk shows in the country, discusses it in infinite detail. Hailed as a "public service presentation" by some admirers, this daily program has presented shows on such social ills as pornography, rape, and incest, as well as shows which feature frank discussions on seldom-mentioned subjects like surrogate sex partners, penile implants to remedy male impotence, and studies of female genitalia which locate specific erogenous zones.

Today's young adults have grown up knowing there is no sexual question which cannot be asked, no sexual fear which cannot be shared, no sexual problem which cannot be solved by experts via mass communications. Sometimes the help they need is only a phone call away.

Whereas their parents would have once phoned the rectory for advice, young adults now dial the TV or radio station.

The impact of this kind of "help," information, and availability cannot be underestimated.

Today, not a twenty-one-year-old in the country has not grown up with or been affected by television. Between the ages of six and eighteen, the average child spends between 15,000 and 16,000 hours in front of the television; whereas school probably consumes no more than 13,000 hours. Semanticist Neil Postman, a professor at New York University, calls it a child's "first curriculum" and believes it molds the intelligence and character of youth far more than formal education. [3]

In the absence of positive and relevant Church teaching on sexuality, the moral development of many of today's young adults has grown out of the options presented to them on the reflecting-mirror of that television screen.

When they look into that mirror, what is the prevailing message they receive about their bodies? Advertising, soap operas, situation comedies, and celebrity talk shows reinforce the same body-message: that to be young is to be powerful; to be young and sexy is to be almost omnipotent.

Young adults grow up seeing their sexuality imaged as both commodity and weapon. Sex sells clothes, cars, luxuries, and fantasies. It can also manipulate, trap, and terrorize, making one vulnerable in a thousand ways.

The main product TV sells young adults is a sense of their own inadequacy. It makes a million promises about their possibilities while feeding their insecurities about their current weaknesses.

Sex and love can be but are not necessarily synonymous. Messages about loving sex and moral values, such as fidelity, trust, patience, and perseverance are at a minimum. Positive values about the human body are, at best, ambivalent. Seminudity or nudity in humorous situations is acceptable and even encouraged, and in "illicit" situations partially-clad bodies are either tolerated or ignored. But when the clothed or naked bodies of lovers are shown in loving, caring relationships, the reaction is one of embarrassment. Many segments of the population are quick to denounce such presentations as "poor taste," as "invasions of privacy," or simply as obscene. The increasing association of sex with violence is not viewed as obscenity, however. The number of fast-paced cops-and-robbers series attests to that. Power, brutality, force, and domination are equated with strength and contol in our culture. In that context, the boundaries between rape and assault and battery tend to blur easily.

Thus, in addition to power broker, young adults see the human body imaged as pawn, victim, and object of gratification. This means that they see themselves as objects of ridicule and as conspirators in "sin" or as playthings and fantasy objects. They are encouraged to indulge, explore, and "experience"—and sidestep moral considerations.

NEWSPAPER CLASSIFIED ADS—PERSONALS COLUMN

• *Mrs. Robinson! Remember the movie! Attractive, discreet single white male, 23, 5'11", blue eyes, 160 lbs., would like to meet attractive older woman. Write or phone. . . .*

• *Couple (male/female) seeks bisexual female. Must be slim, clean and attractive. Call. . . .*

• *Single, successful, attractive white male, 32, blond hair, blue eyes, wants to live out his fantasies! Seeks an exotic black female, a beautiful Oriental lady, or a classy, sophisticated older woman, any race, for good times. Very selective, so please send letter if interested. . . .*

• *Swinging females needed by businessman for parties. Write P.O. Box. . . .*

• *Pretty, healthy-looking white female, 23, seeks Sugar Daddy.*
• *Frustrated male, 25, seeks female 18-40 for discreet affair.*
Must be open-minded. Call. . . .
• *White male wants 1 white new or used 21-35 year old, willing*
to move to Nebraska.

In addition to television as an option for young adults, there is always their one unfailing friend: the radio. Today's young adults grow up with transistors at their fingertips and on their dashboards. As teens they can always count on their local stable of disc jockeys to "be there," waiting to welcome them with their current favorite from the Top 40. Moreover, these disc jockeys let them know that everything they think is important. They actively solicit their ratings on new records; they are full of fun and games and contests which keep them interested and which reward them with prizes.

It's no wonder that one San Francisco television station which programs to the current young adult market talks about "Coming Home to KRON."

One Chicago filmmaker in her late twenties admits to keeping her FM radio on all night to combat loneliness.

"I can go to sleep easier when I feel I have *someone* here with me," she says. "The radio is like a roommate to me."

In order to satisfy the needs of their listening publics, stations who are on the air for twenty-four hours promote program formats that not only provide platforms for experts but also encourage the average citizen to express opinions. In addition to the therapeutic value of this kind of opportunity, they offer listeners a platform for expressing their anger, needs, problems, and pain. In this context, each caller is guaranteed recognition as a human being who has both the right and the responsibility to be heard. Each is treated with courtesy and understanding. Even if the host or "expert" disagrees or chooses to challenge the caller, the person is treated with respect as one who has something of value or interest to say.

Many people think that this kind of media access should be provided by the Church and is desperately needed by Christians, both active and alienated. The opportunity for education, information, reconciliation, and networking is unlimited. Young adults, especially those who are in transition from families, other life-styles, or simply coping with cultural loneliness, might see it as a bridge back to the church community.

What is even more important, that person has immediate access to a platform where, for at least a few minutes, he or she can be taken seriously. There are no committees to be formed, studies to be made, or authorities to consult before one can be recognized. Community is created where caring people gather because they know they will be respected and heard.

What is interesting is that the media have now replaced the Church because the media provide "community." Each person has as much "access" as anyone else; no one is discounted or trivialized or dismissed as being too old or too young, too beautiful or too ugly, too blessed or too broken.

Boston's Janet Jeghelian, who hosts a weekend talk show on WBZ, which is beamed to a million listeners in thirty-eight states, comments on the deep human hunger for communication that she hears week after week from callers throughout the country.

I see myself as both a catalyst and a facilitator who attempts to create a trust level whereby people can communicate not only with me but with each other. Very often, on the air, I will set up conference calls with people in different parts of the country so that they can provide one another with practical help and information.

In addition, I try to provide a witness of trust and caring which not only they but the entire listening audience desperately need to hear.

Thus, a woman who has just had a mastectomy in Canada can receive practical help and understanding from a woman in South Carolina who had the same surgery two years ago. Or a distraught teenage boy on drugs can receive support and encouragement from listeners who understand his trauma.

"If I can't provide an answer, I'll put the caller in touch with listeners 'out there' who can," says Janet. "I have great respect and trust in my callers' sensitivity to respond and care."

Referring to her broadcasts as "family meetings," Janet is called "Earth Mother" by some and "Mother-Away-From-Mother" by many college students. Because intelligence and warmth surround her common-sense answers and because she actively promotes peer ministry, Janet is seen by young adults as having credibility.

"I look forward to being with the 'family' from two to five in the morning," wrote one graduate student. "Sometimes the show helps me get through the night."

And if television and radio do not send enough signals, there is always the local newsstand where, alongside the "pop-porn" publications, there are dozens of popular magazines that claim to provide young adults with still more knowledge and insight into their sexuality and current morality.

Indeed, month in and month out, almost every magazine cover beckons with articles guaranteed to improve one's sex life. And in women's magazines these articles are advertised in the liberated language of the New Age woman, which strongly suggests that sexual satisfaction is a two-way street.

A single issue of *Mademoiselle* (September 1981), a magazine keyed to the young adult market, contained articles titled "Should You Forgive A Man Who Hurts You?" "What Makes A Woman A Good Lover?" "The Faces of Anger," "The Bad and the Bossy: Does Your Superior Make You Feel Inferior?" and "How to Ask for a Raise and Get It!" A monthly column titled "Body & Soul" is written by a female psychiatrist and sex therapist. What is significant is that the prevailing emphasis in each of these articles is *self-trust* and *self-respect*.

As with most publications directed to young career women, issues of equal access to jobs as well as equal pay, assertiveness in the workplace, and legal options for victims of sexual discrimination or harassment are all dealt with on an increasing and continuing basis.

Because these issues affect the professional lives of both men and women, they affect their private lives. Thus, they are clearly seen as issues of sexuality.

These articles deal openly with sexuality. They encourage responsibility and sensitivity in both professional and personal relationships. Sexual needs are seen to be normal and healthy. Trends and alternative life-styles are acknowledged and analyzed; pros and cons are discussed rather than dismissed, ignored, or categorically rejected.

This has not been the experience of most young adults in their attempts to discuss sexuality within the context of the Church.

Theologian Dennis Doherty notes that traditionally "the fence around sexual activity is marriage. Through the centuries all other approaches have become moral mine fields. Even within the enclosure itself one had to tread lightly." [4]

"Trying to talk to the Church about your sex life is like talking to someone whose jaw is set and whose arms are folded across their chest," said a thirty-one-year-old engineer. "It's like, 'My mind's made up. Don't bother me with the facts,' " he said.

Because of the Church's inordinate fear of the body, which prevents it from offering young adults the help they need, these young people make choices about sexual behavior based on the "advice" or point of view they receive from the media.

And even though they might end up making what the Church would consider "ethical" choices, young adults increasingly disclaim any connection between those decisions and the influence of religion.

This is seen by many to be the most critical issue facing the Church of the future. Because of its inability to deal with the cultural upheaval of the sixties, the Church failed to evangelize a whole generation. That generation's spiritual quest did not dissipate but, in fact, intensified. And, in the process, those young adults extended their quest far beyond Christian parameters.

Father Pat O'Neill reminds us that fifty percent of the membership of the Unification Church (Moonies) and forty-two percent of Hare Krishna membership is composed of Catholic young adults. [5]

Thus, though today's young adults exhibit a deep spirituality in their reverence for life—witness their involvement in the environmental and nuclear disarmament movements, in draft resistance, and in holistic health—they make little if any association between their spiritual quest and the institutional Christian Church in America.

This disassociation is not a matter of the Church's willingness or unwillingness to answer their questions. Everywhere they look in their hall of mirrors there are qualified experts who will provide them with any information they want. It is, rather, a matter of belonging to a group of people one feels at home with, where one is valued as being special, and because of that, one is listened to, respected, and taken seriously *wherever one is in one's spiritual or sexual journey.* "You go where you are welcome," said a thirty-year-old nursing instructor. "It's as simple as that!"

Young adults have grown up in a culture where this kind of problem-solving presence and listening has been at their fingertips. They do not care whether the station might be scrambling for commercial sponsorship in a competitive market. All they care about is that they have a place to go where they and others like them who are hurting or who can offer help can be heard. Psychologists, psychiatrists, physicians have regular call-in shows on many stations; they are willing and able to give valuable help to those in need. Where are the moral theologians, the bio-ethicists, and the young adult ministers? Don't they feel that they too have something to say?

What a rich harvest they could gather by encouraging young adults to call in, to write letters of praise or protest, to suggest ways in which the station or program could help them through information, education, or referrals to resources in the Church or community.

Why has the Church been remiss in asking for "equal time" on so many issues related to morality? What does an "informed conscience" really mean? Why is it that in decisions regarding birth control information, pro-choice abortion, test-tube babies, or gay life-styles, both men and women feel freer to ask for what they need from a radio station with a listening audience in the thousands than to approach a priest in a one-on-one encounter in the anonymity of a confessional?

The value judgments young adults make are often the result of such decisions. As Christians, we need to ask why the media have replaced the Church as community.

NEWSPAPER CLASSIFIED ADS—PERSONALS COLUMN

- *Wanted: Surrogate mother—Call between 2 and 8 p.m. . . .*
- *Shy, athletic male anxious to meet shy, athletic female. Write. . . .*
- *Male, 25 years, seeks affectionate woman for relationship. Physically handicapped ok. P.O. Box. . . .*
- *Trim, sensitive single adult male seeks NON-SEXUAL timeshare with a beautiful intelligent lady. Please no kooks, no dollars, no sex.*
- *Handsome male, 26, seeks slim athletic from-the-heart Christian lady. 18-28. Write P.O. Box. . . .*
- *White female . . . 29. Just walk beside me and be my friend. Phone. . . .*

Once upon a time, children were born, baptized, schooled, married, and sometimes buried from a single parish. Indeed, they identified themselves in terms of that parish, as one would identify oneself by a city, a neighborhood, or a street.

Today, in a world where the average American changes residence every few years, we have become a society of displaced persons. As young adults leave home to study or work, they bear the brunt of the loneliness of the uprooted. It is manifest in their spiritual restlessness. Where once the parish church was an extended family where one could count on a hug or a handshake, it has now become a passing-through place where a hurried wave is often the only welcome.

Pastoral theologian Dennes Geaney, OSA, claims, "The strength of the Catholic Church is in the neighborhoods. It wins or loses in parishes or neighborhoods in proportion to the leadership it provides for a community." [6]

Most parishes "regret" that they have no budgets for young adult programs. But *in a church which calls itself Christian, a budget becomes a theological statement.* If the Church sees young adults as a critical part of the human family, then it should find a way to include and welcome them. As most families know, welcome has as much to do with open arms as with open pocketbooks. But in both cases, it is a matter of rearranging priorities.

David Le Shan defined family as "people who, when you don't come home, they go out looking for you."

Jesus said the same thing in another way . . .

I am the good shepherd; the good shepherd lays down his life for the sheep. The hired hand—who is no shepherd nor owner of the sheep—catches sight of the wolf coming and runs away, leaving the sheep to be snatched and scattered by the wolf. That is because he works for pay; he has no concern for the sheep. I am the good shepherd. I know my sheep and my sheep know me. . . . For these sheep I will give my life. (Jn 10:11-15)

crossed hearts

her body unfolds at his touch
like a chinese paper flower
in a crystal goblet full of water,
filling his mind with delicate images
whose names he does not know.
her fingers shimmer over his body
like butterflies,
securing him with fragile bonds
like chains of flowers.
and though he will forget her stories,
whispered shyly with the trust
that comes at dawn,
he will move through his life
haunted forever by a memory
that his heart cannot name.

kim ohanneson

CHAPTER FIVE

WHERE ARE THE LOVERS?

"Deep water cannot quench love, nor floods sweep it away."
Song of Songs 8:7

It is passionate, mysterious, and, as history has proven, irresistible.

It seizes the imagination as much with its audacity as with its tenderness.

It challenges the senses to explore more of their potential for seeing, hearing, touching, yet it also challenges those senses to complete surrender.

It has embraced the lives of countless generations of lovers who have lived and died without truly understanding its teachings but have yielded totally to its mystery.

It has been called the Greatest Love Story of all time and yet the person on whom it centers is seldom defined as a lover. Teacher, Savior, Miracle-worker, Prophet, but Lover seldom, if ever, and then only by implication.

Yet, body and soul, Jesus of Nazareth poured himself out to the beloved community when he walked among them touching them time and time again with overwhelming and transforming love.

Jesus as Lover. Why have we denied him that title? Is it because we are uncomfortable with the thought of Jesus as a sexual, even a genital, being? If so, how does that affect our understanding of his humanness, his wholeness? As his followers, how does this affect his relationship with us? Why are we more comfortable describing him by the power of his miracles than by the tenderness of his heart? Have we, as a

Church, been careful to cast him in bronze so that we would
be able to control his action? Do we allow him to breathe, to
be free?

To call Jesus Lover, we would have to take the manifestations of his humanity seriously. . . . If he appeared
tomorrow, would we choose to walk with him, risk with him,
have him look into our eyes and call us by name? Would we
trust him enough to feel his touch on our eyelids as he cured
our blindness, or his hands on our feet as he washed and dried
them, or his loving arms around us as he helped us stand up
straight and tall?

This is the flesh-and-blood Jesus throbbing with life and
energy, the human being who cried out with frustration and
anger at the money changers in the Temple, and whose terror
in Gethsemane caused him to sweat blood as much from
loneliness as from fear.

It has become easy to relate to Jesus as an historical event,
safely enclosed in a time capsule, or as a perfect specimen,
pinned like a dazzling butterfly against the transparencies of
time.

The textbook Jesus has been prodded, palpated, exhibited,
examined—a process which ensures that our relationship with
him is scientific, orderly, and safe.

But who among our teachers has taught us to love him in a
way that would inspire us to take his hand, wipe his brow,
hold him in our arms and listen for the sound of his heartbeat? Why is the thought so unimaginable? Why do we
celebrate his death with such fervor and yet deny him recognition of the breath of life?

Why does it seem blasphemous to us to think of Jesus
laughing or smiling, hugging or kissing another human
being? These are things that loving human beings do! Do we
believe that Jesus never acted impulsively, spontaneously,

delightedly? We know that women as well as men were with him on his journeys, certainly at all the crisis moments of his lifetime.

Scripture tells us that "Jesus loved Martha and her sister and Lazarus very much" (Jn 11:5). His response to Mary when she told him of Lazarus's death was immediate.

> When Jesus saw her weeping . . . he was troubled in spirit, moved by the deepest emotions. "Where have you buried him?" he asked. "Lord, come and see," they said. Jesus began to weep, which caused the Jews to remark, "See how much he loved him!" . . . Once again troubled in spirit, Jesus approached the tomb. . . . (Jn 11:33-38)

Imagine Martha's and Mary's joy and gratitude when Jesus raised Lazarus from the dead and called him to come forth from the tomb. How natural it would have been for the two women whom Jesus loved to rush forward and hug him, their hearts overflowing with love and their eyes filled with tears of gratitude. From Jesus' own tears, they would have seen that he had acted out of his own compassion. And though he was witnessing to his father through this miracle, clearly he was motivated by his love for them.

Yet the Gospel account suggests nothing about human intimacy and deep sharing. It's possible that moments after Jesus performed the miracle, he was already on his way. It's more likely, however, that Jesus stopped for a while to rejoice and celebrate with Martha and Mary and Lazarus. When we do stop and think about what that scene could have been like, our minds are filled with confusion and uncertainty.

Perhaps it is because we are so accustomed to thinking of the suffering Jesus that it is hard to imagine a joyful Jesus who laughed and took delight in all forms of loving. Shouldn't we believe that Jesus had a human need to be affirmed, caressed, hugged, reassured?

What, in fact, does the record show regarding Jesus' sexuality?

Strangely, next to nothing.

On the precise point of whether Jesus had an active sex life or was sexually tempted, there is no possibility of contradiction since the New Testament says nothing about either. [1]

We do know that the single related issue Jesus addressed was marriage, specifically addressing "departures" from marriage, namely divorce and adultery. His use of wedding guests as symbols, his own attendance at weddings, and his use of the wedding feast as a symbol of the Kingdom of God attest not only to his approval but his celebration of marriage.

We know, too, that Jesus was comfortable with women and enjoyed their company. His friendship with women and his affirmation of them, be they friend or stranger, were a stunning countersign in his own culture, which considered women essentially as property. The clearest example of this occurred when Jesus chose to first reveal his identity and mission as Messiah to a Samaritan woman who was both stranger and outcast.

Certainly his appearance to Mary Magdalene (rather than to his male disciples) after his Resurrection is of utmost significance. Why have we continued to ignore the fact that he specifically chose her to be the "apostle to the apostles" in instructing her to tell Peter and the others that he had risen from the dead? This is the central event of Christianity! For Jesus to have commissioned Mary to be the bearer of this momentous news can only be a reflection of the deep love and trust he had in her as his friend.

Jesus healed women through his miracles. In no way did he denigrate them, trivialize them, or ignore them. He touched them with love. Always and everywhere.

Beyond these few stories, there is little evidence from which to draw about the sexuality of Jesus. But it is widely recognized that the Gospels were not intended to be biographies. Rather, they are a collection of materials used by the earliest Christian preachers and recorded about half a century after Jesus' Crucifixion. This loosely knit sermonic literature only incidentally supplies biographical information. Consequently, *there is no New Testament record for about ninety percent of the span of Jesus' life.*

Other than Luke's vignette, which affords insight into the twelve-year-old Jesus speaking with the elders in the Temple, the silence is unbroken from his infancy to his thirties. [2]

Thus any positions taken by theologians on Jesus' sexuality, and specifically his genitality, are based on an *argument from silence.* This leaves the discussion open to continuing research and development.

The Catholic Church traditionally maintained that Jesus was celibate; it continues that position to this day. One of its arguments is that the Gospels say nothing at all about Jesus' marriage.

In recent years, several theologians have begun to circle that silence and plumb it from a variety of perspectives.

Pioneer studies have been conducted by Protestant theologian Dr. William Phipps, who situates the discussion of Jesus' sexuality in historical, biblical, and theological context. This discussion also includes Jesus' relationship with women. In his two volumes, *Was Jesus Married?* and the *Sexuality of Jesus,* Phipps focuses on historical evidence that illuminates the importance and influence of the cultural setting in which Jesus lived and died.

Phipps maintains that the first step in comprehending the historical Jesus is the full realization that he was raised by faithful Jews and that his Jewishness persisted throughout his life in spite of his rigorous criticism of conventional Judaism. [3]

One of Phipps's arguments supporting his belief that Jesus was married is the fact that had Jesus, who was a good Jew, *not been married*, his disciples and opponents would surely have mentioned it, for it would have differed so markedly from the general custom of that time and place. [4] Marriage was the norm in the Jewish faith-culture. Phipps notes that in early Judaism two of the principal responsibilities a father had to his son were to have him circumcised and to find him a wife. [5] Celibacy, in theory and practice, would have been considered an aberration. [6]

Still other theologians approach Jesus' sexuality in a way that incorporates contemporary understandings of human behavior. Included in this is the realization that sexuality appears to be intrinsically and not accidentally related to one's capacity to love. They argue that the possibility of a sexless Jesus would be unlikely, if not humanly impossible.

John Erskine writes of Jesus, "His character renders it for me utterly impossible that his youth and manhood could have been unmoved by warm human emotions. . . . If he really took our human nature upon him and was human, then he had our equipment of sex." [7]

Tom Driver observes, "The absence of all comment [in the Gospels] about Jesus' sexuality cannot be taken to imply that he had no sexual feelings. . . . I cannot imagine a *human* tenderness, which the gospels show to be characteristic of Jesus, that is not fed in some degree by the springs of passion. The human alternative to sexual tenderness is not asexual tenderness but sexual fear."[8] Jesus lived in his body as other men do.

Likewise, psychiatrist-theologian Jack Dominian reflects upon the necessary connection in Jesus between self-acceptance and genuine openness to others: "This response was unhampered by any need to reject, deny or condemn any part of himself, hence of others. . . . although the evidence is extremely limited, it is hard to see how such total acceptance and availability could have been present without including full awareness of his sexuality."[9]

Richard McBrien claims that "to accept a Jesus who is at once fully human and yet immune from sexual desires is to stretch not only one's imagination but also one's theological convictions about the incarnation, and the fundamental goodness of creation, the human body, and human sexuality."

McBrien goes on to point out that while it does not necessarily follow that Jesus, as a necessary expression of his humanity, actually did engage in sexual activities, neither does it follow that sexual activity within marriage would have been inconsistent with Jesus' divinity. But to think and speak of Jesus as asexual or even anti-sexual may finally undermine the humanity of Jesus and would thereby remove an indispensable basis for redemption and salvation.[10]

The Church Fathers as far back as the fourth century would validate this. At that time they stated, "What was not assumed was not redeemed." (*Quod non est assumptum non est sanatum*).[11]

Don't we really tell ourselves "Of course, Jesus was human . . . but not too human! Of course, he had needs; it's just that he couldn't afford to get involved in relationships." In short, we find it safer, neater, easier to make him asexual. And after saying all that, we set up Jesus as our

perfect model of humanity and try to pattern our lives after
him.

The Body of Christ continues to be surrounded by doubt,
confusion, and controversy. Docetism, which stated that
Jesus only "seemed" to have a body, was early condemned as
a heresy. But has it disappeared? In our day, that Docetism
lingers on in regard to Jesus' sexuality. This means that
Christians are not sure about the humanity of him whom they
call True Man. And this uncertainty confuses us about what it
means for us to be human. One of the signs of this confusion
is the chaos in sexual mores at the present time, which the
Church has not been able to overcome and which it has
actually helped bring about because it has not adequate teaching with regard to the relation between sex and humanity. [12]

If, indeed, we believe that Jesus was like us in all things but
sin, then are we saying that to be sexual is sinful? Are we
saying that in creating our human nature as sexual beings God
made a mistake? How do we reconcile this with our understanding of the goodness and importance of each part of our
body? "If one member suffers, all the members suffer with it;
if one member is honored, all the members share its joy"
(1 Cor 12:26).

Caught in a cross fire which says, on the one hand, that
sexuality is a gift from God and, on the other, that our sexual
needs are a result of our weakness and sinfulness, it is no
wonder that Christians feel confused and guilty, often to the
point of sexual self-hatred. They feel spiritually and bodily
disintegrated at the very core of their beings.

If we are offended at the thought that Jesus was ever
inclined toward a full sexual union, perhaps we're offended
because we suspect that sex is unworthy of the Savior since

it's unworthy of us. Yet, in the process, we project our anger and alienation onto him. [13]

Though the writing and research will continue, perhaps the most critical question for us to examine about Jesus' sexuality is not whether he was genitally active or even married. Rather, we should reflect on the impact that the model of a sexless Savior has had on our Christian legacy over the centuries.

Increasingly, young adults in the Church today refer to the mystery of "the missing body" . . . Christ's missing body. But the body young adults refer to is not the body of the suffering Christ with whose loneliness and alienation they so often relate in their own lives. Rather it is for the missing body of a Jesus who, in the words of one twenty-five-year-old, "surely must have smiled and hugged and had a sense of humor. Why," she asks, "must he always be a study in misery?"

Like Mary Magdalene on Easter morning, young adults go to Christ's tomb looking for his body. With her, they weep . . . "because the Lord has been taken away, and I do not know where they have put him" (Jn 20:13). The emptiness of that tomb echoes in the lives of their generation in a new way.

In faith, they go from place to place praying, believing it is critical that Christ's body be resurrected in the Church today.

"We should be grateful to them," says a priest who teaches in a boys' high school. "We teach them that Jesus is our model for humanity. To them, that includes someone who struggles with questions of sexuality. Increasingly, that issue arises and is discussed when young adults gather. The Church is going to have to deal with it and not dismiss it with a simple 'We'll never know.' All young adults are asking from us is that we be open to discussions about Jesus' sexuality. I think that's both understandable and fair.

"Either Jesus emerges to them as a believable person or he doesn't," the priest continues. "If he's their model for humanity and they can't relate to him in his humanness, then they may stand in awe of him or even be afraid of him, but he'll never be the friend or brother to them that they need. The question is not one of genitality but integrity. Their perception of who Jesus was has a profound effect on their relationships with others in the areas of love and intimacy."

As Christians, we can only speculate on the impact a sexual Jesus might have had on the lives of today's young adults. Many say they relate to him primarily as a person who accepted pain and suffering. Have we received a complete picture of Jesus, they ask? The central message of Christianity is Resurrection . . . the triumph of love! We are an Easter people.

Jesus' overwhelming passion was love, not suffering.

"Why," they ask, "doesn't the Church present the image of the Risen Christ with the same religious fervor that it presents the image of Christ crucified? Wouldn't that event empower people even more?"

Like the apostles on the road to Emmaus, young adults need to be energized by encountering a Jesus who is impossible to forget. . . . One of whom they too can say . . .

Were not our hearts burning inside us as he talked to us on the road and explained the Scripture to us? (Luke 24:32)

We can only wonder how different their lives might have been had they known him on their journeys, whether they would have made different choices or decisions if they had known Jesus as Lover. Would they have felt affirmed in their sexuality, in their ability to say yes or no, if they believed that Jesus embraced that struggle in his own life?

If Christianity is the greatest love story of all time, then we must also ask what kind of love stories have flowed from it? And who has it celebrated as its lovers?

How have these lovers witnessed to the goodness of God's creation . . . "the glory of God is man . . . and woman . . . fully alive!"? In what ways have they praised God with their bodies by celebrating the gift of their sexuality?

How has the Church viewed marriage, the one social institution that Jesus blessed and used in his parables to illustrate the Gospel?

Indeed, what couples has the Church canonized as marriage partners, as eloquent witnesses to that sacrament?

We think immediately of the Holy Family, and yet we have been so overwhelmed with Mary's image as virgin-mother that it has left us little room to think of her as partner or wife. Joseph, the strong, silent protector, seems always to be in the shadow. We must struggle to see his identity in the light.

The annals of church history are replete with men and women whose heroic love for God has lifted them up to the status of sainthood. But more often than not, they have been celebrated for their suffering and martyrdom. Women have a further designation as virgin-martyr, which links their asexuality to their sainthood and sometimes to their suffering. (The Common of the Saints in the official *Sacramentary* lists six categories: Virgin-Martyr, Several Virgin-Martyrs, Virgin Not A Martyr, Martyr Not A Virgin, Several Martyrs Not Virgins, and Holy Woman not a Martyr.)

In two of those Commons, this prayer is said: "O God, one of the marvelous examples of Your power was granting the

victory of martyrdom *even to women*." [14] It is also noteworthy
that many of the women who have been canonized have been
foundresses of women's religious congregations with the status of nuns, thereby signifying consecrated virginity and/or
vows of celibacy.

Womanlist, a compendium of women's achievements,
includes under a chapter titled "Women of Faith," still
another category: Prostitutes Who Became Saints. Once
again, the focus is on a negative image of sexuality, further
reinforcing the stereotype of woman as temptress or whore.
The entry begins: "Who was the Magdalene? The Gospels
tell us very little about the woman who, next to the Virgin
Mary, is the most important female in Christian tradition." [15]

To speak of Christianity's love stories is to summon an
image of twinkling fireflies in the blackness of a summer's
night. We are surprised, delighted, awed at the sight of those
sudden sparks which light up the vast and seemingly unend-
ing darkness. But even as we reach out to touch them, they
are gone.

Where are the love stories and the lovers whose sparks of
fire defy even the blackest night of church history? Why do
they elude us? What truths do they contain that we need to
hear?

If love is the heartbeat of Christianity, then it should be the
Church's mission to share the stories of its lovers from every
pulpit in Christendom.

To follow Jesus in the name of love is to be a friend to
another, and in that friendship to overcome tremedous obsta-
cles and to dream impossible dreams. In a world ragged with
tattered hopes and threadbare faith, Christians need to be able
to draw a blanket of warmth and comfort around themselves,
a patchwork quilt made up of the stories of people who, as

both spiritual and sexual partners, sought to build the kingdom based on the love they shared together.

Like the fireflies in the night, their love stories call out to us. They remind us of the hidden joy and passion that we must begin to claim as part of our Christian legacy. Surely, like these fireflies who surprise the darkness, their stories can ignite our faith in ourselves to be lovers, too.

The shreds of information we have challenge our imagination. What are the untold stories folded into the stark statements made to us by historians?

We read bits of information about St. Olympias, a fourth-century deaconess who was described as "the principal and most beloved of the women who were faithful to St. John Chrysostom after he was finally banished from Constantinople." Seventeen of Chrysostom's extant letters from exile are addressed to Olympias and are filled with gratitude to her, sympathy for her trial, and encouragement and eloquent praise for her enthusiasm. [16]

What arouses one's curiosity about this relationship is that Chrysostom's writings clearly indicate that he was a male supremacist of the first order and his attitude toward women was one of ownership. His antimarriage tracts were written with what has been described as "savage language." [17]

Yet we read of his "unusually deep and tender relationship late in his life with the deaconess Olympias." [18] What was the nature of that relationship? In the struggle and turmoil of their lives, how were they changed by their devotion to one another? What conversion of heart did Chrysostom experience that caused him to reach out to Olympias? And most importantly, what can we learn from him about a person's ability to transcend deep-seated sexism and fear of women?

The relationship between St. Francis de Sales and St. Jane de Chantal, with whom he founded the Order of the Visitation of Mary in the early seventeenth century, has been described as "one of the most perfect in the annals of the saints." [19] Francis said,

"In Madame de Chantal, I have found the perfect woman whom Solomon sought in Jerusalem and found not." [20] And in a letter to her, St. Francis wrote "Know that I hold myself closely bound to you and seek to know no more, save that this bond is not incompatible with any other, whether of vow or of marriage." [21]

The one fact that everyone knows about St. Clare of Assisi is that "she was the one whom St. Francis loved best, and that between them there was a bond of strength such as God alone can forge." [22]

Their story, popularized in the film, *Brother Sun, Sister Moon*, is acknowledged to be one of the great spiritual love stories of all time. The letters written to one another by these two ardent friends should have been made available to every adolescent who searched for models to emulate. Their common vision of joy in poverty might well have inspired the children of the sixties to challenge the Church, as did Francis and Clare, to new understandings of simplicity.

The legacy of their love can be seen in the fruit of their labors. The Franciscan Order of Friars and the Order of Poor Clare Nuns testify even today to their mutual dream of building the kingdom.

In Spain, the deep and life-giving friendship of St. Teresa of Avila, named a Doctor of the Church in 1970, and her disciple, St. John of the Cross, is yet another example. Together they worked tirelessly to introduce reform and new vitality into the disordered religious life of the Carmelites in the latter half of the sixteenth century. Their writings have become classic texts on the spiritual life. As mystics and tireless workers, they left their shining signatures on church history.

The one love story which has come down to us is, not unsurprisingly, a story of passion clearly etched in scandal and sorrow. It concerns Abelard and Heloise. Peter Abelard was a French philosopher and churchman of the twelfth century and was acknowledged to be a bold and original thinker; students came to him from everywhere in Europe. Abelard fell in love with Heloise, who was the niece of Canon Fulbert of Notre Dame. When news of their love reached Fulbert, Heloise, who had borne Abelard a son, denied their marriage since she did not want to stand in the way of Abelard's advancement in the Church. Fulbert in his rage, however, had Abelard castrated. [23] Heloise became a nun and Abelard a monk. The Church later condemned him as a heretic. When he went to live in Nogent-sur-Seine, his students followed him.

Heloise and Abelard wrote letters to each other until he died. They are described as among the most moving expressions of love ever written. When the two lovers died, they were buried at each other's side. [24]

Perhaps one of the reasons this love story continues to claim our interest is because we cannot accept the fact that love and marriage are still seen to be impediments to ordained ministry in the Church. Only by denying, negating, and finally rejecting the legitimacy of their love relationship were these two lovers able to "absolve" themselves of its mutually life-giving nourishment. The gift of love these two people shared with one another came to be seen as a kind of crime.

Do we not have the right to marry a believing woman
like the rest of the apostles and the brothers of the Lord
and Cephas? (1 Cor 9:5)

Despite the fact that biblical theology affirms that everything is created good, the most gnawing heresy in Christianity
continues to be that the sensual is evil and that decontamina-
tion is effected by pommeling the pleasure drive to death.

Yet, according to the Gospels, Jesus' anguish was over
human recalcitrance to extend love more broadly, not over
whether to renounce love of a woman. [25] Jesus was a lover.
He lived and died so that we would be lovers, too.

The deepest and most profound experience of relationship
is to be found in friendship. Jesus taught us the total meaning
of friendship not only in his own healing ministry to others
but in the gift of his very life.

Yet we seem to think that Jesus was above the need for
friendships in his daily life. Why do we deny Jesus the
possibility of having a loving friend he could turn to? What
greater gift could we wish to give him? Indeed, what greater
gift has he given us than our own love relationships?

If today's young adults, whom some have called the Love
Generation, grew up without an understanding of Jesus as
Lover, then perhaps the Church at this time should provide
them with the model of revolutionary love Jesus came to
bring. Jesus touched with love because he touched with
perfect integrity. His touch was without violence, without
manipulation, without an intention to compromise, to seduce,
or to abuse.

But does this mean that Jesus did not know what it was to
be human, to feel desire, to feel longing, to feel overwhelmed
with a need to be held in the arms of someone who
understood?

We need only imagine Jesus in his final agony, looking down from the cross at his dear friend Mary Magdalene, remembering how she cared for him in Galilee, how she accompanied him to Jerusalem and, at the risk of her life, stood with him here.

> The Lord God said: "It is not good for the man to be alone. I will make a suitable partner for him." (Gn 2:18)

Over the centuries, we have gradually stripped Jesus of his humanity. We have done this by denying that he had human doubts and fears and needs. And in the process, we no longer even take his temptations seriously.

As Christians, we have come to a place where we profess a human love story . . . the Incarnation . . . without a human lover. We speak of Jesus as being fully human, but we cannot speak of him as a sexual being.

How long can we continue to present Jesus as the Believable One unless we image him as a Lover? As a Church, we must search our hearts to find out why this thought makes us so afraid.

James Nelson reminds us that our ways of knowing are always wedded to our ways of loving . . . love is always an affair of the body-self and not just the mind . . . love and sexuality can never be separated, for both are the impulse toward communion. [26]

> Then, taking bread and giving thanks, he broke it and gave it to them, saying, "This is my body to be given for you. Do this as a remembrance of me" (Lk 22:19).

Can we imagine Jesus saying to us, "Remember that, being human, I needed to give love and receive love through my body, in accordance with my Father's plan for creation. Remember, each time you touch one another with love, you touch my Body. And whenever you witness to me as Lover, you truly remember me."

SLUMBERSONG

Some day, when I lose you
will you be able to sleep without
my whispering myself away
like a linden's crown above you?

Without my waking here and laying down
words, almost like eyelids,
upon your breasts, upon your limbs,
upon your mouth?

Without my closing you and leaving
you alone with what is yours,
like a garden with a mass
of melissas and star-anise?

Rainer Maria Rilke

CHAPTER SIX

BURIED TREASURE

Pages from a journal. . . .

Last night, I really got scared. I realized that Bob and I may no longer have a relationship. And I feel so lost and alone and isolated. But at the same time, I'm realizing this morning that I have to *not* need him in order to relate to him in a healthy way. He has not made any attempts to get together with me or find out how I'm doing. That does not fit into my definition of what friendship is all about. I must stand on my own two feet.

There's a lot of anger in me right now over this whole relationship—anger and hurt. I do not want to continue in an unhealthy, one-sided emotional relationship. How much can I give—give in—without expecting anything in return? How much longer can he expect me to be "understanding" and "patient" as he repeats that he loves me and needs me? He assures me that his priesthood does not need to "get in the way". . . .

. . .

Bob has been calling me and has been so responsive to me lately. I'm off balance. What does he want, what does he need from me? What part of myself can I risk in the relationship? Help me, God, help me! Take my hand, show me the way.

. . .

Had a terrible time yesterday and today but especially last night. I wanted Bob to come out here so badly. We were both playing so many games, it was pitiful. I wanted to be

near him, to touch him, but I can't allow myself to be that
vulnerable anymore. Sometimes I feel so good about our
relationship—other times, so sad. I need to talk to him.

. . .

I seem unable to concentrate on the Scripture readings this
morning. Thoughts of Bob keep running through my head
and heart.
I hold him up to you, God—as well as my fear and
confusion about our relationship. I ask for healing, for an
open, nonclutching, nonpossessive heart. I ask for the grace
to allow him the freedom to be who he is, to love whomever
he wants to love as intensely as he is loved by someone like
me.

. . .

I'm feeling rotten right now. I feel empty and very
depressed and lifeless. I feel like crying, but the tears won't
come. My unreal expectations about my relationship with
Bob always surface after we've had a sexual encounter. I'm
angry about the secretiveness of our relationship. Why can't I
accept the fact that he's a priest before he's a person. It's a
dead-end, one-way relationship. Help me, God, help me to
breathe.

. . .

Let go, Ann, let go.
Trust in God.
It's okay to:
  be afraid
  feel lost
  love Bob
Let go, Ann.
Let go.

You're okay, Ann. You're loving, growing, hurting,
striving, wanting.
Rest. Sleep. Trust.
Tomorrow is another day.

. . .

Bob called and told me how much he missed me, how
much he needed me and that he doesn't deserve me and
wouldn't blame me if I never saw him again. He sounded so
tired, so lost, my heart went out to him. He said we needed to
be together, next weekend maybe we could go away.

. . .

Dear Loving Lord . . .
I am writing you to tell you that I am no longer bargaining
with you about my relationship with Bob. I am asking you to
give me the courage to let go . . . to LET GO FOREVER
of whatever this thing is I have for Bob. Give me the guts to
CUT IT—the grace to love myself enough to know that I do
not need anyone to complete me—that I am good and
beautiful and sensitive, even if I have made mistakes in
relationships.
Help me to be patient with myself, compassionate. Don't
let me turn in on myself in the wrong way.

. . .

Bob called last night and after just a few minutes, he said,
"I have to go now to visit a friend." Half an hour later, as I
was leaving to go to the library, I opened the door and he was
standing there. He was exhausted and we sat and had tea and
he kept holding my hand and wouldn't let go of it. But it was
a gentle holding, too gentle.
This morning I feel lost, alone, scared, frustrated, angry,
hurt, shy, vulnerable.

Bob is so tied up inside himself and living everything inside himself and living everything out in his head. He goes round and round incessantly. More than anything, I was surprised to hear him say that he is scared of and feels guilty about his sexuality. I was not aware of just how deep the fears go. No two people who are so scared should get together, it seems to me. Would we just reinforce each other's fears and guilts, or would we enable each other to become freer and freer? And why do I keep thinking it is possible with priesthood in the way?

. . .

"Rely not on your strength in following the desires of your heart" (Sir 5:2).
Lord, I believe, help my unbelief. . . .

. . .

My eyes filled with tears yesterday when I thought of the children we will never have. I think we would have made very good parents.

. . .

Let go, Ann, let go. Say, believe, accept the fact that by going away, you will never see him, hold him, touch him again.

. . .

" . . . birds build—but not I build; no but strain, Time's eunuch, and not breed one work that wakes. Mine, O Thou lord of life, send my roots rain." [1]

Gerard Manley Hopkins

SATURDAY'S CHASTITY

That one lost rib
pains me
on celibate evenings
when even the breeze
seems godless.
Failing
in a restless attempt
to clothe
this naked knowledge,
I am exiled
from my paradise
by a flaming sword
of lonely fear
which forces
this clay vessel, unglazed,
to the edge—
and regretful smoke
in the abyss
pulls me down.
   (Praise comes painfully
   while one is being fired.)
Just to be united
for a moment—
but the earth
is an altar for sacrifices
and the weak,
like ashes,

are scattered
by the hollow breeze
into the dark night.

Albert Haase, OFM

CHAPTER SEVEN

CELIBACY

A Clash of Symbols

Celibacy: 1) the state of not being married; 2) abstention from sexual intercourse; abstention by vow from marriage.

Webster's Dictionary

"There is no true love in an atmosphere . . . of the collective; for the collective is the impersonal. If love is to be born and to become firmly established it must find an individualized heart and face." [1]

Teilhard de Chardin, SJ

One of the lenses through which today's young adults could view sexuality is through Pope John Paul II's illuminating words on virginity and celibacy.

"Virginity or celibacy, by liberating the human heart in a unique way . . . is that pearl of great price which is preferred to every other value no matter how great, and hence must be sought as the only definitive value.

"*It is for this reason that the Church throughout her history has always defended the superiority of this charism to that of marriage,* by reason of the wholly singular link which it has with the kingdom of God." [2] [Italics mine.]

. . .

By their symbols you shall know them.

For some celibacy is a curse, for others, a blessing. It has been described as a trust, a trap, a smokescreen, a status symbol. It has been lived out as a grace, a charism, a mystery, a call. The term most people would agree on is that it is a never-ending struggle.

"I know it has a value, a worth," said one religious, looking back over forty years of priesthood, "and I've tried to live it. But I wonder, in retrospect, is it worth it? It's all well and good to talk about 'responsible loving,' but what does that really mean in terms of people's needs and lives?"

"Celibacy is a mystery, all right," said a nun in her early forties. "Just when you think you've figured it out, the ground shifts. You do the best you can to balance your needs against your sanity. But somehow you're never sure; it's always a guessing game."

Game is a word which seems to surface often when talking to vowed religious.

Some liken celibacy to a chess game, one that began centuries ago, but whose effects continue to this day.

The symbol with which they most identify in that game is the pawn. Though the dictionary describes a pawn as one of the chess pieces of least value, a pawn is extremely important in that it can be used to further the purposes of another. It can block others. It is especially useful when it is used to protect the king's position, though it can never be a king itself.

And what is perhaps most important of all, a pawn can be sacrificed easily.

Chess is, of course, played by two forces who are in opposition to each other. Naturally, the object of the game is to win.

This particular chess game, celibacy, is no exception. The forces compete under a variety of titles. There are the Black and White forces, the Body and Soul forces, and the Men and Women forces. There are many versions of the struggle and many consequences as a result of the struggle.

One version, with far-reaching consequences, took place in fourth-century Spain at the Council of Elvira. The Council's basic intention was to present a Christian ideal, to keep the faithful in the fold, and to combat idolatry and apostasy. The Spanish clerics, in their attempt to find communal identity, looked for a way to create a clerical image that would have a strong hold on the faithful.

The way the Spanish clergy chose to assert its power was by controlling the sexual behavior of its own members. Thus we have the account of Church's first demand for sexual continence of its *married clergy* and one which forbad the begetting of children. Unmarried clergy were prohibited from living with anyone but a sister or a daughter, but even these blood relatives had to be vowed virgins who had consecrated their virginity to God (Canon 27). [2]

The Church, it is said, then spent the next 700 years trying to legally enforce the rules which it had set down. Marriage for priests, deacons, and bishops became unlawful in the Western Church.

Dutch theologian Edward Schillebeeckx, OP, believes that the law of celibacy was the conclusion of a long history in which there was, at first, simply a law of abstinence applying to married priests. It appears that the dominant reason for the introduction of a law of abstinence was "ritual purity." [4]

In ancient times, the Eastern and Western Churches of the first ten centuries never thought of making celibacy a condition of entering the ministry: both married and unmarried men were welcome as ministers. From the fourth century on, church law, which was at that time new, contained a *lex continentiae*. . . . This was a liturgical law, forbidding sexual intercourse during the night before communicating the eucharist . . . (when) the Western churches began to celebrate the eucharist daily, in practice this abstinence became a permanent condition for married priests.[5] The ritual law of abstinence is the only decisive and the only determinative element in ecclesiastical legislation. It is, therefore, historically incorrect and ideological to regard the law of celibacy as a means used by the Church to acquire power, at least in antiquity and the Middle ages. *In later times, once the law was established, it began to function in the context of a struggle for power; but this has nothing to do with the reasons why it came into being.*[6] (Italics mine.)

Hans Küng notes that the Church took charismatic celibacy, which had its original place in monastic communities and was an express prohibition of marriage, and extended it to the whole clergy. "It was imposed," said Kung, "with often cruel and harsh measures."[7]

An example of this was the penalty of *enslavement* of the *offspring* of *clerics* (Council of Toledo in 655), a canon that was later incorporated in general law as well as the penalty of *enslavement* on the *wives of clerics* who violated the law of celibacy.[8]

Richard McBrien notes that when bishops began to be recruited from among those with some monastic training, they tended to bring with them some of their monastic mores, which included celibacy and "a certain disdain for ordinary human experiences."[9] He also cites the fact that celibacy was imposed on the Latin-rite clergy as a way of dealing with the alienation of property (the passing of church property into the private hands of a bishop's or priest's offspring). [10] Since many of the clergy were members of nobility, even royalty, the question of inheritance became a central issue. If a priest were married, who would inherit his land and worldly goods—the legal heirs (that is, the children) or the Church? Celibacy precluded the possibility of the former.

Schillebeeckx also confirms this interpretation, although he cites it as a motive of "very secondary importance" in the medieval law of celibacy. He does agree that "there was the medieval confiscation of the goods of 'priests sons', through which the church fought itself clear of the tutelage of secular powers. *In fact celibacy considerably increased the church's resources* (and thus the independence of the church over against princes and emperors.)" [11] (Italics mine.)

. . .

The crackdown came in the twelfth century at the first and second Lateran Councils when marriages of members of the clergy were declared to be illegal for the universal Church.

The position came to be justified and surrounded, in part, by statements from Paul, primarily in 1 Corinthians, chapter 7. But Paul was not antimarriage (7:5), nor did he believe celibacy was for everyone (7:7). It was only in the light of Christ's impending return that Paul called for celibacy. He believed the time was short (7:29), and he wanted the Corinthian Christians free from care (7:32). [12]

Yet for almost 800 years, that law has been essentially cast in concrete in the Roman Catholic tradition.

. . .

"Sorry," says one pastor in a rural Montana parish. "I try to keep my vow but to me the arguments for celibacy just don't stand up. There are just too many contradictions. How can the hierarchy talk about celibacy as a glorious tradition of the Church but sidestep the fact that the apostles were and remained married men?"

Scripture is full of evidence of that (italics mine in each reference):

- Jesus entered Peter's house and found *Peter's mother-in-law* in bed with a fever. He took her by the hand and the fever left her. She got up at once and began to wait on him. (Mt 8:14-15)
- A bishop must be irreproachable, *married only once.* . . . He must be a good manager of his own household, keeping *his children* under control without sacrificing his dignity. (1 Tm 3:2,4)
- Do we not have the *right to marry a believing woman like the rest of the apostles* and the brothers of the Lord and Cephus? (1 Cor 9:5)

"How can they allow married men to be ordained in some of the Eastern rites but not in the Western (Latin) rite?" the Montana pastor continues. He also questions the recent decision to accept a group of married Episcopalian priests into the active Roman Catholic ministry with the understanding that they would remain priests and retain their wives.

"They claimed they acted in the cause of ecumenism," comments the pastor, "but ecumenism, like justice and charity, begins at home."

Columnist Gary Wills says, simply, "In other words, the church is saying that what is forbidden to those inside is allowed to outsiders." He also notes that this "recruiting gesture comes after a time when one of America's most prominent married Catholics, John Cogley, was forced to become an Episcopalian in order to become a priest." [13]

"It's the Vatican version of the shell game," says one law student in Boston. "It's also sexual politics at its most sinister since the Anglicans requested to enter the Roman Catholic church in response to their church's decision to ordain women."

Gary Wills adds that "Church 'conservatives' are willing to welcome any allies against the threat of females polluting the sacristy." [14]

"If celibacy is a game," says a Baltimore priest who is a seminary professor, "then like any game, it has certain rules and restrictions for those who want to play. Nobody forces anyone to take the vow of celibacy unless they want to. If they accept the challenge and want the privileges of priesthood, they should be mature enough to accept the responsibilities. Priesthood, like marriage, doesn't offer anyone money-back guarantees."

"I wouldn't call celibacy a game as much as a gamble," offers a red-haired nun in a nursing order. "It's like any choice you make: you take your chances. Sometimes you win, sometimes you lose. The important thing is to keep working at it with faith and trust in God's love and mercy. You have to *decide* to live it as a positive value, as a freeing way of loving, both for yourself and others. Good friendships help you to keep your balance. Otherwise, celibacy becomes a necessary evil which you tolerate. It's something you learn to cope with, like a chronic infection or a rash."

"Celibacy's freeing, all right," says a priest in his early thirties. "It frees you to be a workaholic because you're always supposed to be available to everyone every hour of the night and day.

"In the seminary, I'd look at the guys working in the parishes and swear that I'd never fall into that 'over-booked calendar' trap. But things are different when you're in the system. Now I wonder if I look on a full calendar as a security blanket rather than a cover for my own loneliness. If I'm booked up, it must mean I'm needed, I'm important, I'm sought after. I keep having this fantasy that I go to the doctor and *he orders me to slow down*, or *he* won't be responsible. It's like I need a double reason for saying no!"

"Celibacy can be anything you want it to be," says a religious brother who teaches in a New Orleans high school. "In that sense, I guess you could call it a game. Some religious feel that simply by not having sexual intercourse, they've fulfilled their obligations to celibacy. But I think it's much more than that. I think it begins with a sincere desire to work through your fear and distrust of sexuality. In a sense, to overcome your religious formation. That's not easy to do in a system that surrounds you with signposts that say Beware! Be careful! Danger! You get so you feel there's either a cloud or a question mark over every friendship you have with a man or a woman."

"It's a Catch-22," a Jesuit theologian admits. "You can't be a celibate unless you understand your sexuality, and you need people for that."

A priest in his thirties who is involved in support groups that contain both men and women explains, "while I find celibacy freeing in my life, I think it can also be used as an excuse for avoiding people and sidestepping friendships that could be very enriching. I think it's important for a minister to be both a functionary and a friend.

"One has only to look at Jesus," he continues, "and see how he was continually in the midst of people, giving to them and receiving from them. And he always had women with him. Women were his friends!

"I think that needs to be pointed out to people who bought the theory, either through fear or training, that for Jesus women were not 'occasions of sin.' "

In the Church, sin and sexuality were somehow seen to be silent partners. Even in marriage, genital sexuality was referred to as an obligation that was imposed, a duty. In canon law, sexual intercourse is referred to as "rendering the debt."

Yet even when genitality is renounced or transcended, as in the vow of celibacy, a haze hangs over it. Until very recently, celibacy was defined in the negative in terms of what one "gives up," rather than as a positive choice of one's creative power to love. In time, that negative energy seems to build boomerangs. Priest-psychologist Martin Pable writes:

> In my experience, the most frequent syndrome I have found among priests and religious is what I would call a "low key hostility." These are not angry people: they are quietly and passively resentful. They resent the burdens of celibacy, the ineptness of religious leadership, the confusion of theology, and the ingratitude of the faithful. Their prayer life, or lack of it, will often reveal that the low-kept hostility is also directed at God; somehow, He has let them down. Henri Nouwen called them the "grumpy children of God."
>
> My own belief is that the problems . . . are sociological and cultural. Religious men and women have experienced a stunning loss of status, a painful deglamorization of religious life. As a result, a good number of religious are no longer proud of their profession. They have a terrible feeling of being outsiders; they so much want to give, but nobody seems to need them. This is that painful experience of "non-validation" spoken about in the document on the spiritual renewal

of the American Priesthood: "It is a cruel suffering to feel useless, out of date, not needed, rejected; to experience the conflict of having to preach a Gospel the people do not want to hear." [15]

What is ironic is that for many young adults, both in and out of the Church, celibacy has been reappropriated. Some call it the new game in town. But it is hardly the brand of celibacy taught in the past in seminaries surrounded by real or imagined barbwire fences. It is, rather, celibacy as a "vacation" from sex, an escape from peer pressure, a way of saying "I'm not interested," "I'm not available," or "I don't want to put out the energy it takes to get involved."

"That's a game that's played all the time in religious life," says a nun-artist from Iowa. "Only it's not cool to talk about being a celibate. Instead, they talk about 'my vocation' in religious life or 'my priesthood': it's always the role, never the vow. Whether they admit it or not, they like to keep a little sexual energy out there for their ego, but they want to be safe and protected in the process. That's because most of them are either afraid because they're so out of touch with their feelings, or they're threatened by the women they know they need. So they do this little dance where they give out mixed messages. And if they get in deeper than they planned to, they act surprised if you take them seriously. They head back to the rectory, protected by their Roman collar and you find yourself sitting there asking yourself what happened and why.

"But if you try to talk to them about it, or ask them to take part of the responsibility for what happened, they act either crushed or aghast or furious. It's as though you're confronting them with the unthinkable: choosing between you and God."

"Everybody seems to talk about celibacy in terms of genitality, but what about celibacy as mind control?" asks a nun in public relations. "I think you can violate the vow of celibacy just as much by manipulating a person's feelings. By encouraging dependencies and playing emotional mind games, you can use a person's emotions as carelessly as you use their bodies."

"I feel strongly about the creative power of communication between celibates who are trying to honor their vow of chastity as well as celibacy," says a priest who works in media. "I've learned to trust my instinct on this and take the risks that need to be taken in order to maintain my integrity. Sometimes, you just have to say to someone, 'You know, I'm really attracted to you and I want you to know that. I also want you to know that I have a commitment that I want to keep.' "

Is it possible to be a loving human being and an effective minister without developing dependencies?

"It's possible, I guess, but I wouldn't call it healthy," says a nun who teaches psychology. "People need people. In religious life, dependency on God is professed publicly, but we also live in community."

Yet for religious, "community" takes many different forms in response to a variety of circumstances and needs. Relationships with one's own sex or the opposite sex are always in process; they range from casual dependencies to intimacies.

For some, the dependency takes the form of a daily phone call. For others, it is nourished by the devotion and loyalty of a faithful colleague in a professional setting. For still others, there is a sharing of one's life journey through the deepest forms of friendship. The demands of that friendship may vary, but the hallmark of such friendships is fidelity.

"It is possible, but never easy," volunteers one priest. "It's like trying to walk a tightrope or a high wire with both grace and discipline. You have to be alert and calm and centered. You have to look straight ahead, never backward. You have to be able to stand on your own two feet with confidence, yet know that you are vulnerable. Your arms must be outstretched at all times, to keep your balance; yet they must be kept free and floating to respond to sudden dangers and emergencies.

"On the high wire," he continues, "where you are responsible for a partner, the danger is obviously doubled. The partner is carried on one's back or stands on one's shoulders. Each of you must have perfect trust in one another. In a sense, you are two-in-one-flesh.

"On the high wire, the partners can never, for a moment, be unaware of one another. If the weight is shifted suddenly, the high wire's two support poles can easily be shaken. They can also be easily sabotaged from below.

"One should carefully consider the risks involved in walking the high wire. It is a very public place to be. The partners must conduct themselves with perfect poise since they cannot help being the subjects of scrutiny.

"For people who choose the high wire, there are two possibilities," the priest said. "They can enjoy the challenge indefinitely, until they decide that the strain is not worth it and it's time to climb down and get their feet on the ground.

"Or they can stay up there and take their chances on being careful, not careless; of not losing their footing or getting worn down.

"But they must also live with the fact that under the high wire, there is no net to catch them if they fall."

Reflecting on her past relationship with a priest, one thirty-year-old woman says that the most important thing she learned was not to be afraid of her loneliness. "I also learned that it's okay to know I'm needy, to be aware that I crave affection, to acknowledge that I found this priest attractive on a variety of levels. But the critical thing is to keep myself honest about what I need! Only then can I take repsonsibility for my feelings. Once that happens, I am free to make decisions. I own myself, after all!"

"I think one of the secrets of celibacy is to work actively at either finding or creating a support group," claims one priest, who spends as much time with married couples and their families as he does with the priest friends with whom he hikes and vacations each year. "The important thing is to be open, to realize that most crises can be averted if you check out what's happening in your life with people who know you and love you. Even if you seem to be growing in different directions, at times, you have to keep reaching out for help, and that's risky. But if you don't have faith in God and your friends, then where do you turn?"

By their symbols you shall know them.

A twenty-seven-year-old young adult who recently returned from overseas duty for the United Nations speaks of celibacy from the perspective of his memories. "In my experience," he says, "the Church itself doesn't take celibacy seriously. I am a product of Catholic education, grades one through twelve. The moment of truth came for me in a Catholic boys' high school in the sixties. I remember being taught all the way along, but especially by the brothers, that celibacy was a call, a sacred vow that religious took publicly to profess their dedication to God and the Church.

"At one point, I was seriously thinking of entering religious life and mentioned to some of the guys, some of my classmates, that I wasn't sure I could carry out celibacy. They looked at me as though I was crazy.

" 'Do you really believe all that stuff?' they said, shaking their heads. 'Believe me when I tell you that they're no more celibate than we are,' said one guy, laughing.

"What really blew me away was when I mentioned the same concern to one of the brothers who taught me and got essentially the same reply.

" 'Well,' he said, 'let's face it, Joe, we'd never have anyone going for vows if we took it *that* seriously, now would we?' And yet they stand up in those religion classes and teach it. Why? I remember feeling stupid and angry at the same time," he says. "I guess I really grew up that day."

"Sexuality is confusing enough when you're a teenager," says a young adult woman who is a city planner. "But when you surround it with religious double messages, you compound the problems for an adolescent in the midst of his or her psycho-sexual development."

"And if that adolescent is a seminarian, you are compounding the problem even further," states a seminary professor. "You can't put a kid in a same-sex 'incubator' at the beginning of such a critical growth period when his body is in such an uproar and expect him to be unaware of his sexuality."

Celibacy seems to be only one of many "confusions" for young adults who are growing up in a culture that is becoming increasingly sexually aware.

"If you ask me, I think the Church's whole choice of sexual symbols is weird," says a twenty-four-year-old medical student. "They talk about 'Mother Church,' who is the 'Bride of Christ.' Then they talk about nuns being 'brides of Christ,' but where does that leave the brothers? Are they 'brides,' too? And what does it say when an all-male priesthood dedicates itself to serving a church called 'Mother'? It sounds like the Church has a sexual identity crisis to me."

Celibacy as a life-style can have dramatic, critical moments.

"I think I came to terms with celibacy in the doctor's office," says a bright, talented nun in her early thirties. "I remember that the doctor took off his glasses and leaned back in his chair and looked at me.

" 'Sister,' he said, 'your breasts are a veritable garden of tumors. And as for the dull ache you describe, it is a condition I can only describe as advanced pelvic congestion. It's as though your body has ganged up on you.' "

She holds her face in her hands and looks away, her eyes suddenly brimming with tears.

"All of a sudden, I was aware of what was happening," she says softly. '*I want the child I will never have*,' my body was screaming back at me."

Many young adults recall the fascinating aura of mystery which surrounded priests and nuns. They saw the celibate religious receive "instant respect" and were impressed with their obvious status. Some saw the mystery of celibacy as protective covering. Others found it a sexual challenge.

"It's the old 'forbidden fruit' theory," says a psychologist from New Jersey, who spent the sixties in the seminary in his late teens and twenties. "Celibacy, by its very prohibitions, guarantees a preoccupation with sexuality. You always want what you don't have or think you can't get."

A priest who left the active ministry during that decade admits that "I was never so attractive to women before or since. The priest as 'mystery man' or the nun as 'untouchable' surround religious with an aura of secrecy which can be both appealing and challenging. It can also provide them with a shield, or protection, from accountability: self-disclosure to others and self-revelation within."

One thirty-five-year-old priest spoke candidly about his coping mechanisms for celibacy, which he was in the process of examining.

"So I'm not Superman. I learned to live with that long ago. I may wear a Roman collar, but I'm an ordinary human being, plus or minus a few talents I've been given by the grace of God.

"It's just that I'm so tired of feeling full of self-hatred for the needs I have and the fantasies that I seem to spend more and more time indulging in. Sometimes I wonder if that's my real world or my sanity.

"My support group is great but they can't do it for me. I've either got to decide whether I'm going to spend the rest of my life using women to take the edge off my loneliness or whether I'm going to claim the fact that I feel incomplete in my priesthood and need to move on.

"The thought of growing old in a prostitute's bed doesn't appeal to me. Neither does the thought of getting my jollies with other men's wives."

"I wish there were a magic answer," muses a nun who directs a retreat house for religious. "All of life is a struggle; nothing is perfect. If you choose religious life today, then part of that choice is celibacy. But you have to work at it just like you have to work at a marriage. Life is a trade-off. If you can't honor your vow in a life-giving way, then I think you need to reevaluate your commitment. The important thing is to keep on growing. If celibacy keeps you from that, then I think the only honest thing is to move into another way of loving. I don't believe that in the process of serving God we're supposed to suffocate."

Donald Goergen, author of *The Sexual Celibate*, believes there is more repressed anger than repressed sexuality among celibate people. "It is easy for a celibate person who is striving to be deeply Christian to deny negative feelings," he asserts.

"Adults frequently find it unacceptable to express anger openly. Nevertheless, anger eventually comes out. . . . Admitting anger does not necessarily mean immediately expressing it: admitting the anger, however, is necessary to the constructive handling of it. It is worthwhile for every celibate person to take anger seriously. Because anger was considered one of the seven capital sins, we are afraid of it. Anger can be un-Christian; it can also be Christian. Jesus himself showed the ability to express anger when he felt it necessary." [16]

"Celibacy?" says a parish priest who is still referred to as the top athlete in his seminary class. "Yeah, I'm celibate. I can look you straight in the eye and say that and stand before my God and say it, too.

"For me, it's no call or gift or anything as fine sounding as that," he says. "It's a matter of obedience. It's that simple. And I can also tell you that if they changed the rule tomorrow, I'd be down at that marriage bureau like a shot."

Most church-watchers agree that celibacy for religious seems to have shifted from clear-cut, black-and-white categories to twenty shades of gray. "In the old days, we used to be given bromides like 'You'll never miss what you haven't had,' " says a vocation director. "But if things continue as they are now, those days are gone forever.

"Today it's almost impossible to get candidates who haven't been either heterosexually or homosexually active," he continues. " 'It's the Church's problem, not our problem!' they tell us. 'My concern and yours should be whether or not I'm going to be a human, loving minister who can relate to people with understanding and honesty.'

" 'But I can't do that by myself,' they say. 'I need other people—all kinds of people!—to walk with me, care for me, love me enough to call me to accountability. I just can't limit my love to a single community.'

" 'Maybe I can live without genitality but not without intimacy. Beyond that, I'll just have to trust myself.' "

The only choice vocation directors have, they say, is to trust that the candidates will honor their vow.

"When I look back," says a silver-haired religious, "I realize how scared I was of women. Those were the days when 'particular friendships' were forbidden, where you were not 'allowed' to have a best friend in your class or community, and you certainly couldn't have anything to do with women. All those rules and regulations and scruples, those sessions with your confessor," he sighs, shaking his head. "Control was synonymous with holiness. You had nowhere to put that love, no one to share it with, so you turned in on yourself and just kept praying. The hardest thing was to wake up one day and realize that when all was said and done, you didn't know how to love."

Fortunately, medical professionals in the Church are attempting to counteract the results of such training and to rechannel destructive, negative energy into enabling, positive strength.

James J. Gill and Linda Amadeo, in an article in *Human Development*, stated that while celibates enjoy no exemption from most of the ordinary experiences of life that provoke anxiety among married persons, there are, nevertheless, many reasons why celibate religious persons run a higher risk of experiencing anxiety. One reason is that their "pursuit of perfection" is pitted against the constant possibility that their impulses, wishes, fantasies, thoughts, or behavior are less than what their relentless superego is demanding.

Trying to live a life of vowed obedience is another reason for anxiety. According to these writers, "Only a person who truly believes that doing God's will is all that matters and the superior's final decision represents His preference can hope to keep this anticipatory anxiety to a minimum."

The problem of intimacy in relationships is still another reason for celibate religious to experience anxiety. Gill and Amadeo state that many priests in a psychological study revealed a growth-paralyzing anxiety over their relationships with both women and men.

"If I become a close friend of a woman, will I risk becoming sexually involved? If I share life too deeply and emotionally with another male person, is it going to reveal a homosexual tendency in myself that I can't accept or handle?

"Not only positive (tender, affectionate, sexual, loving) inclinations can produce conflicts and anxiety in celibates; negative responses in themselves can prove just as stressful to them. Repressing anger, fear, disappointment, and other similarly painful affective states—as many celibates do, since they think it wrong to feel or express those emotions openly— sets up the stage for intense and prolonged tension and anxiety."

While stating the high success rate among countless celibate religious and clergy who have sought help through individual or group counseling and psychotherapy, Gill and Amadeo also point out that "the emotionally flexible and expressive Jesus was a perfect model of free, not uptight or anxious humanity." [17]

How do today's priests and religious feel they could have been better prepared to live as celibates? In their seminary training and religious formation, what do they wish they had been taught or told?

"*Anything!*" says one blond, blue-eyed nun who is a dance therapist. "We got hours and hours and hours on poverty and hours and hours on obedience and about twenty nervous minutes on chastity."

"I would have appreciated more guidance on developing a creative prayer life," says a priest who is a diocesan director of education. "We had spiritual directors, but that somehow turned into more of a counseling situation than an experience of prayer."

Were spirituality and sexuality ever seen to be synonymous?

"Are you kidding?" a priest in his early fifties laughs, adding, "If anything, they canceled each other out."

Moral theologian Philip Keane, SS, suggests that part of the reason why celibacy and virginity are fairly often lived poorly is that many celibates and virgins have not really *chosen* celibacy or virginity. Rather, they have accepted celibacy or virginity as a necessary evil.

"They have perceived their real choice as being for priesthood (even women can have this perception, theologically speaking) and put up with celibacy as part of the bargain. Or they have perceived their real choice as being for radical Christianity and tolerate virginity because, unlike the radically Christian sects in Protestantism (such as Mennonites, Hutterites), the only form of radical Christianity open to Catholics is a religious life which includes virginity.

"In any case," Keane continues, "the point is that the forced choice of Catholicism's present legislation can contribute to the clouding over of the gospel values which celibacy and virginity are supposed to proclaim." [18]

And what of those celibates and virgins who have made a positive, creative decision to be celibate? The light and life of their important witness is so often diminished or lost in the "package deal" of mandatory celibacy.

Presenting a realistic picture of mature celibate loving as a life-style would be aided by considering it as "the work of a lifetime," not as an instant charism of grace.

"Today," Keane explains, when we see celibacy and virginity as styles of loving we are aware that celibates and virgins must face and transcend different facets of life at different times. In one's twenties, for instance, the big question may be learning to live without a spouse. In the thirties and forties, the question may be learning to live without children. In older years the question may be learning to live without the security of one's own home or supportive context. Loving for virgins or celibates, as for anyone else, is an ongoing task rather than a fully accomplished reality." [19]

"I don't believe anyone can talk about choosing celibacy unless they've experienced other possibilities," says Sister Marjorie Tuite, OP. "If you have loved deeply and have known what the potential for growth and integration would be in such a relationship . . . and *then* have chosen celibacy as an expression of faithfulness to mission, then I think you are qualified to say you have made a *free and informed choice.*

"Otherwise," she continues, "no matter how noble the decision, the choice is made in a vacuum. Celibacy can only be fully tested against the experience of a love relationship," says Sister Marjorie. "Then the choice to be celibate becomes an active one, a daily choice, year in and year out, over the course of lifetime. It is never easy, but in another way, you are never alone in the same way again. You are called to both embrace your memories and move beyond them. But forever after, whatever way you reach out to the other, whatever love you show others, flows from those memories.

"Celibacy then becomes a gift you give to others because with it comes the wisdom of an understanding heart," she says.

"If Jesus were celibate, and we do not know this for certain, then it would seem to me that celibacy would have to have been a continuing choice for him, as well. How is it possible to be human and not to have loved another?" she asks.

The concept of freedom surfaces with predictable regularity in all discussions of celibacy. The balance between what celibacy frees one "for" and frees one "from" appears to be the central issue. It is a question which each religious must answer in terms of personal needs and integrity.

It must also be measured against the legacy of love that Jesus brought to all people. "I came that they might have life, and have it to the full" (Jn 10:10).

For some, celibacy has provided freedom for service to others. For these people, celibacy has been lived out in a lifetime of loving that has been a source of blessings known fully only to God.

For others, it has been a faithful, tear-stained stumbling . . . a never-ending struggle. As they have attempted to minister to others, they have lived with a terrible loneliness within.

"If I did not believe that 'God is always close to the broken-hearted,' " says a gay religious, "I could not continue on."

"For me, ten o'clock at night is the worst time," says a thirty-five-year-old priest who is a recovering alcoholic. "The day is over and you haven't stopped running since morning when you said six o'clock Mass.

"You open the cupboard . . . 'One little drink, just a thimbleful!' you say. 'After the day I've put in, I deserve it.' Besides, you rationalize, it's safer to wrap yourself around a bottle than to wrap yourself around a woman."

"And then there are the love stories," begins a nun who has been a spiritual director for almost three decades. "The untold love stories of people in religious life could fill a million volumes in a thousand libraries. In a sense, those stories are the buried treasure of the Church. All that suffering and longing and sacrifice in the name of celibacy. I wonder what Jesus would tell us to do if he were here?"

The chorus of voices calling for optional celibacy continues. The People of God believe they have a right to be heard.

In 1976, the Detroit Call-to-Action Conference, an assembly of 1,340 official representatives of 155 dioceses, including 110 bishops, called for the American bishops to petition Rome to change the present law on celibacy.

More than half of the 59,000 celibate priests in the United States believe celibacy should be optional. By 1989, according to statistics, forty-one percent of the celibate priests in our country will be at least fifty-five years old.

In a 1975 resolution, the National Federation of Priests' Councils supported the full utilization of married priests in America. The National Conference of Diocesan Vocation Directors has called for the use of the talents of married priests in an official ministry. Parishes are closing in many areas due to a shortage of priests, and in some places the people are deprived of Sunday Mass. Parishioners are questioning their bishops whether the law of mandatory celibacy is more important than the Church's evangelical mission and the people's spiritual needs. [20]

The Southeast Asian bishops recently requested of the Pope clearance to ordain married men as priests. [21]

By their symbols you shall know them.

In Rome, optional celibacy continues to be a non-question.

Pope John Paul II called celibacy the "lofty inheritance of the Church," a witness which must at all costs be preserved. In this, the present Pontiff echoes his predecessors.

In reading their words, we would do well to test their language and values against the historical record. Since it was first uttered in the fourth century, how successful has the first commandment of celibacy been? *And what has been the cost?*

Have the laws which forbade priests to marry or have sexual intercourse or beget children been honored? Has celibacy helped Christians to be better lovers? Has celibacy helped to bring all members of the Christian community together, or has it kept them carefully apart?

In 1954, Pope Pius XII wrote that "according to the teaching of the Church, *holy virginity surpasses marriage* in excellence" [23] . . . since "*works of charity* are for the most part *the field of action of consecrated* persons." [24] (Italics mine.)

He extols virgins, proclaiming that "you pass through the world without suffering its contagion. In preserving chastity, you are the equals of the angels of God. . . . *Married people and even those who are captives of vice*, at the contact of virgin souls, often admire the splendour of their transparent purity, and feel themselves moved to rise above the pleasures of sense." [25] (Italics mine.)

Parents of today's religious were no doubt influenced by His Holiness when they read, "Let parents consider what a great honor it is to see their *son elevated* to the priesthood [spiritual] or their *daughter consecrate* her virginity [sexual] to the Divine Spouse." Citing the Bishop of Milan, he continues, "You have heard, parents, that a virgin is a gift of God, the oblation of parents. . . . *The virgin is a mother's victim, by whose daily sacrifice divine anger is appeased.*" [26] (Italics mine.)

In 1967, Pope Paul VII referred to celibacy as "a brilliant jewel." [27]

"The true, deep reason for dedicated celibacy is the choice of a *closer and more complete relationship with* the mystery of *Christ and the Church* for the good of all mankind: *in this choice there is no doubt, that those highest human values are able to find their fullest expression.*" [28] (Italics mine.)

In a Letter to Priests on Holy Thursday 1979, Pope John Paul II continued that tradition, calling celibacy a "gift of the spirit," a "special treasure."

Why is it a treasure? Do we wish thereby to reduce the value of marriage and the vocation to family life? Or are we succumbing to a Manichean contempt for the human body and its functions? Do we wish in some way to devalue the love, which leads a man and a woman to marriage and the wedded unity of the body, thus forming "one flesh"? How could we think and reason like that, if we know, believe and proclaim that marriage is a "great mystery" in reference to Christ and the Church?

"Priests, by renouncing this fatherhood proper to married men, seek another fatherhood and, as it were, another motherhood. . . . The heart of the priest, in order that it may be available for this service, must be free. [29] Our sisters and brothers joined by the marriage bond have the right to expect from us, priests and pastors, good example and the witness of fidelity to one's vocation until death, a fidelity to the vocation that we choose through the sacrament of Orders, just as they choose it through the sacrament of Matrimony.

"Every Christian who receives the sacrament of Orders commits himself to celibacy with full awareness and freedom, after profound reflection, prayer and training lasting a number of years. . . . Only after he has reached a firm conviction that Christ is giving him this 'gift' for the good of the Church and the service of others, does he commit him to observe celibacy for his entire life. . . . It is a matter of keeping one's word to Christ and the Church." [30]

In his visit to West Germany in 1980, Pope John Paul II acknowledged that "hours of distress, exhaustion and perplexity, excessive demands and disappointments also occupy the daily life of priests.

"What medicine can I offer you in this matter?" he continued. "Not greater amounts of exterior activities, not convulsive strivings, but deeper penetration to the core of your calling, to that friendship with Christ and one another. . . ."[31]

"But this friendship calls for more. It calls for that brotherly openness toward each other, that bearing of each other's burdens, that common witness in which prejudice, thoughts of prestige and distrust are overcome. I am convinced that if you do your service in the spirit of friendship and brotherhood, you will obtain much more than when each of you worked on his own."[32]

. . .

In encouraging such bonding, Pope John Paul is obviously aware of the possibility that "brotherhood" and "sisterhood" has many names.

As a loving Father, he knows his responsibility is to speak to his children in a way that communicates his truth and experience, his wisdom and understanding.

But as any father or mother who has raised a family can testify, in time, each of their children will reveal his or her own gift of wisdom, a gift which will both surprise and enrich the entire family. Yes, each child will absorb and treasure the parents' legacy of love and wisdom. But in time, the children will add that legacy to their own revelation of truth which *they* will have been given by the Spirit to share at their moment in history.

The moment at which parents realize that they not only have much to *teach* their children but much to *learn* from them can be one of the holiest moments in a family's history. It is an act of faith, an act of surrender, an act of trust in the Spirit beyond ego and understanding. It is the moment when the father and mother realize that, as parents, their family's tradition only passes through them, that there is no static point in time where that family's tradition begins and ends.

Who will decide the question of mandatory celibacy?

Who will decide whether the value of mandatory celibacy is, indeed, "worth it"? And, most of all, whether it is worth the *human* cost in terms of people's lives?

Though there will be always men and women who will choose to live celibate lives for the "sake of the kingdom," is it the *only* choice the Church can offer to its people? As a Church, we must continue to ask "Why?"

Perhaps the Spirit is already in the process of answering the question. But the answer might very well turn out to be an unexpected response to Pope John Paul's call for brotherhood.

"Some years ago," says a priest in his mid-forties, "I attended a three-day reunion with my classmates from the North American College in Rome. There were thirty-five of us from all over the country. Three of the men were there with their wives. We shared deeply, and out of that sharing it was clear that, except for a few who chose not to reveal their experience, the overwhelming majority of priests present were not celibate.

"Yet, at the end of our time together," he says, "*everyone of us* stood around in a circle and pledged to each other that we would go back to our individual dioceses and work and pray for optional celibacy."

Each of those priests is ministering in the Church today. Should we pray with them or against them?

"Any religion which cites tradition as the reason why it cannot change is using tradition as a sedative," says Sister Margaret Ellen Traxler, SSND.

But what is even more dangerous is that a sedated Church is deaf to the cries of its children. And in time, it may roll over and smother the lives of its young.

AFTER DUSK

asleep
the firefly
is fueling

sparks
however small
light lovers

our bodies
listen
to light

Raymond Roseliep

CHAPTER EIGHT

SEXUALITY AS PROPHECY

"The unfolding of sexuality is also the unfolding of the human spirit—or at least it can be . . . The stunting of sexual development which happens when sex is kept separate from the rest of life means that people often remain curiously immature spiritually." [1]
Rosemary Haughton

"People journeying and searching, people wrestling with questions of how they can be more deeply human, are really asking how they can be God's people in terms of intimacy and relationships." [2]
Reverend Patrick H. O'Neill, OSA

"Sexuality is not a problem to be solved—it is a life to be lived," said Dr. Dan DiDomizio to a class of Midwest college students.

"But what does it mean to *be* a sexual person?" he asked. "Is the issue still the traditional one, namely, whether I go to bed or not, with whom, and when?"

Dan asked the questions somewhat rhetorically. As he looked out at the students, he knew that they, like most of their peers, had probably worked out their stance to those questions some time ago.

What their questions now seemed to indicate was a dissatisfaction with their current experience of so-called sexual freedom. More and more, they reported, they were discovering that genital expression, isolated from a deep, human exchange of trust and care, was *ultimately* unacceptable and destructive of growth.

The new questions were these: Is intimacy possible? Is there a deeper meaning to sex and therefore to life itself? Before two bodies touch in sexual union, what must—or should happen between two people?

"When we ask ourselves what it means to be a sexual person," Dan said, "we are looking at an experience that demands a set of words to make this experience accessible to us. The thought and language patterns that we use are immensely important, not only in communicating with others, but even in understanding our own personal stance.

"A friend of mine often says, 'How do I know what I think until I say it?'

"In speaking of an experience, we in a sense relive that experience. And so, the words are not insignificant," he said.

"I'd like to spend some time trying to do what language must always do: interpret experience—experience in this case being ourselves as sexual, spiritual people who are trying to move toward an integrated sexuality."

INTIMACY

"To be a body-person," Dan began, "I must be in relationship with others.

"The first question then becomes this: How have I struggled to make myself available and present to another as honestly and fully as I can?

"How has intimacy entered into my life?

"What does the experience of intimacy do to my sexuality?"

Describing intimacy as a gradual process of revelation which involves the whole person, body and spirit, Dan said, "In this context, intimacy, not intercourse, becomes the goal of sexuality.

"If one were to look at cultural values, however, what

would one see as the goal of sexuality? It isn't intimacy; it's sex, it's intercourse. But I don't think that's what we're searching for here. I think we're interested in intimacy.

"To have begun the process of intimacy with another person is a transformation experience, a conversion experience, a breakthrough to a new level of seeing life which happens as a result of my relationship with this person.

"In intimacy, a power is released which frees us to give ourselves and to be present to another. When this 'conversion' takes place, we enter into the very mystery of Incarnation, the God-being-present in human experience.

"Sexuality, when it strives for intimacy, becomes sacramental. It's an attempt to encounter the depths of life. If sexuality touches the marrow of our life, then it opens us up to an encounter with the Holy Mystery itself, the Mystery which pervades all human life.

"When I use the word 'sacramental' here, I'm not using it in the limited sense of ritual ceremonies; I'm using it in the sense of an encounter with the depths of life. And in that sense, all of life is indeed sacramental, all of life is sacred. There are no zones in which we can divide sacred from profane. "But in these terms also, nothing in human life . . . nothing . . . is more sacred than the dynamics of our sexuality.

"In some ways, sexuality would seem to be *the experience* which underlines all other sacramental moments, all other crisis moments in life. Why? Because the Christian way is intrinsically relational. To be a body-person is to live in relationship with other body-persons. To be a Christian body-person is to live in relationship with the Lord of life.

"But," Dan continued, "intimacy involves paradox, because intimacy is always incomplete. Intimacy always involves an experience of both 'togetherness' and 'otherness,' or separation.

"Every intimate relationship must face this somewhat unpleasant fact: Two people cannot, indeed should not, merge totally into each other. To do so would be to dissolve the differences which provide the richness of their relationship and, thereby, to impoverish it.

"In a sense, then, intimacy is always a quest; it is never complete.

"We learn this only too well through the hard test of human experience. As we attempt to give ourselves to another fully and honestly, we come face to face with our limitations, the depths of our spiritual poverty. In attempting new depths of sharing with the intimate-other, we often discover new depths of selfishness, new tendencies to be manipulative.

"Thus, intimacy often brings us to real self-knowledge of our strengths and weaknesses as no other experience can. It calls us to ask, how much of myself am I willing to give in compromise or surrender?

"Intimacy, then, is precisely that strange paradox of only being able to be loved into existence by realizing the extent of our inadequacy. And so, even though we celebrate the ecstasy of sexuality in the experience of intimacy, whether through genital expression or not, intimacy is never, never complete.

"Intimacy always comes up against barriers, and it thus calls for a letting-go, a new openness, a dying, a self-denial. Hence, we have to affirm that in real Christian spirituality, there is indeed an authentic basis for a tradition of asceticism. Not an asceticism that denies the human, but one which pushes us beyond our tendency to live comfortably with our selfishness: an asceticism which says, 'You have not let go of enough, you have not allowed the "living water" of God's grace to flow freely.'

"And it's important for us to know that this asceticism is part of our journey, a journey which seeks an ever fuller integration of our humanness which is, in fact, our quest for transcendence."

RECONCILIATION

"In a broken world, we ourselves and the broader world can only be healed and brought to wholeness through reconciliation. The recognition of the place of self-denial in the process of reconciliation has always been fundamental to an understanding of Christian transformation.

"Another reason why intimacy is always incomplete is that in a relationship between two equals who are becoming intimate, conflict is inevitable. Because we do not merge into one, my 'I-ness' and your 'you-ness' are going to clash with each other. It is an inevitable tension.

"There is no deep relationship which is without conflict. But I would suggest that the deeper and more intense the relationship, the more *creative* the possibilities are for conflict. Let me explain.

"Part of the difficulty we have is that we are used to seeing conflict as destructive. Why? Because conflict implies 'I-win-you-lose.' In a win-lose syndrome, conflict simply cannot be creative because if I lose, nothing very good is going to happen.

"What I'm suggesting is that to the extent to which we face conflict and look for a mutual resolution, to the extent that we're willing to be healed and to heal, intimacy can grow. This doesn't mean that there is no pain. Sometimes we take the attitude that, well, if it's creative, then maybe it won't hurt.

"Conflict has within it the potential to hurt. Yet the pain can be a creative crisis. All sacramental moments confront us with the opportunity to grow. There is no intimacy without reconciliation. Indeed, reconciliation is always an ongoing task between people who seek intimacy.

"And so, if spirituality seeks the integration of life into wholeness, then *intimacy is a major sacramental accomplishment*. If human life is truly sacramental, then intimacy stands for the journey into the sphere where God embraces our human existence wholeheartedly.

"Thus, within the paradox of intimacy there are tremendous possibilities for healing and reconciliation. Why? Because intimacy can call forth our generosity as well as our selfishness. When I acknowledge my limitations, I am then opened for healing. When I fully accept my emptiness and inability to love with abandon, then it's possible for me to be *loved into existence*, which is what healing is.

"And when that reconciliation happens, it becomes a profound experience of grace in our lives.

"Not that we have loved first, but that God has loved us first," that's the reality!"

HOSPITALITY

"How far should intimacy reach?

"If we say that it is sacramental, we are saying that it is an encounter with the depths of life and therefore with God. In this way, intimacy can never be confined to two people. It must reach out, in some way, to include the community. There is no sacrament, no encounter with the mystery of life, which is truly private. This is, I know, a hard saying in a country which values individualism and privatism and encourages each of us to build picket fences, literally and psychologically, to keep out a world we don't want to face.

"But just as we have been spiritually nourished by an experience of intimacy in our own relationships, so are we called to share that intimacy with others by reaching out to them in an attitude of welcoming. If we are capable of loving and being loved, then we cannot limit ourselves to the loved one only.

"From the beginning, our tradition has taught us that love is a way of life, an expansive virtue. If love is restrained or withheld, it shrivels and dies. If I say I love you and you only, I will ultimately not even love you. Whenever we attempt to enclose love within strict boundaries, it dies.

"Intimacy, then, becomes more than a means of personal friendship or personal fulfillment. It must broaden into hospitality, the willingness to allow others access to my life-space, my time, my talent, my possessions.

"I think one of the enormous dangers of the human potential movement in the last ten years is that it has recreated another kind of privatism, another kind of individualism, because we fail to ask, after we've gotten ourselves together (which no one ever does), then what? What do we do now? Is that all there is?

"The notion of hospitality for middle-class Americans often is to set up comfortable boundaries for ourselves. Yet hospitality demands that we extend our welcome to all—that we, in fact, take the risk of being used. That we risk the depletion of our material and personal resources because hospitality proclaims a radical sense of justice—namely, the right of any person on the face of the earth to shelter, nourishment, protection. These are things which are given in creation as a common resource for everyone.

"Seen in this context, sexuality involves far more than what happens between spouses and friends. Sexuality then expands and deepens to become a total way of loving from which no Christian is exempt.

"This, then, moves the connection between sexuality and spirituality to an even broader context—namely, to the context of the world of human justice. To integrate our sexuality with our capacity for intimacy is to commit ourselves to many others besides the loved one.

"Not only does hospitality complete the experience of intimacy, but it is only when I experience the give-and-take of love and intimacy that I am nourished enough to *risk* real hospitality; only then can I experience the real poverty of opening my time and possessions to others.

"But the moment I open my time, my life-space and my possessions to others, I am utterly poor as well as supremely rich. Why? Because I have nothing to lose . . . I've put it all out there. I have no props, no supports . . . my existence depends on and needs only the insurance of love, the assurance of trust, and the experience of intimacy, and, ultimately, the guarantee of grace. That is not only real poverty but true freedom.

PROPHECY

"Now, this is heavy stuff. This is the stuff of prophets, of Dorothy Day, of Francis of Assisi, of Damien of Molokai, of Mother Teresa of Calcutta; these people embody, in their own existence, our Christian tradition. They are utterly poor, but they are so rich in their poverty because their ability to relate deeply with others has given them the freedom to say, 'Everything is yours.' And, in that poverty, they are tremendously rich.

"Again, the degree of intimacy we achieve is never finished, never full, because we are always building the Kingdom by reaching out to the community. To seek to integrate our sexuality with our capacity for intimacy is to commit ourselves to many others besides a loved one.

"The prophets, as we know, were strange and unique persons. They were the off-beats of their societies; they were the men and women who accepted the challenge to 'swallow the word of God.' When they, in turn, spoke the word of God, it became an event for the people, an event for the community—an event of justice, of judgment, of challenge. And for the prophets, it also became a powerful, wrenching experience of alienation from their societies: They were disliked; they were homeless; they were put to death because the word of God rarely, if ever, lives at peace with the values of any society.

"Yet, I think it's significant that the prophets used sexual imagery to express the relationship between God and his people. Josiah, Isaiah, Jeremiah—all allude to the marital relationship between God and his people. The prophetic idiom, like the Jewish people themselves, was basic and earthy. The prophets used the language of sexual relationship, of intimacy and intercourse, to describe the powerful union of God and his people.

"Today, more and more, we are coming to see the prophetic dimension of an integrated human sexuality. Sexuality witnesses to the importance of relationship in each human person's quest for wholeness and to intimacy as the flowering of relationship. There is no better way to respond to life, to others, to the Lord of life than as body-persons, as man or woman. And therefore, to experience the healthy integration of our sexuality through life-giving intimate relationships is indeed to taste the transcendent dimension of our lives.

"Yet the society within which we live and within which each prophet must function is always fraught with threats and dangers to an intimacy and hospitality which, in justice, extend to and include the entire community.

"What, then, is the role of the prophet in these situations? To proclaim the power of creative love, of welcoming relationships over alienation, of community over privatism. The prophet strives to love concretely in a manner that accurately reflects the healing, unifying love of God.

"For the prophet, intimacy is only possible when love, justice, community, and hope can flourish among us. In this way, the attempt at a truly human sexuality would be prophetic. It would proclaim to singles, married, and celibates alike what our culture seems to prevent: namely, the possibility of intimacy born of real, self-giving love.

"Thus, when intimacy in a so-called sexual revolution is seen only within the context of a one-night-stand, then *sexual fidelity* becomes not only a countersign but a bold prophetic statement.

"When fear of others moves people to build social, economic, and political walls of isolation, to construct colossal means of personal and global destruction, then the open embrace that invites touch and acceptance and the intimcy that nourishes creative relationships become politically and culturally subversive. Such ideas represent a threat to the status quo. Thus to espouse a posture based on trust, sharing, and even vulnerability is to take a truly prophetic stance.

"Institutions which are spawned in selfishness, be they financial, political, or otherwise, are extremely threatened by the kind of intimacy and creative love we are advocating.

"Therefore, the integration of our sexuality, be it married, single, celibate, carries with it a profound social as well as political and personal implication. In the struggle for true intimacy, the personal and the universal, in a sense, become one.

"I believe the ground is shifting. The question is no longer whether one goes to bed or not, when, and with whom.

"The question instead becomes this: What are the possibilities for wholeness and intimacy for myself, for others, and for the universe? How can the open embrace be a sign of a real, self-giving willingness to be vulnerable?

"This is the question which links spirituality with sexuality.

"This is the stance which moves the dialogue regarding sexuality away from a sphere of limited moral categories to a new sphere of the realm of spirituality where the totality of our lives is at stake. To live out sexuality in this full sense is truly to be about evangelization.

"This, indeed, may be the true sexual revolution of our time."

. . .

In the back row of the lecture hall, a man turned to the woman sitting next to him and shook his head.

"Well, there it is," he said. "Sexuality as past, present, and future tension. Everything from the next date to the current relationship, to the body politic as part of the global sexual community."

He glanced down at his notes and read aloud . . . "Sexuality as intimacy, reconciliation, hospitality, and prophecy. Man, he just took those options and unrolled them like a carpet down the middle aisle of our lives."

Again, he shook his head. "I just don't know. . . ."

The woman smiled as she gathered up her backpack.

"I guess it depends on the way you look at it," she responded. "It's not so much a question of whether you're willing to deal with those options but what your alternatives are if you don't."

LOVESONG

How shall I withhold my soul so that
it does not touch on yours? How shall I
uplift it over you to other things?
Ah willingly would I by some
lost thing in the dark give it harbor
in an unfamiliar silent place
that does not vibrate on when your depths vibrate.
Yet everything that touches us, you and me,
takes us together as a bow's stroke does,
that out of two strings draws a single voice.
Upon what instrument are we two spanned?
And what player has us in his hand?
O sweet song.

Rainer Maria Rilke

CHAPTER NINE

GAY, BY GOD

"For the heterosexual, it is better to marry than to burn; for the homosexual, there is only burning." [1]

Dr. Daniel Maguire

"Many are coming to the realization that God loves them as they are and that He invites them to open out in concern for others. This movement of grace cannot be ignored or discounted. Many are seeking the opportunity to grow. . . . We have to see gay people, then, not as an enemy to be battered down, but as persons worthy of respect and friendship." [2]

Archbishop Rembert Weakland

"Think back," said the handsome, well-groomed man to the woman sitting with him at a table in a quiet cafe. "Think back to the first time you looked at a man, maybe as an adolescent, and felt a sudden excitement, an irresistible attraction that made you instinctively want his attention. Think about all the times you looked at a man during your teens when you were so aware of your changing body. Then think of your college days when you were away from home for the first time and were able to explore relationships with sexual freedom, maybe for the first time.

"Think of all the times since then, all the times you have looked at men on the street or at work or at parties and fantasized about what it would be like to be with them, make love to them, wake up with them. Think of the thousands of times you longed for these men and then imagine what it would be like to feel that each time you did, you felt there was something drastically wrong with you, that you were abnormal, that you were sick, *that you were a sin.*

"This is how it was for me," he said, "from the time I was a teenager, and I realized I was gay. Even after years of therapy, the guilt still lingers, and I'm in my thirties."

. . .

Marty Koshuba grew up in a working-class Ukrainian family that lived in a Pennsylvania mining community. The family's solid Catholicism surrounded them with security. Marty has an appealing wholesomeness, highlighted by the natural color in her cheeks. One senses shyness when she speaks. It belies her life experience.

As a teacher, she traveled to Africa with the Peace Corps, to backwoods Saskatchewan, Canada, and to an all-Black high school in Washington, D.C. She did graduate work at Princeton and holds an MA in social science.

"I was," she says, "absolutely terrified to 'come out' to my parents. I never planned to tell them. I still can't believe I told them on the telephone. Almost from the beginning, you know that people really don't want to know, they desperately want you to remain closeted. When I tell men I'm a lesbian woman, they say, 'Now why did you have to tell me that?' Others feel that just knowing you're gay makes your gayness contagious. So you add that to your list of what it means to be a lesbian woman in this Church and this society. To be a gay and to be a woman," says Marty, "is double jeopardy.

"I never 'lived it' until I was able to link up my identity with liberation theology and social justice issues," she continued. "Fortunately, I came to know brilliant and assertive women in the field of international law who affirmed and strengthened me. I dealt with criminal justice and hunger issues when I worked as a staff person on the Commission of Social Justice in the Archdiocese of San Francisco. I then gravitated to the National Assembly of Women Religious, for whom I now serve as the Southwest regional representative. Because of the public stands they had taken on social justice issues, I saw the position as one of empowerment which would allow me to confront economic injustice for women and also to work for the rights of women in the Third World.

"Gayness is the litmus test for Christianity," says Marty. "It is at the heart of every challenge, every justice statement the Church ever makes. Are gay men and lesbian women entitled to civil rights and human rights in a church which preaches justice?" she asks.

"I want to say to the Church, 'Look at me! I'm a human person. My lesbianism is part of me. *It can't be put out, because it's my life!*' After all the rust and corrosion I've gone through, I've survived and I'm delighted to be alive! My dream is that someday, as Church, we will be able to celebrate differences . . . whether it's for the Third World oppressed or for sexual minorities right here at home."

. . .

"As a child, Jim was," says his mother, "different. In a houseful of six children, I saw it. The way in which he looked at things, made decisions, approached life. Looking back, he was perhaps the most lovable of all the kids. He was everyone's favorite! But he did things differently than the other boys. A parent, a mother instinctively sees these things in the ebb and flow of a family.

"The Church always meant a great deal to us. We always prayed a lot, and there was always a strong faith dimension that the kids seemed to absorb and share. They were always active in church groups and went to everything. Out here in the plains, the Church provides a real community.

"During Jim's first year away at college, he wrote and told us he discovered he was gay. In a way, we didn't know how to respond to it. But in another way, it was as though I could finally put a name on the feeling I'd had watching him grow. Not better or worse, not good or bad, just different. He was still the same outgoing, sharing, affectionate kid he'd always been. Only now, suddenly, he was gay.

"We tried as best we could to deal with it. When we visited him, we met all his friends and the gay rights group he was working with on campus. Then the second letter came. In it, he told us about his new lover. He was a Catholic priest. Jim said he was planning to leave college to work with him. When we met the priest, it was obvious that he thought the world of Jim. We have exchanged letters and visits over the years, and we feel the priest is doing wonderful work and that Jim is enabling that ministry. It's still hard for us to accept the relationship, but we try to be grateful that there has been openness and honesty. Mostly, I'd say, we've given up trying to understand; we just let it be. It's easier to pray that way. Jim is our son and we will always love him. The fact that his lover's a priest is something they have to deal with. It's between them and God."

. . .

"The Church isn't ready to accept human sexuality, much less lesbian sexuality, because women aren't supposed to be sexual in the first place," says twenty-six-year-old Joanne, a photographer from San Antonio.

"To me, lesbianism isn't necessarily sexual. I know lesbians who don't have sex. But they love women, and they love the person they're with.

"When it comes to love, I think the Church is very

two-faced," said Joanne, who grew up in what she describes as the Catholic ghetto of Chicago. "It's a church which talks about love endlessly and yet refuses to accept the fact that it is humanly possible for people to love in different ways. I think love is love whether you love a man or a woman," she continued. "When you experience that outpouring of spirit and feeling, whether it goes to a man or a woman, it's a special gift which needs to be expressed. There is nothing more important that one could live for! What is more important in life than loving? I simply choose to love women.

"For years," she said, "my priest-brother has put me down as a mere earthling because I needed physical love. He's been trying to tell me that spiritual love is more than sufficient and, in fact, far superior. I, in turn, have been trying to tell him that you can't truly experience spiritual love unless you experience it in the context of physical love because only in that context are you able to be totally vulnerable to another person. To me, that is the height of all experience and I wouldn't give it up for anything.

"What really bothers me is that my brother counsels people on sexuality every day in his priesthood. He heads the office of marriage, family, and divorce counseling in his diocese. Yet he feels he is spiritually superior to these people. He actually admitted that to me!

"Well, recently he got physically involved for the first time, and he really got burned. He called me and he felt awful. He was hurting badly.

" 'I think,' he said, 'we'd better go back to square one when we discuss sexuality' he said, 'and start all over again.' "

. . .

According to Father Paul Shanley, a homosexual is a person who is predominantly erotically attracted to the same sex, though that does not mean that the homosexual person acts on that.

It has been estimated that there are twenty million homosexuals in this country and that one in twenty Americans is homosexual or gay, he says. [3]

Shanley, who served on the first National Young Adult Ministry Board in 1976, was assigned by Boston's Cardinal Humbert Medeiros to a full-time ministry with homosexuals and bi-sexuals, the first priest in the country to receive this appointment. In the sixties, Shanley received national prominence in his work with teenage drug abusers, juvenile runaways, and gays.

"I worked with them, prayed with them, counseled them on the streets of Boston as well as on the West Coast, in places like Big Sur where 'outlaws' like draft resisters gathered at that time," Shanley says. Describing himself as a priest who was trained in the "pre-Vatican-II Church," he nevertheless appeared on the street in the sixties in long hair and jeans.

"When I spent time counseling homosexuals," he said, "I knew I'd spend half my time counseling the kids and half my time counseling their parents. And when I'd learn the parents were Catholic," he said, "I knew I'd have to spend two hours counseling them for every hour I'd spend with their kids."

After ministering to homosexuals for more than a decade, he believes that almost no one chooses to be a homosexual any more than one chooses to be a heterosexual. He further believes that sexual identity is established between the ages of three and five, an opinion which is borne out by studies conducted by Dr. John Money from the Gender Identity Clinic at Johns Hopkins University in Baltimore.

"How do you condemn a three- or five-year-old for a condition they didn't choose?" Shanley asks. [4]

While homosexuality is a subject that is being discussed as

much by physicians, psychologists, and politicians as it is by moral theologians, very little is known about the *causes* of homosexuality, though theories abound.

What is understandable, however, is the kind of self-image a homosexual is likely to have after being classified as "sick" by the medical profession, "criminal" by the legal system, and "sinful" by popular religious beliefs. It is a burden which few of us could bear without severe and permanent emotional damage. [5]

It might be enlightening for all of us, whether homosexual or not, to consider the following:

• A homosexual orientation (feelings, attractions, and fantasies) is morally neutral (not sinful).

• Jesus said nothing about homosexuality that was recorded in the Bible.

While Scripture scholars continue to study and interpret, the American bishops must deal with the question of homosexuality from a pastoral perspective. Pressure to do so surfaces from every segment of church and society, from the most liberal to the most conservative.

There are two church documents which address the homosexual specifically and are most frequently cited: One is from Rome and the other from the American bishops.

• *The Declaration on Sexual Ethics* was issued by the Sacred Congregation for the Doctrine of the Faith on December 29, 1975. It is careful to define the persons for whom homosexuality is a choice and those for whom it is a given.

A distinction is drawn, and it seems with some reason, between homosexuals whose tendency comes from false education, from a lack of normal sexual development, from habit, from bad example or from other similar causes, and is transitory or at least not uncurable; and

homosexuals who are definitely such because of some
innate instinct or pathological constitution judged to be
incurable.

The Declaration warns, however, against concluding that
homosexual activity is natural for some people, and it says
that no pastoral method can be employed which would give
moral justification to these acts on the grounds that they
would be consonant with the condition of such people.
"Homosexual acts," according to the declaration, lack an
"indispensable finality" (namely biological potential) and are
judged to be "intrinsically disordered," and can "in no way be
approved."

But the Declaration also states that homosexuals must be
assured of pastoral care. They "must certainly be treated with
understanding and sustained in the hope of overcoming their
personal difficulties and their inability to fit into society." The
Declaration also states that culpability for homosexual behavior "will be judged with prudence." [6]

• In their 1976 pastoral letter, "To Live in Christ Jesus," the
American Catholic bishops wrote: "Homosexual activity,
however, as distinguished from homosexual orientation, is
morally wrong." This is the first church document to give
official recognition to the distinction between homosexual
behavior and homosexual orientation. Their advice: "To give
witness to chastity, avoiding, with God's grace, behavior
which is wrong for them, just as non-marital sexual relations
are wrong for heterosexuals."

The American bishops recognize that some persons
"through no fault of their own" have a homosexual orientation. They state that, as with everyone else, homosexual
people "should not suffer from prejudice against their basic
human rights," that they have "an active role in the Christian

community." Although they are unable to enter into marriage like their heterosexual counterparts, the Christian community should provide them with "a special degree of pastoral understanding and care." [7]

In still another document titled "Principles to Guide Confessors in Questions of Homosexuality," published in 1973 by the National Conference of Catholic Bishops, confessors are advised to treat homosexual persons with compassion and understanding, taking into consideration occasional "lapses" such as habit, ignorance, compulsion, impulse, an erroneous conscience, and any other factor which can lessen personal responsibility for homosexual activity. [8]

Thus, the official church attitude is essentially to "condemn the sin but love the sinner."

Others argue that there is another "sin" that must also be addressed, and that is the "sin" of homophobia, which has been defined as a fear and hatred of homosexuality, both in others and in ourselves.

"The basic issue is really not about 'them,' " says James Nelson, "but about all of us. How can we live less fearfully and more securely in the grace of God? What is the nature of the loving humanity toward which the Spirit presses us? And what does it mean to be a woman or man in Jesus Christ?" [9]

The quintessential underlying fear, says Father Paul Shanley, is that I might be a homosexual or that it is possible for people, in general, to be seduced into being homosexuals. [10]

Professor Robert N. Bellah, considered to be the foremost authority on American civil religion, approaches the subject of homophobia from another perspective. "The hidden assumption . . . is that homosexuality is really so exciting, thrilling, marvelous, you know, intensely sensual that, if anybody really had that as an option, why, they would madly choose it. That's what happens when you have to work too hard to repress something. My sense is quite the opposite. If it were demystified and accepted as one of the possibilities of human life, it would have less impact. If some people choose it as their option, okay, but it's not something one needs to get hysterical about.

"In any case, I do think that contempt, anxiety and fear about homosexuality is directly linked to contempt, fear and anxiety about women. And I think lessening the anxiety about it would be healthy all the way around." [11]

After attending a 1978 Strategy Conference on Homophobia in the Churches, Dr. Georgia Fuller reflects on her feelings as the Chairperson for the National Committee on Women and Religion for NOW (National Organization for Women). Her insights integrate her experience as a married woman and mother.

"The Conference has given me a greater understanding of my own sexuality. I believe that God has created us as sexual beings and gave us this mysterious gift for reaching out and joining with other people. This gift blends on a continuum among us and within us: celibate and non-celibate; heterosexual and homosexual. It is similar to the blending of male and female qualities that we are just beginning to appreciate. A man who recognizes his own tenderness and caring for children, formerly thought to be women's characteristics, is no less a man. Sexuality, though more internal and innate, is somewhat the same. Being with whole, responsible, spiritually alive Gay people has enabled me to recognize the Gay dimensions* of my own life. Affirming those dimensions has helped me to value my heterosexual preference.

*I am defining gay dimensions, gayness, etc., in terms of sexuality . . . a continuum of reaching out, relating to, being with and enjoying people of the same sex. Sexuality can include, but is not limited to genital contact. Fear of this continuum has produced rigid sexual role stereotyping.

"In questioning and finding that part of me which is Gay, I have also found, growing right next to it, a strongly-rooted heterosexual preference. My life-style with a husband and child is a primary way of living and relating that comes from deep within me. My life-style and preference are not conventions which I accept only because that's what all the story books say and all the teachers model. They are not conventions that I accept simply because the alternatives are bad and I'm afraid.

"By recognizing gayness within me, I can understand myself more fully and bond more freely with other people . . . women and men, Gay and non-Gay. I do not need to draw back for fear that they will trigger some hidden motive or urge deep inside my being. By realizing that gayness is a minor part of myself, I have no fear of changing or being changed. I do not need to worry that recognizing and affirming more of my sexuality will automatically compel me to act it out in promiscuous or exploitive ways. In fact, increased understanding has brought about increased respect, responsibility and stewardship towards God's mysterious gift.

"Exploring, searching and questioning our own identity, especially our sexual identity, is certainly risky. My Gay brothers and sisters are forced to take this risk in order to gain the internal strength necessary to stand against a hostile world. Non-Gay and non-lesbian people have a choice. In taking that choice, I won't pretend that I haven't become unsettled and scared, but I have survived. And in surviving, I have begun to rid myself of fear.

"We are called by Jesus to be a reaching, risking people. Our fears keep us held in and focused on security. Contrary to the teaching of Jesus, the church fosters fear and insecurity, particularly regarding sexuality. Preoccupation with sexuality has diverted the institutional churches from their true mission.

As non-Gay people, . . . fear, particularly fear of our own
sexual identity, has prevented us from challenging that
diversion." [12]

. . .

Just as discussions of homosexuality surface with greater
and greater frequency in the public forum, so, too, they are
appearing with parallel frequency in the Church. Ministry to
the gay and lesbian population is a grassroots phenomenon
undertaken by groups like Dignity, which was founded in
1969 in Los Angeles by an Augustinian priest who gathered
together a few gay Catholics for small group classes and
discussions on being gay and Catholic. Today, Dignity is an
organization of 4,000 members in ninety chapters in the
United States and Canada. Specially appointed committees in
Dignity deal with matters pertaining to women's concerns,
prison ministry, handicapped gay persons, social action, spiritual development, and aging gay people. Individual chapters
in most major cities meet for weekly Mass and social gatherings as well as for retreats, sacramental celebrations, workshops, counseling, and recreational activities.

New Ways Ministry is a small, Catholic-oriented group
located in metropolitan Washington which has engaged in
ministry of education, counseling, writing, research, workshops, and retreats since 1977. It is an important resource
facility for individuals, groups, and organizations in the
non-gay and non-lesbian community.

Sigma (Sisters in Gay Ministry Associated) is a support
group for religious women and other women ministering to
the lesbian and gay community. Founded in 1978, Sigma has
grown to a membership that includes 100 women religious
from seventeen communities working in twenty states. The
goals of the group are "to reach out to the lesbian and gay

community with love and acceptance . . . to help legitimize gay ministry within our communities . . . and to support each other by sharing ideas, fears, dreams and hopes."

Communication is a private network of gay religious women and men, including religious brothers and diocesan clergy, who communicate by means of a privately circulated monthly newsletter (*Communication*). The purpose of the newsletter is to provide a private forum where gay and lesbian oriented sisters, brothers, and priests can engage in a dialogue about topics and experiencess of common interest to them with the assured privacy and sensitivity of generally anonymous contributions in forms of articles and letters of response. [13]

. . .

The presence of gay men and lesbian women in religious life is receiving more and more attention through press reports of national retreats held for gay and lesbian religious (or suppressed, as was attempted by the Sacred Congregation for Religious in the case of a retreat for lesbian women religious sponsored by New Ways Ministry).

A National Symposium on Homosexuality and the Catholic Church was held in November 1981 in Washington, D.C. and, according to New Ways Co-Director Father Robert Nugent, more than one-third of the 180 participants were major superiors, vocations directors, or information directors for their religious communities. [14]

Can persons who are irrevocably homosexual or lesbian or give evidence of it be candidates for the priesthood or religious life if they are convinced that they can be celibate?

"In this context," says theologian Philip S. Keane, SS, "truly celibate life means that the true homosexual person can avoid all explicit acts and live in the mature harmony and non-exclusive type of loving pattern that are the characteristics of the celibate life-style. . . . In answering," says Keane, "it must be admitted that the case we are considering is quite rare. Celibacy, to begin with, is a rare gift among all people of whatever orientation. In addition, the homosexual who wants to be celibate needs a special type of maturity to deal with the social pressures he or she will face. Hence the conclusion that a given true homosexual can live a genuinely celibate life-style is not a conclusion to be jumped to easily.

"However, when it is clear that a true homosexual can live a life of genuine celibacy, such a person need not be excluded from the priesthood or religious life simply because of his or her homosexuality." [15]

Another opinion is expressed by James J. Gill, SJ, MD. He reports that recently "in view of the fact that from time to time religious superiors find it necessary to take administrative action in response to overt homosexual behavior of some members of their community, a group of Jesuit priest-psychiatrists prepared some recommendations, or guidelines, that superiors might usefully keep in mind. These seven psychiatrists were unanimous in their conviction that overt homosexual activity is incompatible with faithful observance of a life of celibacy. They regarded the behavior itself as sexually disordered and generally representing impaired personality development. Because homosexual behavior in a religious person frequently manifests serious emotional disturbance, they emphasized that it warrants a psychologic or psychiatric evaluation. They felt that a vocational decision should not immediately follow the discovery or disclosure of homosexual behavior; it should await the outcome of professional evaluation and treatment. They remained in complete agreement in their belief that a religious person who is either unable or unwilling to resolve this problem (repeated homosexual behavior), for whatever reason, is unsuitable for life in an order or congregation that understands the vow of chastity or celibacy in the same way the Church does.

"These Jesuit psychiatrists, all experienced in the treatment of homosexuals, were quick to state that they regard externally expressed homosexual behavior no more morally objectionable than overt heterosexual activity that is deliberately chosen by vowed celibates. They also pointed out to the superiors to whom they addressed their suggestions that homosexual behavior was, in view of their professional training and clinical experience, evidence of arrested psychosexual development." [16]

Father Paul Shanley sees the homosexual's choice for a religious vocation as a life-giving one.

"Imagine," says Shanley, "that you are eighteen years old and you believe you're gay and any acting out of that gayness is mortally sinful. You're aware that you cannot marry (your gayness is an impediment to marriage). You feel second-rate. If you came out, you feel your family would disown you, your friends would no longer be your friends, you couldn't get a job . . . living as a gay in society would be living at the bottom of the barrel.

"What," asks Shanley, "would be a way out? If you became a priest, the church would love you, society would love you, your family would love you. You would have a profitable ministry to people; you would be welcomed, received, respected. You wouldn't be committing sins against your sexuality." Shanley suggests that it is understandable to see how, in such a case, "the seminary beckons, and that such a consideration might be part of the motivation for entering the seminary." [17]

Humanly speaking, what suggestions might be considered

which would allow the homosexual to cope with his or her needs for intimacy?

According to Father Robert Nugent, SDS, a growing number of reputable theologians, including a prominent Vatican moral theologian, allow, on the pastoral level, for the formation of "stable, faithful homosexual relationships for certain individuals, relationships that would embody some of the more traditional values associated with heterosexual marriages, such as fidelity, monogamy and permanency." [18]

Father Charles Curran stated that "homosexuality can never become an ideal. Attempts should be made to overcome this condition, if possible. However, at times one may reluctantly accept homosexual unions as the only way some people can find a satisfying degree of humanity in their lives." [19]

The Catholic Theological Society of America's report (Human Sexuality: New Dimensions in American Thought) stated, "Faced with a problem of promiscuity, a pastor or counselor may recommend close, stable friendships between homosexuals, not simply as a lesser of two evils, but as a positive good." [20]

Of all human rights, certainly the right to friendship should be the last to be denied. Friendship was the heartbeat of Jesus' ministry.

> This is my commandment: love one another as I have
> loved you. I no longer speak of you as slaves. . . .
> Instead, I call you friends. . . . (Jn 15:12,15)

Jesus' call to us to "love one another as I have loved you" carries with it certain clear implications about the cost of loving. He reminds us of the risk dimension of love. Reaching out to another places us always in a position of vulnerability, a position of possible rejection. The life of Jesus calls for

commitment. Loving is no superficial venture. The reassur-
ance that comes to us from Jesus gives strength. His life says
to us, "I have done this and so I know that you can do it,
too." [21]

What is it like to work in gay ministry.

Ten years ago, Sister Jeannine Gramick, SSND, began
working with gay Catholics while ministering in Philadelphia.
With Father Robert Nugent, she is currently a co-director of
New Ways Ministry. "My attitudes toward gays (then) were
typical," she recalls. "I had had no contact with them before.
I felt a compassion, but it was condescension because I
thought there was something wrong with them. I felt sorry
for them."

Her attitude changed through continual contact with gays
and after she had studied the issue and gained "correct
knowledge."

"I thought if gays wanted to, they could change their
sexual orientation," she continued. "I thought if I exposed
(gay) males to contact with women, it would help. That
notion was naive. It goes beyond behavior. You can't ignore
the emotional component," she said.

Addressing parents' fears that a gay teacher or other homosexual role model can affect a child's sexual orientation, Sister
Jeannine pointed out that most of today's gays grew up with
heterosexual role models, and research on lesbian mothers
found that an overwhelming majority of children raised by
them turned out to be heterosexual. [22]

When asked what was the most difficult aspect of her
ministry to lesbian women, Sister Jeannine stated that it was
the lack of support and misunderstanding from her own
religious sisters who are close to her.

"For too long coldness and emotional distance have been
the signs of celibacy," wrote Sister Jeannine in *Probe*, the

publication of the National Assembly of Women Religious. "If we are to share Christ's love, we must love without fear. If we fail to trust others, out of our own goodness or our motivations or if we fear losing control, we live without the warmth of true chastity. . . . We as women need to reflect, theologize, pray, share and dialogue from our own experience as sexual celibates living together and loving each other. From the bondedness of women a new ecclesiology will emerge in which human sexuality will be a means not of control but of love." [23]

"Ministry to homosexuals," says Father Paul Shanley, "is surrounded by fear. People are afraid that if they stand up for the human rights of gays, people will think they're gay. They fear they will be tarred with the same brush that tars the people they are trying to serve." [24]

What I am doing is sending you out like sheep among wolves. . . . Be on your guard with respect to others. They will hale you into court, they will flog you in their synagogues. You will be brought to trial before rulers and kings, to give witness before them and before the Gentiles on my account. When they hand you over, do not worry about what you will say or how you will say it. When the hour comes, you will be given what you are to say. (Mt 10:16-19)

Brother Cosmas Rubencamp has been ministering to young adults in the Diocese of Richmond, Virginia, for over a decade. The diocese contains sixty-eight colleges and universities. He is the Diocesan Director of Campus Ministry there.

"We try to deal with the moral issue of homosexuality from the same perspective of ethical responsibility as we would apply to heterosexual standards. This includes the whole area of promiscuity."

Brother Cosmas believes young adult gays have hope in and commitment to the Church once they experience the Church's caring presence. "But," he noted, "I am also aware that more gay men than gay women keep faith with the institution. For gay women, the Church is doubly incredible.

"We see all sexuality as a gift," says Rubencamp, "but we speak of homosexuality as a gift which brings greater pain."

As a minister to young adults, Rubencamp sees that pain in many places: in the lives of the gay young adults to whom he ministers and in the lives of their families. "Parents of gays desperately need the Church's support," he says.

"There is pain in still another place: pain in people's hearts in the form of fear and anger," says Brother Cosmas, remembering a diocesan retreat for gays that would have included Mass and prayer sessions but was canceled because of strong objections from the community.

"The Chancery office said they received calls that 'extreme measures' would be taken to prevent the retreat from being held," says Brother Cosmas. "And the Retreat House received threats that ranged from blocking the driveway to burning the place down." [25]

In a statement to the press, diocesan priest Father Richard Dollard said, "The Church's ministry to homosexual people is because of Christ's concern for all people, whether they be prostitute, tax collector or thief. Like Christ, the Catholic Church does not condone active homosexual conduct. . . . In supporting people in prisons, with alcohol problems and in hospitals, the Catholic Church is not condoning crime, use of alcohol or ill health. . . . Christians are called to reject sin, but as Christ was found among sinners, Christians have to care for sinners. We are all sinners," he said. [26]

"There are four to six thousand 'hustlers' . . . male prostitutes . . . in Los Angeles," says Father Paul Ojibway, SA, who is director of the Office of Young Adult Ministry in Hollywood. "They leave home between thirteen and fifteen. They are on the streets from sixteen to twenty-two. By twenty," he says, "they are in their 'declining years' on the street. Most of them whom we see in our ministry are bright, above average, not from broken homes. They are looking for something and they've found it on the streets," he said. A disproportionately high number of them are Catholic or fundamentalist. Over half are into the drug experience. Counselors indicate that more than half seem to be homosexual.

"Most of them are caught up in role identity. They say they are hustling for the money. But we have to ask them if they are setting themselves up for it because they are gay. Psychologically, hustling gives them an out.

"We get them on the 'wane side,' " says Ojibway. "Usually, they're past their prime, in their mid-twenties, and they are wondering what to do with their lives now. We try to follow up, to get them back into school, to help them with things like the registration process.

"A typical 'hustler' would be someone like Joe. He's twenty, he's been on the street for three years. Originally he pimped. He got into it, he says, for the money. He averaged $400 to $800 a night. He had Catholic education through grammar school . . . a bright guy, who now lives with a gay man who experimented with leather and S&M (that's sado-masochism). We helped him to get back into junior college. It worked for a while. He went back on the streets for six to eight months . . . and then came back. . . .

"Another was a runaway from a home with a strong Catholic background. He had been arrested for assault and rape. He was twenty, had been on the streets for three years but didn't see himself as gay. We worked with him weekly for three months, got him back into school and classes. Then he was arrested for breaking and entering. . . .

"Another is sixteen, gay, involved with a gay man in the area. He was gang-raped and tortured, and later escaped and sought help from friends. That's where we heard about him and tried to help."

While Ojibway admitted that "more fail than succeed" and that there are "low payoffs in this ministry," he believes deeply that there is a value in "pulling them out of that place, even for a while, and giving them a new experience of community, of 'grouping.'

"We try to encourage them to a place of new growth where they see that, as a gay person, each one has something to offer the Church, and that together it's possible to build a new form of Christian community," he says. "The first step in the process is to help them move past their self-hatred and self-loathing. They need to be able to see that spiritual surrender is possible, one that includes both their choices and orientation. It's not good enough for them always to be calling from a place of hurt and struggle," says Ojibway. "Young adult gays need to accentuate and define a peer ministry where they can help each other. They need to develop counseling skills among themselves. We have a contemplative prayer group and try to help them develop a cogent spirituality.

"Ministering to young adults, whether gay or not, is a ministry of reconciliation which supersedes and cuts through preconceived notions and legality. The Church must look to these marginal people and take their plight seriously," Ojibway says.

Healing and integration are the key concepts in Father Vincent Inghilterra's ministry to gay young adults in the

Diocese of Trenton, New Jersey.

To date, Trenton offers the only concrete model of ministry
for gays in the United States and was the first in the country to
issue a Pastoral Plan for Sexual Minorities.

As Director of Campus and Young Adult Ministry,
one-third of Inghilterra's ministry is devoted to the young
adult gay population, which includes students as well as
young professionals and deals with alcoholics, married gays,
custody cases for lesbian mothers, gay Cuban refugee sponsorship, and family counseling for parents of gays. The
thirty-nine-year-old priest, who has been in ministry to sexual
minorities for eight years, works with a staff that includes
physicians, a psychologist, a married couple, and six fellow
priests, all of whom work as a team to provide pastoral care
and counseling to young adult gays.

The stated goals of the Office of the Diocesan Liaison for
Sexual Minorities, which Inghilterra founded two years ago,
are to provide education for clergy and laity regarding sexual
minorities, to work for the eradication and exposure of eccle-
sial and social structures and attitudes which discriminate
against gays as persons, and to work with gays themselves to
secure basic rights in employment, housing, and immigration.

"Because young adult gays feel alienated from family and
friends, they break off from the mainline culture and go into
the subculture of the gay bars and bathhouses," says Inghilterra. He feels it is part of the Church's responsibility to see that
all young adults are welcomed and integrated back into the
church community.

As the Bishop's representative to the twenty-one organizations in the state of New Jersey, as well as the three chapters of
Dignity, Inghilterra conducts workshops in such campus
communities as Princeton University. There he works with
dorm monitors to teach them skills and attitudes which will

be helpful in working with gays in that environment.

When asked what he believes to be the Church's fear in dealing with gay sexuality, Inghilterra replies, "It's the fear of dealing with gay clergy and religious within the Church. Unless the Church deals with this agenda within its own ranks," he claims, "it won't be able to address it honestly in the larger church community."

. . .

"What you have to understand," say the gay young adults who had gathered to pray, "is that to be gay is to struggle against the belief that, humanly speaking, you are a freak, and that even the Church wished you would go away."
• To be gay is to freeze or rage or sigh or die at certain words . . .

Words like *queer* or *faggot* or *dyke* used by someone you like or love or had hoped would be your friend . . .

• To be gay is to never be able to say other words . . . Words like *my lover* . . .

Knowing that, all your life, you'll never speak about the one you love, the way other lovers do.

• To be gay is to pray you will never grow old and that while you're young, you'll sidestep the statistics . . .

"The leading cause of death among teenage gays is suicide."

• To be gay is to sense the averted eyes, the stepping back, the sudden barrier . . .

"But you loved me ten minutes ago, you said I was
wonderful!
"Please tell me the reason you're firing me.
Do you deny my gifts and talents now because I'm
gay?"

• To be gay is to see young shadows in the parking lot . . .

   " . . . The thirteen, fourteen, fifteen year olds hanging
   around the gay bars, looking for action, knowing they'll
   get it with the older men."

• To be gay is to see the hurt and surprise in someone's
eyes . . . The denial which says,

   "It's just a phase. . . ."
   "You can be cured. . . ."
   "I'll change your mind in bed, you'll see!"

   The anger that says,

   "Don't do this to me!"

• To be gay is to always feel that you're on the run . . .

   "The Nazis put pink triangles on us. . . ."
      "In San Francisco, you wear a whistle, to call for help
   if you're jeered at or jumped on the street for being a
   'fag.' "

• To be gay is to stand before your parents, feeling guilty for
something you didn't "do" . . .

Ashamed of something you never sought. . . . The
victim of combinations of cells or genes or hormones or
chromosomes over which you   had no control and
which nobody has yet figured out. . . .

• To be gay is to see your parents' guilt flaring up like a fire
that can't be put out, not ever, not even with a father's or
mother's tears . . .

And part of you says, "It will take time. . . .
In time they'll accept the fact. . . ."

And the rest of you says, for the billionth time, "Why,
God . . . *why?* Why *me?*"
• To be gay is to want to forget, just once, the feeling, the
longing you have

*to wake up one day
and not be gay.*

• To be gay is to keep on believing you are good, you are
loved, you are precious in the eyes of the God who created
you!

. . .

Bishop Francis J. Mugavero of Brooklyn encourages gay
men and women to value themselves as whole human beings.
"We urge homosexual men and women to avoid identifying
their personhood with their sexual orientation. *They are so
much more as persons than this single aspect of their person.* This
richness must not be lost . . . It is not homosexuality which
should be one's claim to acceptance or human rights or to

being loved by us all: it is the fact that we are all brothers and sisters under . . . God." [27]

Many gay young adults feel that "wholeness" for them means "coming out."

"For me, coming out was coming home to myself," says the Reverend Lois Powell, a thirty-one-year-old ordained minister in the Church of Christ. "Till then, I was walking around in little pieces. It was, in the classic sense, a resurrection experience. I already understood brokenness. Coming out helped me to stay in the Church because I could relate in a new way to the Good News, to liberation and freedom and wholeness. I knew at last who I was and was called to be.

"When we are broken and gathering up the fragments, we must believe that the grace is there and that there is healing. And most of all, that God doesn't let us go."

"I had a personal relationship with Jesus before I came out publicly," said Brian McNaught, a journalist who was fired by the Detroit diocesan newspaper when he "came out" as a gay in 1974. "And that relationship enabled me to come out. Church, for me, was everything. I wanted to be God's best friend; a saint. I wanted Sister and Father not only to like me but to approve of me. I realized that if they knew I was a homosexual, they would reject me. So I had to develop my own relationship with God. It was this personal spirituality which enabled me to come out.

"In fact, I came out for spiritual reasons. I had no idea what was going to happen politically. . . ."

But McNaught admits that many gay people who grew up Catholic didn't have the advantages he had. "I'm concerned about the people who were in the Church long enough to be convinced that their salvation was through the Church and now the same Church condemns them. Where do they turn?

"Most gay people I know want a growing, loving relationship," said McNaught. " . . . I'm not looking to the Church to endorse my relationship. I want the Church to encourage heterosexuals and homosexuals alike to take responsibility for their sexuality and to express it in selfless ways," he said. "I don't want special rules for the gay community." [28]

"I was not able to come out and deal with my gay sexuality until I left my community," said Frank, who was a religious brother for seven years. "When my religious superior asked me, 'What sexual problem do you have for leaving?' I just looked at him and said, 'I can't breathe here anymore.' I was suffocating with 'defending the Church's defenses.' For postulants, the maxim was to 'overcome your feelings.' . . . 'If you don't see what you want, want what you see.' " he said. "There were homophobic men on one side of the community and gay men on the other. I began to look at community as a war men make. Outer events are metaphors for inner events. The end result of the games, the denial, the pretense, was a slaughter of the personality.

"All I wanted out of religious life was to know how to love!" he said. "I had spent my whole youth searching for God through my sexuality. I always felt that my life was off balance. I saw religious life as a way of calming my spiritual terror. I was looking for order, not anarchy. I believed that religious life would allow me to live with some degree of creativity. It was just the opposite for me.

"All I saw were men carefully armoring themselves with protections so they wouldn't find out who they were and what they needed. I saw men struggling with 'black and white' sexuality. I had hoped men could live together with some kind of joy and spontaneity. But creativity was seen not as a gift but a pastime.

"The option they offered was 'Stay and there's power.

That's the transformation of sexuality we can offer in terms of creativity.'

"At the end, my decision to leave came gently and effortlessly," said Frank. "I trusted it because it embraced both my spirituality and sexuality.

"I was sitting in the library on an autumn afternoon, and I glanced over at one of the other brothers, who was a special friend of mine. I thought how beautiful he was, completely absorbed in a book, totally unaware of anything around him. Just at that moment, rays of the afternoon sun came through the window and flooded his face with light, changing it suddenly. My sexual feelings for him spilled over into spiritual tenderness. I felt tears in my eyes, so overwhelmed was I with what I can only describe as a kind of clarity. It was, for me, a real moment of 'knowing.' I knew, then, that my being required my leaving. I knew in that instant, beyond a shadow of a doubt, that change was possible; just as the sunlight had changed his face, it would change mine, too.

"I have learned since then that it is possible to be with a man in a relationship which is gracious and loving. Wanting to be cared for by other men in more than sexual ways is, to me, a sign of my deepening spirituality and a coming to terms with intimacy. I have learned that love is being transparent. And there is, in my life now, a loving which keeps happening to me."

"I had lots of my own stereotypes about who could be a lesbian and who couldn't be," said Jane Howard, a twenty-five-year-old high school teacher in California, "and whether one could be a spiritual lesbian and even if spirituality entered into it at all.

"A friend, a man, helped me by challenging me. He said, 'Jane, you can't use Jesus to stay in the closet. You also can't use the fact of offending people to stay in the closet because

Jesus offended people; we will all offend people.' He challenged me to get more in touch with the Jesus that I had
always known, and as I grow, I see how all these things
connect spiritually.

"The more I came out, the more I felt oppressed. I wasn't
angry for a long time because I said, 'Well, it's okay that a
particular thing was said to me because they just don't *understand.*' Well, it's not okay, and it's becoming not okay for me
more and more. I used to say that 'It's okay that the Church
oppresses gay people because they're just not up-to-date yet.'
But, again, it's not okay, because who is going to bring it
up-to-date? Who is the Church but us? So silence to me is
non-Jesus. Camus said, 'Not to tell is immoral.' And I really
think that's true.

"I am teaching in a homophobic institution, in a
homophobic Church which is a product of my own early
homophobia, in a sense. And I could be fired at any time.
And yet, I'm saddened by a lot of my lesbian sisters who have
rejected spirituality in general, because of oppressive structures and institutions. I don't know why I work within this
institution. My only answer is that these are my roots and I'm
not going to let them be taken away from me. This is where I
came from and where I received so much good because this is
where I got to know Jesus. I didn't get to know Jesus as a
Methodist or a Presbyterian; I got to know Jesus as a Catholic
and I have to claim that, but also correct it and support it
where I can. The greatest gift I bring to the Church is my
lesbian spirituality. It's the gift of my life because it is the way
God created me. Body and soul, this is how he wanted me to
be."

. . .

Because we possess this ministry through God's mercy, we do not give in to discouragement. . . . We proclaim the truth openly and commend ourselves to every man's conscience before God. . . . We are afflicted in every way possible, but we are not crushed; full of doubts, we never despair. We are persecuted but never abandoned; we are struck down but never destroyed. Continually, we carry about in our bodies the dying of Jesus, so that in our bodies the life of Jesus may also be revealed. . . . We have that spirit of faith of which the Scripture says, 'Because I believed, I spoke out.' We believe and so we speak. (2 Cor 4:1-2, 8-10, 13)

. . .

The Church is in a state of siege about human sexuality, homosexuality. And fear has seized the heart of the Body of Christ. But as the People of God, *what* do we fear? And *why* do we allow our fear to keep us in bondage?

We are members of Christ's body: as heterosexuals and homosexuals, as priests and religious, as men and women, we are Jesus' brothers and sisters.

Are we afraid of Christ's body? Are we afraid of what it might reveal to us . . . and to others . . . about where we have been, who we are now, and what we are called to understand?

DID THE WOMAN SAY . . .

Did the woman say,
When she held him for the first time in the dark dank of
  a stable,
After the pain and the bleeding and the crying,
    "This is my body; this is my blood"?

Did the woman say,
when she held him for the last time in the dark rain on a
  hilltop,
after the pain and the bleeding and the dying,
    "This is my body; this is my blood"?

Well that she said it to him then.
For dry old men,
Brocaded robes belying barrenness,
    Ordain that she not say it for him now.

Frances Croake Frank

CHAPTER TEN

THE BODY POLITIC

"Do not stifle the Spirit. Do not despise prophecies. Test everything; retain what is good."

2 Thessalonians 5:19-21

The story is told of a certain tree in East Africa in whose branches is placed a statue of Mary, the Mother of God. Before that tree, the barren women of Eritrea dance, their graceful bodies swaying to the music which, like the community, inspires and surrounds them. Theirs is a prayer that flows outward through their outstretched arms, their open hands, hands asking the Mother of God to intercede for them with her Son that their wombs might be filled with new life. Their prayer of longing is visible in every movement, every gesture of petition. For these women, the bringing forth of new life is basic to their identity. In dancing before the statue in the tree, they are offering their bodies to God in an outward expression of petition and supplication.

And yet, we are told, though this plea is the most important prayer they make, never once do these women bend and kneel before that tree, for to do so would be the sign of a slave. Instead, the barren women bow. In bowing, they do honor to to person before whom they stand while retaining their dignity as women and as human beings.

. . .

The call to human liberation which Christ, as brother, came to bring us is contained in the gracious bow of the East African woman. By that gesture she is offering her body to

God as gift, one all the more precious because it is given in freedom and with dignity. "This is my body," she is saying to her God, "the body you ransomed with your own body. Because of that act, I must carry myself with nobility and walk with grace. To do less would dishonor you."

The East African woman is a metaphor for all women in the Church who hear the last two words of the commandment "Love thy neighbor *as thyself*" in a new way. They have come to realize that Christ's call to human liberation is a call to self-respect. They, like their African sister, *believe* that their bodies are temples of the Holy Spirit and must not, in any way or by any person, be profaned.

To walk with grace means to be a reflecting mirror for the Creator. It is to reflect the source of one's gifts and talents. To allow those gifts to be dismissed, ignored, or trivialized is to dishonor the God who entrusted them to us.

The winds of change are blowing through the Church in the breath of the Holy Spirit. Women are coming to see that they have unknowingly been involved in an act of betrayal: They have betrayed their bodies by letting them be used against themselves.

They have been seduced into their own invisibility. Though they comprise over half the membership of the Church, a church which they have, as women, carried on their backs for centuries, they are expected to see nothing, do nothing, require nothing. Nothing except, in one person's words, "keep their mouths shut and chill the beer."

They look at the organization of the Church as the Body of Christ and see only a male body. And they are told that because they do not have this male body, they are ineligible for ordination. (Thus women may receive only six of the seven sacraments.) To have ordination would give women the "official" authority to make decisions which directly affect their lives—their minds and their bodies, their hearts and their souls. It would include decisions by which they live, love, and make their living. It would, in short, give them voting power. As it stands now, they may canvass the districts, run the campaigns, get out the electorate, and stay up all night counting the ballots. The only thing they cannot do is vote.

When they protest that they were taught by the Church that male and female bodies are equal . . . "There does not exist among you . . . male or female. All are one in Christ Jesus" (Gal 3:28) . . . they are told that this interpretation is *their* problem. The way things are is the way the family business has been run for centuries, and churchmen see no *real* reason to change things now.

And when women continue to protest, when they say that "Only Male Bodies Need Apply" turns Christianity into a phallic religion, they are dismissed with an accusation of having penis envy.

Elizabeth Janeway points out that the locus of punishment put forward by the theory of penis envy and fear of castration is male. Which sex is frightened by this? Surely the sex which has a penis to protect. Women don't fear a *loss* of something which is for them physically impossible.

Fear of castration is a male reaction projected onto women with a perfectly sensible purpose: "Protect yourself and keep women inferior. Your penis, which she doesn't have, is the sign of your superiority. Its lack marks women as inferior, and if they accept this inferiority, they will feel guilty for having done something wrong and having been punished, and it will be easier to deal with them." [1]

Increasingly, both men and women are looking critically at a male-centered church as separatist. Dr. Phyliss Chesler is one of them. "I favor integration and would like to see the sex war end and genuine 'heterosexuality' begin. . . . I call it a male homosexual culture when men prefer to congregate only with other men for the 'important' things: religion, making war, making money, making peace. I call it a male homosexual culture when women are supposed to provide men with their definition of male sexual pleasure," she says. "This is illustrated, to some extent, when men share 'their' female property with other men; they are expressing the desire to satisfy forbidden homosexual longings in a socially approved and profitable way. Thus do fathers traditionally award their daughters to men of their choosing; thus do men often pay for economic and political favors with women, that is, with prostitutes; thus do an increasing number of men in America, whether politically 'right,' 'center,' or 'left,' express 'brotherhood' by sexually sharing wives and girlfriends.

"As I listen to men talk about male bonding and male violence, I wonder to what degree male hostility towards feminist aspirations has to do with male fear of being abandoned by women—so that males would be left to themselves, in an all-male society?

"Patriarchal civilization is, from a psychological point of view, a male homosexual culture because of its exclusiveness," says Dr. Chesler. "Yet it requires the renunciation of *overt* homosexuality." [2]

How does the Church, which celebrates the *spiritual equality* of the sexes, attempt to integrate and transform this kind of culture? Indeed, is such integration and transformation even possible in a church which allows only males to be ordained and segregates women and men who aspire to religious life into same-sex communities?

In this regard, Nancy van Vuuren suggests that an examination of the position of Mary, the mother of Jesus, in the Catholic Church might be illuminating.

The worship of a woman in a completely male church may be an attempt to compensate for the unreal emphasis on masculinity. Such compensation, however, cannot be viewed in terms of the needs of women but must be viewed in terms of the needs of men, for Mary was [as mother] thought to be especially efficacious in behalf of men and the church. . . . But as Jesus was stripped of his sexuality, so Mary was stripped of hers, before the church would allow them to be worshipped or at least to be the subject of prayers.

For men spirituals [religious] to speak of a sexual love for Jesus left them open to accusations of homosexuality, and the clerics were especially sensitive to this, for there was some truth in the accusations. And since the church had decided that homosexual relations were sinful and unnatural, it was even worse to be labeled homosexual than to be accused of not keeping the vow of celibacy. In this contest, Mariology became a major part of the liturgy of the Roman Church. [8]

"I really resent trying to have to make sense out of all this sexual confusion, and more than that, trying to defend the Church's double talk," says a twenty-seven-year-old young adult, who is a computer programmer. "We're taught in Catholic schools that the Incarnation means that Jesus was God-made-man, that He was *like us in all things but sin.* But if he's like us in all things but sin and he's asexual, does that mean that sexuality and genitality are sins?

"Why doesn't the Church teach a version of the Incarnation that makes Jesus a flesh-and-blood person, not someone abstract, like The Force?" he asked. "Young people need a Jesus to relate to whom they can turn to and whom they have every reason to believe *understands.* I wish I had been able to pray by saying, 'Jesus, tell me what it was like for you when you were thirteen years old? Tell me about sex in ways which will help me!' Why doesn't the Church help us to understand that Jesus, through his relationships with women like Mary Magdalene, was a Lover in the way he cherished and affirmed her? Why doesn't it highlight the fact that this was the real message he left about how we should act and what we should do?

"I feel we've been shortchanged twice and through both sexes," he continued. "The main male and female figures in our Catholic religion are asexual: Jesus is presented as a eunuch, as the son of a mother who never had sex either because she's a virgin.

"How am I supposed to relate to that as a human being struggling to believe in God's love for me and my own goodness? How do these models of sexuality speak to me in terms of my life, my needs, my biological makeup? Is the Church really saying that God made a mistake in the way He created me?"

For those who have been labeled both "The Body Generation" and "the spiritually homeless," these questions rise up in young adults like angry tears.

"As a teenager," said a twenty-five-year-old advertising copywriter, "I remember reading in *The Diary of a Country Priest* that it was 'the church's mission to recover the source of lost joy.'

"Are they still looking?" she asked, with upraised eyebrows. "I'd like to ask them: If we're not supposed to find joy in our bodies, in our persons, which is all we really have, then where are we supposed to begin to look for it? If we don't believe we've found joy in ourselves, how can we give it to others? Where does the Church suggest we go?"

Some young adults believe that the Spirit surprises us with unexpected answers, unlikely places.

Others say simply that it is a matter of faith. "We know that all things work together for the good of those who love Him, who have been called to his decree" (Rom 8:28).

For one Catholic priest, a liturgy honoring the Gifts of Mary was an unexpected source of consciousness-raising about sexism. The liturgy was one of many which took place at a CCD Congress sponsored by the Archdiocese of Los Angeles in Anaheim, California.

Father Ed Fronske, OFM, had every intention of concelebrating at the Marian liturgy. He vested along with his fellow priests who were also concelebrating liturgies at the congress, but when he arrived at the door of the Marian liturgy minutes before it was due to begin, he was refused as a concelebrant. The door was closed.

The explanation given, he learned later, was that it had been agreed by all of the planners beforehand that only one priest would celebrate at that liturgy, which was designed to highlight the presence of women. And since only one priest's presence is "officially" needed to celebrate, the planners agreed that only one priest should be present.

Father Ed admitted that he was "crushed, hurt, and angry." What made it even worse, he admitted, was the attitude of his brother-priests who couldn't understand why the refusal bothered him. "I went on to concelebrate at another liturgy, but I was completely distracted. When the anger and hurt subsided, I felt incredibly sad. I later learned that 300 people were turned away from that liturgy for lack of space. It seems that even the planners did not anticipate how many people wanted to attend a liturgy that celebrated women through Mary."

Father Ed said that he later shared his hurt and confusion with a close friend. "She shared my pain with me," he said, "but she did even more than that by helping me to look deeper. She helped me to see that the hurt and powerlessness and anger and confusion I felt on that one occasion is shared by thousands of my sisters throughout the world everyday. They, too, feel called to concelebrate, to share their spiritual gifts, but unlike me, the door *always* remains closed to them.

"Now I can more easily identify with their feelings of pain, frustration, hurt, discouragement—which they have carried down through the centuries—because of their not being able to get in, to belong, to take part fully, to feel welcomed when they were so sure they would be. I had heard it before, and now I could feel it, taste it, suffer it. Now I have a keener insight into why it's critical to work for greater freedom for everyone." [4]

What will it take to "free" the body of Christ from the bondage of fear which causes competition and distortion? What will it take for the People of God to accept responsibility for the gift of their sexuality?

Our sexuality is not frightening or uncontrollable; it is not an idol or a slave. It is a mystery at the heart of our familiar selves; it is ourselves as we live with other people we love—parents, friends, children, lovers, husbands, wives—in individual relationships and communities. [5]

If we are to claim the image of the Body of Christ, we must also claim responsibility for what is happening in each part of that Body. We would do well to begin by acknowledging that a body is not something we have, it is something we *are*. Thus our bodily energy and spiritual energy are inseparable.

Ken Dychtwald suggests that one path to self-awareness is to "read" one's body, "to allow yourself to enjoy the way your muscles and limbs have to tell the stories that are alive within you, stories that tell of experiences past, passions present, and dreams future. By becoming more aware of the distinctions within your own Body-Mind, you will find yourself in a position of greater self-awareness and greater self-responsibility." [6]

Dychtwald also notes that while most people would agree that feelings, attitudes, and emotions have an effect on the conditions of the Body-Mind, he believes further that the body begins to form around those feelings that animate it, and the feelings, in turn, become habituated and trapped in the body tissue itself. [7]

He cites specific places such as the neck, which he likens to a telephone switchboard, which links incoming and outgoing calls, and where tension may gather for the person who has taken on more responsibilities than he or she is able to handle; [8] the heart, which tenses up in an attempt to protect itself from feelings of warmth and nourishment; [9] and the diaphragm, which is critical to the full functioning of the lungs and internal organs and which stiffens itself to protect the body from assertive and expressive emotions which might have been held down for a long time. Dychtwald cites the diaphragmatic area as the region which often suppresses severe anger and rage. [10]

He goes on to state that when we experience emotions we don't want to acknowledge or express, they do not just disappear. We like to think that we can instantaneously remodel everything. When there is something about our lives we don't like, we believe we can simply remove it or make it disappear.

"But nothing can be simply detached and removed from the Body-Mind and nothing really disappears. So when I work with people," he continues, "I try to transform their unmentionables into mentionables, bringing what they have put back out of sight into the forefront, into view." [11]

As Christians, what observations can we make about the

feelings and emotions that have become habituated and trapped in the Body of Christ—the Church? What emotions are unexpressed or unacknowledged? What attitudes would we like to see brought into full view and transformed?

Where in the Body of Christ do we experience communications problems? Where does the switchboard overload? What conditions cause it to jam? What persons in the Church are forced into states of over-self-protection in order to insure that the heart and its emotions must be covered by protective armor?

Are the lungs of the Body of Christ able to breathe freely and deeply, or are they always in danger of collapsing? Does the Body of Christ continually withhold severe emotions such as pain and anger, which might cause it to suffocate?

Medically speaking, death is defined as the absence of brain function, even though the heart can be kept beating with resuscitation equipment. In the human body, laws about when death occurs are as problematic as when life begins. If the pulse and the heartbeat grow too weak in the Body of Christ, who will be held responsible? How long is it wise or possible to keep the Body of Christ on a "breathing machine"?

Maryknoll psychiatrist Dr. Maria Reickelman reminds us that our call is to *life*, to the preservation and celebration of life, in all its possibilities! "No more can the dead give praise than those who have never lived; they glorify the Lord who are alive and well" (Sir 17:23).

· · ·

Change shivers the world, says Elizabeth Janeway. It occurs both at the large, general social level and also within the individual psyche, which must try to evaluate the new situation and adjust to it. In addition, it threatens the personal side of life, the precious, unthinking trust and affection and assurance which one has learned to count on within old, habitual role relationships. *It creates loneliness.* [12]

No one is more aware of the linkup between loneliness and change than those who minister to young adults in the Church. Through Young Adult Ministry, these ministers hope to help young adults transform loneliness by building community.

They believe transformation is possible through action, commitment, and spiritual renewal. They believe that young adults should accept change as a challenge to grow, a step which will enrich *all* the People of God.

For the past five years, a group of young adults has gathered to dialogue, pray, and discern their direction in Young Adult Ministry. They begin by acknowledging the loneliness of the young adult in Church and society. With that as their starting point, they work as a community to explore ways to heal loneliness.

This leadership training program for those committed to Young Adult Ministry is called the Aura experience. The program adopted as its symbol the aura: a glowing multicolored magnetic energy field that surrounds each person, an outer reflection of the goodness, wholeness, vitality, and health of the person within. Young adult ministers believe the aura is "a symbol of the inner Christ who shines brightly and steadily, asking that we extend ourselves to another in ministry."

A recent Aura meeting focused on the theme of spirituality and sexuality and was titled "The Healing Process: Broken Like Bread, Poured Like Wine." It gathered young adults from around the country who spent ten days building a community that approached the questions of spirituality and sexuality from such various perspectives as Body Awareness,

Community Organizing, Sexual Politics, Gay Sexuality, the Eucharist, Community Mentors and Models, the Minister as Artist, and Theologizing from Group Experience. Participants shared stories and discussed experiences of sexuality and spirituality as ministers, healers, dreamers, and artists.

Nancy Hennessey Cooney, nationally recognized author, lecturer, and member of the United States Catholic Conference's Committee on Family and Human Sexuality, challenged the group to explore the experiences in their lives in which sexuality and spirituality are interwoven. For example, the woman who goes to the abortion clinic never goes "alone"; even if no one knows, she is always "connected" to the rest of the Body of Christ. Likewise, the starving child who, in the deepest sense, is a victim of rape. "Our sexuality flows through our lives and never stops," she said, "because the goals of sexuality include both intimacy and communion and occur in relationships with others. These are human needs which never end."

Grace McGinniss Lamm brought her background as anthropologist and community organizer to questions of faith and community.

"Theology is trying to find words to express what we already know. A lot of theology is disembodied intellectualism," she noted, adding that "much theology strangles us." Defining power as "the ability to act effectively," she reminded the group that they "are in the process of redistributing the power of decision-making and also the power of ownership." The development of a people in process is as important as anything that takes place at city hall, but there is no talk about power without talk of conflict. "Conflict is a creative necessity" in the power process, she said. One should expect, she added, to confront a "certain kind of arrogance which comes from those who have *unearned* power." She called the group to apply principles of community-organizing to the process of theologizing. "You cannot know a thing unless you know the positives and negatives," she said. "Then you are prepared."

"We cannot know our people unless we know their metaphor system," she continued. "We must begin by asking: 'Is sexuality our metaphor for intimacy or is intimacy our metaphor for sexuality?' "

She reminded the group that *faith also empowers*. "Since the Incarnation, there is nothing human that does not speak to us of love," Grace continued. "The heart of the Good News is that because of the Incarnation, nothing is too profane to be touched."

Professor Scott Hope of the San Francisco Young Adult Network told the group that "to not hold, to not touch out of fear is a perversion of our sexuality." We live in a society that encourages intensity but not depth. We need rituals that celebrate our sexuality.

"Are we more afraid of our strengths than our weaknesses?" he asked. "If we define sexuality and spirituality as separate, are we saying that one is better than another?"

Scott spoke of ministry as a balancing act and addressed the many forms of loneliness which stalk the young adult minister. Reminding them that "a prophet is not without honor except in his or her own country," he noted that often "in our own psyches as prophets, trying to proclaim the needs of the alienated and lonely, we are lonely, too.

"We see the repression of sexuality as well as the repression of our spirituality as the burying of our talent," he noted.

"We have only to ask ourselves, 'Are we more embarrassed when someone comes up to us and asks us how our sex life is than we are when they ask us about our spiritual life?' If so, we must ask ourselves why. What are the differences?"

For ten days, members of the group pursued and prayed about these questions, collectively, individually, in formal workshops, and in conversations which lasted into the dawn.

Each of the members had invested his or her time and energy and faith in this process, Each represented an important segment of the young adult community. There were graduate students in psychology and theology. There were artists and musicians who wrote songs to accompany the group along the ten-day journey. There were members of the military, as well as a man whose work was in the Peace Movement and in draft resistance. One man's ministry was picking up drunk marines along the road on the weekends and returning them safely to their barracks. There was a pediatrician who had decided to enter ordained ministry. There were social workers and students and accountants. There was a woman whose mother was pressuring her to marry a priest; a man who loved the right woman at the wrong time; a priest who admitted he could no longer live without being nourished by a dream. There were those who healed simply by listening and celebrating liturgy. But all the persons in this diverse group admitted when they left that they would never be the same. They felt they must share this intense and deeply moving experience with others. They did so by issuing a declaration. It was a declaration of love which called them to responsibility. It was the fruit of their collective experience as a theologizing community. It dealt with the critical issues in young adults' lives. . . .

Issue: Powerlessness - Personal Helplessness - Loneliness
• in the face of church hierarchies
• in political, economic, social and church crises
Enablements:
• to redistribute power through shared ministry

• to promote a vision of Church which calls for *accountability to people* rather than to power structure
• to encourage people to be aware of their deep need to listen to their bodies and spirits and to trust the messages they receive
• to struggle for integration of their spirituality and sexuality in supportive communities
• to name our needs, to own our needs, and to deal with them

Issue: Credibility of the Laity in Church Leadership Enablements:
• to recognize that young adult ministers are the present heartbeat and future hope of the Church
• to challenge Young Adult Ministry to be both creative and accountable
• to encourage all people to challenge the Church to live up to its own mission
• to recognize and *support women* as lay ministers
• to dignify and affirm the importance of Young Adult Ministry by providing its ministers with a *just wage*; to recognize that Young Adult Ministers are grievously underpaid
• to work for the *elimination of all elitism* whether among the ordained or among laypersons
• to affirm the right and need to freely and intelligently explore all aspects of our spiritual and sexual lives
• to seek lay recognition of the fact that *any decision or action* of the institutional Church (the People of God) has *political and sexual implications*
• to promote the knowledge that when we speak of and envision the Church, we are always looking to an ecumenical ideal
• to support the need to put "yes" in the vocabulary of the institutional Church

• to recognize that no religious awareness is possible without equal social justice awareness

Issue: The Goodness of the People of God
Enablements:
• to believe that we are *good* and that in order to care for the People of God, we do not have to wear hair shirts or Super People costumes
• to recognize that our loneliness is something to be dealt with and not denied
• to realize that when we label people as "deviant," we divide and dis-member the People of God
• to realize that we have all been victims as well as oppressors as single people, divorced, sexual minorities, Hispanics, Blacks, veterans, women, the unchurched, the mentally ill and physically handicapped, the poor, the Third World, single parents, and celibates
• to establish national, regional, and local support networks for those engaged in ministry to young adults
• to form a nationwide organization of young adult ministries which would facilitate training of young adult ministers
• to issue a national publication and create a resource bank where issues of particular interest to young adults would be addressed, including sexuality and spirituality, social justice, creativity, careers/vocation/life work, models of ministry, psycho-social development, social problems (alcoholism, drugs, etc.), and community organization

Issue: Accountability
Enablements:
• to recognize that we are all accountable to the institutional

Church, as it is to us; *as Church, we are accountable to each other.*

• to acknowledge the need to change metaphor systems in the Church in order that they be more all-encompassing

• to recognize the need for a ministry that is more androgynous and, therefore, more integrating

• to be aware of the importance of calling forth the gifts of those other than the majority culture

• to recognize ministry as a process as opposed to simply information-dispersal

• to promote a sense of personal and group ownership-partnership of the Church

• to recognize the need to invite rather than to coerce

• to recognize that tension and dissension can be creative

• to be willing to be uncertain as an act of faith

Summary: The Church as Eucharistic Community

• to work and pray for a church community to which each person can bring his or her story and know that it will be taken seriously and reverently

• to recognize that the Church needs to be a community that allows itself to be challenged and changed in its understanding of itself as the symbol of the Body of Christ

• to challenge the Church to be a community which encourages in each individual a sense of responsibility to act in faith and trust as a member of Christ's Body and as an indispensable link in the Church's history

. . .

And the hands, having written, moved on. But the words

were engraved in the hearts of those who heard them and those who would be called to listen.

And the Word dwelled among them. . . .

Let no one look down on you because of your youth, but be a continuing example of love, faith and purity to believers. . . . (1 Tm 4:12)

Prophecy has never been put forward by man's [and women's] willing it. It is rather that men [and women] impelled by the Holy Spirit have spoken under God's influence. . . . (2 Pt 1:21)

5 RIDERS IN CARDINAL RED

5 riders came from the North. There were 2 women, one
   holding a small child. Cardinal red was their color and
   there were leaves everywhere.
They all seemed to be warriors, and when they came to
   the town well, the women drank first.
It was only later that the silence was noted.
There were no kids.
And it had gotten very cold.

It is like this without you,
forever riding from town to town,
through leaves, waiting to drink.

William Bradd

CHAPTER ELEVEN

CROSS FIRE

The Vietnam Veteran and the American Conscience

"I believed in Jesus Christ and John Wayne before I went to Vietnam. After Vietnam, both went down the tubes," said one. . . . "I fought for God and country," said another, and then laughed cynically. [1]

William P. Mahedy
Vietnam Veteran, Former Army Chaplain

Today's young adults were teens then, and many of them were on the road.

In the sixties, they came to San Francisco's Haight-Ashbury with packs and ponchos on their backs, sandal-shod, their souls caught up in a blend of rebellion and innocence. But their hearts and minds were at war over questions of peace.

In the city of seven hills beside the Bay, they spread out their questions in the parks and coffeehouses and public places, crowding into basements overburdened with sleeping bags from Maine, Montana, New Mexico. They curtained their windows with peace-sign posters and fluttering banners, which in some cases turned out to be tattered American flags.

Peace had a hundred names in the Haight in those days. And in some of the youthful hands of the Body of Christ, peace held a gun, and in others, a flower.

By 1973, many of these "flower children" were among the 60,000 who said no to the Vietnam War and fled to Europe and Canada. In time, they were joined (and some believed, outnumbered) by persons leaving military service before or after being ordered into combat.

And also there were among them some of the 2.7 million who went to Southeast Asia to fight a war they still don't understand.

More than a few years have passed since then. Time and money have washed over the Haight, restoring, among other things, the faded facades of the once-wonderful Victorian houses who, like the youthful seekers they once sheltered, have turned another page of their history.

Some things have changed but others have stayed the same. The carpeted corridor of trees and green grass known as the Panhandle still has its share of stumblers and seekers. The coffee houses still flourish, now refurbished with ferns and calico curtains, tended by young entrepreneurs who, though they still wear batik shirts and headbands, now have demanding bank loans to meet.

And the questions of war and peace which were once sky-written in the Haight in the sixties by teenagers are now being asked in the Haight by young adults. Only now they are being asked in retrospect in the aching privacy of a storefront Vietnam Vets Counseling Center where the answers are spread out on the canvas of the survivors' lives.

The prevailing colors in the canvas are blood red and agent orange. The impressions they left have tattooed these survivors' psyches. They have become indelible in their lives.

Statistics:
2.7 million Americans served in Viet Nam
57,692 died
57,000+ have since committed suicide
300,000 were wounded

75,000 were permanently disabled
Average age: 19 years old

Vietnam was a teenage war.

Those teenage warriors are young adults now, many in their early thirties, and comprise a sizable portion of this country's population. They set out for Southeast Asia believing they were fighting for their country, trusting that this is what their country wanted them to do.

But while they anticipated bullets and battlegrounds, they were not prepared for the cross fires in which they would be caught . . . the sudden, wrenching realizations that they had been pulled into personal and political wind tunnels from which there was no escape.

Jack McCloskey, team leader at the Haight Vets Center, describes the impact that the experience had on the psycho-sexual development of the teenage warriors.

"What happens if you're an eighteen-year-old person trying to find your personhood and you are put into a situation of total survival and what that total survival means is killing. And along with the killing, the raping: raping the land, raping the women and children, raping the whole experience—and being raped in return.

"Now what happens when you go through that experience and you are told that it is normal; in fact, you are rewarded for doing it. You are rewarded with medals, with the promise that if you get these many 'kills,' then you will be rewarded with R and R and will be able to get away from the fighting for a couple of days.

"You are rewarded by your peer group. 'Hey, he's *bad*! He killed ten yesterday!' What happens when you go through that for a year, when you are taught that it is normal, when you are taught that it is good?

"Then seventy-two hours later, you are back in the streets of America, without any debriefing. And welcome home, guy; here's the world again! The norms for survival in Vietnam are not the norms for survival back here. And there is no transition.

"It was almost like having dinner with your family one night, fighting for your life the next, then returning home.

"You went over to Vietnam believing that that was one way you were going to become a man. And back here, by your own group, you are spat upon and called a baby-killer. By older veterans, you are considered less than a veteran because you did not win your war."

"I felt like some kind of a freak—a cross between a leper and a spy," says a veteran from Boston. "It's as though my old buddies didn't know what to do with me, so they either avoided me or got behind this screen of small talk. Even when we were drinking, there was a strain, an edge to everything. I found myself avoiding the old hangouts where I might bump into them. I realized one day that it would just be easier to take off, to move away."

No matter where they turned, there were cross fires. They were unexpected and they were everywhere.

That's when they realized there were two combat zones: one over here, one over there.

Psychiatrist Arthur S. Blank, Jr., states that "sanction, praise, appreciation, and festive welcoming are important elements in beginning a returned warrior's healing of the emotional trauma of war. These were absent from the reception accorded most Vietnam returnees. Much of society was diverted from attention to the veteran by vigorous controversy over the war, which tore at the structures of our nation for over a decade. Pro-war and anti-war civilians alike had developed anger and disgust over the war itself, which was sometimes displaced on the veteran. It was not rare for returnees from Vietnam to be shouted at and ridiculed in airports and other public places. *This led, among other results, to the remarkable phenomenon of soldiers hastily changing into civilian clothes and throwing away uniforms, en masse at disembarkation points.*" [2] (italics mine.)

That war is a memory now. The young, strong lives which once swayed in the wind like glistening stalks of wheat have been mowed down in a harvest of infamy. They sleep in peace in somewhere-soil, 57,000 of them, most of whom were still in their teens, never to reach the then-legal age of twenty-one.

Yet here at home, the Body of Christ which is the Vietnam veteran is still on the battlefield, only now it is hemorrhaging internally. In small towns and metropolitan cities, in the ninety-one storefront counseling centers set up by the Veterans Administration, men and women sit in newly formed squads, haltingly exposing the scabs, the pockmarks, the scar tissue. It is their Vietnam legacy which no surgeon's scalpel can ever touch.

"This is," says one, looking at his raw, rash-covered hands, "my stigmata. It never lets me forget."

Even though years have passed, many of these men and women find they can no longer forget or repress their nightmares. Diagnosed as "delayed stress syndrome," their memories flare up like brushfires and, once again, Vietnam threatens to destroy their lives.

Over and over, they speak of their spiritual anguish: their despair, their powerlessness. They use words like "my need for confession, for absolution, for atonement." But many choose not to trust the churches which, they feel, participated in their schizophrenia and betrayal.

"In 1968, when Cardinal Spellman blessed the bombs in Hanoi, I was totally shattered!" says one "cradle Catholic" veteran, shaking his head over and over, still incredulous. "I remember saying to myself, 'So now it's Kill a Commie for Christ.' "

Robert Lifton describes the scenes of betrayal:

> The men had a special kind of anger best described as ironic rage toward two types of professionals . . . chaplains and shrinks. They talked about chaplains with great anger and resentment, as having blessed the troops, their missions, their guns and their killing. Whatever we were doing . . . murder, atrocities—God was always on our side. . . . In that sense, chaplains and psychiatrists formed an unholy alliance, not only with the military command, but also with the more corruptible elements in the soldiers' psyche. . . . We can, then, speak of the existence of the counterfeit universe, in which pervasive, spiritually reinforced inner corruption becomes the price of survival. [3]

But others remember chaplains who were there and who were "just as numb with disbelief as we were." Says one nurse, "All I can tell you is that over and over I would see them bend over the beds and bodies, their eyes stinging with tears as the dying boy would gasp 'May God have mercy on our souls.' "

Margaret Walker remembers that often she and another nurse were the only ones who attended services the chaplain held. "Nobody went because by then they didn't, they *couldn't*, believe in a God that allowed that slaughter to happen.

"Everything you had been brought up to believe, the rules you were taught to live by, were shattered, blown apart," she says. "You would look around and ask yourself, 'Is this reality? Is this truth?' There was no right or wrong. . . .

"In Nam, nothing made any sense. Everyone knew that what they were doing was absolutely, totally hopeless. For what were they fighting? There were no beginnings, no endings, no rules and regulations, no boundaries, no *normal*. All they could say they were doing was simply staying alive. . . .

"What you have to understand," says Margaret, "is that when you looked around, all you saw were bodies and stumps. I had worked in emergency rooms in the Chicago ghetto and had seen every kind of trauma, but I still wasn't prepared for Nam. Fifty, sixty, one hundred people . . . all fifteen-, sixteen-, eighteen-year-olds, coming in blown apart. There was no sense to it, *none*. It's like you died there, too. Part of you had to, in order to survive.

"There were so many times when you'd think, 'Can you go on another minute? What if they bring in more and you're too tired to respond immediately? What if the choppers come in and it takes you two seconds longer to respond? What if, in that two seconds, you don't clamp an I-V and someone doesn't get resuscitated?' What if . . . what if . . . day after day . . . week after week . . . month after month, for what seems like a thousand years."

It is a feeling that Episcopal priest William P. Mahedy, a Vietnam veteran and former Catholic Army chaplain, knows well. He describes it as a "spiritual numbness which occurs when one's sensitivity and compassion have become dulled, and the reservoir of one's spiritual resources has begun to run dry. Besides alienation from one's own feelings, there is also an alienation from one's spiritual center," he says.

"At the beginning of the Vietnam War, a peculiar national mythology was invoked to bolster support for our military endeavor. As a people, we seemed to be convinced that God had called us to a special destiny. The feeling that America has a divine mandate to evangelize the world on behalf of the American political and economic systems has never been far from the surface of our national self-perception. . . . For many American veterans, the American political system seemed invested with an ultimate value. It had been religionized.

"Most veterans embraced the theology of our foreign policy. They went to Vietnam with great fervor to stop the onslaught of godless Communism. Most were products of homes which were at least culturally Christian. Many former altar boys were among them. War, glorious war, that cultic act of civil religion, was unquestionably part of the mythology which gripped them as they went off to Southeast Asia. They were 18 and 19-year-olds for the most part; they were, by and large, black, brown, rural white, blue-collar types, high school graduates and high school drop-outs and college drop-outs, as well. . . . I almost never heard the Vietnam War discussed by any veterans in anything resembling the 'just war' theory of Christian tradition. Some saw the war as the lesser of two evils, but the conceptual frame of reference seems always to have been the war ethic of the crusade. . . . The justifying motives were religious and ideologic, and the task of the soldier was seen as a holy one.

"To this day, most Vietnam veterans see themselves as having been involved in a noble profession if not a noble war. And that is the root of much of the veteran's problem; the soldier bears the burdens of his people, makes great sacrifices and deserves the respect of his people when he returns home. He is a hero; he represents his people under unspeakable conditions. But the hero's welcome never happened, of course, to the Vietnam veterans. There was no ritual of return, no respect. Instead they were reviled." [4]

Cross fire. . . .

There were even more factors.

"As the anti-war movement developed," notes Mahedy, "the mythology of the holy crusade was challenged. Much of the anti-war feeling, however, also seemed to be rooted in the same premise of a quasi-religious national destiny. The nation had sinned against its special covenant by becoming involved in Vietnam and the voices of the prophets were raised against it. The soldier was caught right in the middle of this crisis of civil religion." [5]

For Vietnam nurse Peggy Tuxen the reality of war was immediate. "I had not been in Vietnam twenty-four hours when I encountered a classmate of mine from junior high school who had stepped on a land mine and had his legs blown off," she said. Her wounded classmate was the first of a never-ending stream of patients she would care for whose bodily pain was matched by their spiritual terror.

"Their eyes haunt me to this day," she says.

Peggy's pain was her sense of helplessness, her realization that she could never do enough, be enough, have enough supplies to ever put them back together again. "They had all the helicopters and guns and ammunition they wanted," she notes, "but we never had enough respirators or medications or supplies.

"Your whole life was there . . . every minute, every second. There was no one else there for them, so you tried to be everything to them. You'd work a twelve-hour day and then go back to the wards at night to sit and read to your patients or write letters home to their families. It was important to me that their parents knew that someone was there who cared for them because a lot of them died."

Peggy states that, from the beginning, she had to make a decision that as long as she was there, she could not allow herself to cry.

"If you began to cry, you'd never stop," she says. "Over there, you shut down your feelings. For a whole year, you took care of really sick people and saw them die and could not allow yourself to grieve for them. And yet," she says, "I don't think I ever knew a nurse over there who left because she couldn't handle it. Even now, as a woman, it's hard to talk about hurting. You keep giving and giving and giving because you are expected to be the nurturer and the comforter. But there's no one there to grieve with you.

"And then you come back, and people either don't want to hear about it, or all they want to know is whether it's really like *MASH*," she says.

"It's only after I joined the group that I could speak about these things," she says. When Peggy first appeared at the Vets Center and met Jack McCloskey, he told her that she'd have to join a woman's group, but she refused. "We're Vietnam veterans, just like you are," she told him. And he realized that she was right.

But it took patience and time.

"The first group I joined was composed of combat veterans who couldn't understand why a woman could be hurting. 'You weren't in the field! You didn't carry a gun!' they told me. That's what it took to qualify as a Vietnam veteran in their eyes. And so," she says, "they voted me out.

"It really hurt me," says Peggy. "These were the men that we took care of and tried to support and encourage and help put back together again."

In the next group, Peggy was joined by other nurses, and the men in the group were more accepting. It took a little time for them to realize that we weren't there to fall back into the nurturing role that we were in Nam, she said, but that we needed help and a safe place to be. We needed to be able to cry the tears that we had choked back for so long. Some of the men in the group admit that the women's tears have helped them to confront their own inability to cry.

"Everyone cries," says one husky veteran. "It's just that the tears take different forms. I must admit that I get a little nervous in the group when the tears start, but I think it's more from a sense of feeling powerless and out of control," he says.

"I *want* to cry," he continues, "but I don't think that the circuits are there anymore. I feel sad, but maybe it's just that I cry on the inside now. But," he adds, "it doesn't make it any easier."

For many, this is their cross. They cannot live with their memories, but they cannot live without them. Vietnam was, in many ways, the high of their lives. Never, say some, had they felt so wildly alive. The prayer-chant they had learned in Marine Corps boot camp had been fulfilled.

God bless my drill instructor
God bless America
God bless the Marine Corps
Pray for war, pray for war. . . .

"I extended for a year," says one veteran, who went on to get a degree in anthropology. "I found it very exciting! But I also found myself becoming very much of a pacifist since my return, and it's something I really concentrate on. Since I came back, I watch friends of mine driving fast cars or hang-gliding for excitement, but I don't need it. I used up all my lives in Nam; I've walked the line, I've been on the edge," he says.

"There is," says one nurse, "a sense of wanting to be back there because there was a constant high that is hard to explain. It's like you never felt so challenged or needed or called to your fullest creative capacity as a human being. It was a constant adrenalin high . . . constant crisis . . . with the choppers coming in, casualties coming in, constantly making life and death decisions. . . ."

But for others, that experience remains a burning memory of anger, of being placed in a position of "making decisions about who should live and who should die." "It was a high, all right," says another nurse, "but it's a high I never want to have again as long as I live."

And for still others, many others, there is the realization that there is a dark shadow which will stalk them forever: the memory of their own capacity for violence and tolerance for atrocity. For them, to be in Vietnam was to experience the embrace of demons . . . demons who, without warning, had risen unbidden, seducing their souls.

"They would come to, calling and crying, still in the clutches of hand-to-hand combat, of battles that made them half crazy with killing . . . and in the midst of it all, getting off on that," say the nurses. "For many, their first conscious act was to reach and make sure that they still had their genitals."

"Is all war sexual, a sort of sexual perversion or a complex of perversions?" [6]

Phil Caputo defines courage as "the urge to rid oneself of fear by eliminating the source of it. This inner emotional war produces a tension almost sexual in its intensity. It is too painful to endure for long." [7]

Veterans themselves talk about "getting off when they pulled the trigger." One says he thinks that American males have been raised to believe that there is a connection between violence and sexual gratification; he cites the fact that the penis is referred to as a gun.

"That's why, since Nam," he says, "a lot of guys have guilt 'getting off.' "

"But when is a gun for fun and when is it for killing?" asks another veteran. "When I was in combat, all I could hear were the words and music of John Lennon's song 'Happiness Is a Warm Gun' in my head, and I used to think I was flipping out, man, going crazy. It all came back to me on the day that Lennon was shot down by an assassin's gun."

What is real, and when does reality take the form of a nightmare or a fantasy? Vietnam continues to be a war with blurred edges. It has been called by some a national nervous breakdown; by others, a kind of coast-to-coast schizophrenia with nothing to show for the spilling of blood but the body count.

The intense national conflict about the Vietnam War directly affected troops and was an integral stress for them, as well as for many civilians. This sometimes reached into families, where one son was serving in Vietnam, and another was stateside, militantly opposed to the war. Whatever side an individual soldier was on—whether pro-war or anti-war—a substantial portion of the American people were on the other side. The same was true in Vietnam because of sharp divisions about the war among the troops themselves.

Cross fire. . . .

"We talk about these things in the group," says Jack McCloskey, "and something happens. I can't explain it. All I can say is that when we share together, it is holy ground."

"What is so healing is that it takes so few words to get your message across," says a veteran from North Carolina. "You sense, almost immediately, that just by having been in Nam, everyone understands."

In time, and with patience, the veterans are able to slowly empty their emotional pockets. Even when they become vulnerable, they feel they are in a safe place.

Each one in the group is different and comes for different reasons. For one, it was the sudden terror of nightmares from nowhere, flashbacks which occurred, without warning, even

after ten years. ("I could hear the choppers, I could smell the
fire.") For another, who feels he has coped and is fairly well
adjusted ("I saw the dead and the gore, but I lived through it;
I'm a survivor!"), there was the unfolding publicity about
agent orange.

"I sprayed it; I was drenched in it over and over. I never
wore a mask. None of us did. Now," he said slowly, "I just
live day by day."

For others, there are the unrelenting memories of
powerlessness. "When somebody dies in your arms, you
know what life is about and how precious it is," says one
veteran. "They plead with you, out of their pain, 'Please,
please, save me!' . . . and you know that you can't. So you
come back and you try to tell people, but they don't want to
understand," he says. " 'You,' they say, 'it's *you* who's abnormal. Don't try and put the blame on us.' "

In his essay "Ecstasy and Violence," Rollo May speaks of
the psychic loneliness of modern man, a loneliness that is only
compounded in the life of the Vietnam veteran.

Now when we consider contemporary man—insignificant, lonely, more isolated as mass communication
becomes vaster . . . aware of his identity only to the
extent that he has lost it, yearning for community but
feeling awkward and helpless as he finds it—when we
consider this modern man, who will be surprised that he
yearns for ecstasy even of the kind that violence and war
may bring?

We are going to have upheavals of violence for as long
as experiences of significance are denied people. Everyone has a need for some sense of significance; and if we
can't make that possible, or even probable in our society,

then it will be obtained in destructive ways. The challenge is to find ways that people can achieve significance and recognition so that destructive violence will not be necessary. [8]

Others argue that the roots go even deeper and that every war is essentially a "holy war."

Lewis Mumford points out that the urban institution of war is actually rooted in the older "sacrificial magic" of tribal societies.

"If anything were needed to make the magical origins of war plausible, it is the fact that war, even when disguised by seemingly hardheaded economic demands, uniformly turns into a religious performance; nothing less than a wholesale ritual sacrifice." [9]

"It's ironic," says Jack McCloskey, who is a former national president of Vietnam Veterans Against the War. "When I was young, I wanted to be a priest. For ten years now, I've been doing this work and I'm exhausted and I don't know how to stop. They come in and plead with me . . . 'Please help me because I hurt people, I hurt myself!' Yet you know inside that it's not okay because you killed someone and you know you didn't have to. You took a life for nothing! It wasn't even for survival! And worse than anything," he says, burying his face in his hands, "is knowing that you were raised to believe that going to war and killing is what it took to be called a man! Sometimes," he said, "you listen and it's hard to know which side of the confessional you should be on."

For all of them, there are the recurring nightmares. . . .

A medic from Philadelphia speaks of one he has been having for years. "I keep having this dream that I reach into my medical bag for battle dressings and the battle dressings turn out to be a body bag. Over and over, no matter how often I keep reaching in, I keep producing body bags instead of battle dressings."

"I've tried to explain it to women," says another veteran, struggling to find the right words. "I tell them, 'What if you were nineteen years old, if you came from a small town and went away to college and all of a sudden you were always in danger of being raped, raped at every turn. All your friends have been raped, every one, every day! No one knew who was doing the raping or why it was happening. All you knew was that you were the next one and it would be happening to you, like it did to them every time you would turn around, You could not be an exception because there were no exceptions. There was only your turn.'"

And for some of them, there are reminders within reminders. . . .

Glenn "Ras" Raswyck, a thirty-four-year-old vet who is now a self-employed contractor, recalls the scene in the movie *The Deerhunter* in which the soldier plays Russian roulette by putting the gun to his head.

"When I was watching the movie, I kept saying to myself, 'This is crazy, this is awful!'" says Ras, "and then I remembered. . . .

"I was a flight-platoon sergeant and had to fill out the roster of names of helicopters that would go out each day or night. We all slept in these semi-tents, bunkers with sandbags, and there were all these cots on either side in a row. A helicopter wouldn't come back and then there would be this empty cot. But the empty cot always moved around. The first thing I thought of when I saw the roulette scene in the movie is that, indeed, we had played roulette. The empty cot moved, and there was always a new guy to fill it. But then where would the *next* empty cot be? Which one would it be? Would it be mine?"

While most veterans' memories take various forms, there is an abiding memory on which most seem to agree. It involves the question of intimacy.

"When you're in combat, you learn very fast to become very intimate and very close to people because your lives depend on it. But you set up a barrier, too, because they could get blown up tomorrow, and if they got blown up, in a way, part of you could die, too. So your survivial, they say, depends on being both detached and intimate."

Cross fire. . . .

And yet, in his book *Rumor of War*, Phil Caputo writes, "In war, the communion between men is as profound as between any lovers." [10]

Ras Raswyck says simply, "In Nam, I learned about sex without love from a prostitute and love without sex from my buddies."

Statistics:
48 percent of the people in this country had a close family member who served; 27 million men were eligible; only one-third of them ended up going into the military.

Dr. Hanna Levenson, a psychologist at the Veterans' Medical Center in San Francisco, speaks of the experience of the Vietnam veteran as "an individual experience, in many ways, because they came there independently and left independently from others. They did not come with a group, fight with a group, and leave Nam with them. Especially on his return, the veteran feels a terrible sense of isolation and separateness because of that, and as we have seen, that feeling of aloneness was compounded when he received no support on his return."

Dr. Levenson goes on to note that in her work of counseling wives of Vietnam veterans, she experiences that same

feeling of aloneness from another perspective. "So many feel
a lot of hesitancy in talking about their anger with their
husbands' inability to share their Vietnam experience with
them. For them, there is the additional feeling of
guilt . . . 'He's been through so much already and I feel I'm
only adding to it, but if I don't know what's going on inside
him, I feel so helpless about understanding what's happening,
about knowing what I can or ought to do.' "

Thus the wives must embark on a parallel journey with
their husbands. Like them they learn that only by sharing
their pain and their anger can they break through their
loneliness.

There were other insights . . . insights that came painfully and often at a great price. One of them dealt with
racism, which left a trail of scars in Vietnam.

For one veteran, confronting racism in Vietnam in the light
of life-and-death situations provided him with "one of the
most profound insights of all." He says, "Coming from where
I was, a small town in New Jersey, and being thrown in with
Iowa farm boys, big-city black guys from Chicago, guys from
California, I learned an unforgettable lesson. *All blood bleeds
red when it's on the killing floor.* When it's a fine line between
life and death, all people are alike, we're all the same human
beings. When you share the same fear, you become the same
people. In human terms, it's as simple as that."

"I see that blood even now," says Jack McCloskey. "The
wound is still open and still bleeding. The pain of being used,
being lied to! I can't cure the bitterness. I'm seeing doctors
and lawyers as well as street people. We've all been corrupted
by war," he says.

Peter Marin writes of the veterans' moral pain, an issue
most analysts shy away from because they feel it opens up
areas of pain for which there is no cure.

"The mistakes one makes are often transmuted directly into others' pain—there is sometimes no way to undo that pain—the dead remain dead, the maimed are forever maimed, and there is no way to deny one's responsibility or culpability, for those mistakes are written, forever and as if in fire, in others' flesh. This," he admits, "is a terrible and demanding wisdom. . . . They become suffering pariahs not only because of what they have done but because of the questions it raises for them—questions which their countrymen do not want to confront, questions for which, as a society, we have no answers." [11]

Who can take back the "dark night of the soul"? And more importantly, what will be the consequences for Christians who do not even attempt to minister to the moral pain?

> You, then, are the body of Christ. Everyone of you is a member of it. If one member suffers, all the members suffer with it; if one member is honored, all the members share its joy. (1 Cor 12:27,26)

"The veteran cannot heal himself," says Jack McCloskey. "Local America has to go through a purification rite before we can deal with the Vietnam veteran. Unless America can deal with Vietnam, we can't deal with the veteran."

In this regard, the anguished voice of the Vietnam survivor may prove to be prophetic for both Church and society.

If we are to be healed of Vietnam, then we must take responsibility that it doesn't happen again, say the veterans. Our legacy must be that we are the *last* generation to go to war.

We must take responsibility for the fact that we have used our power to betray one another. We must confront the ultimate betrayal: the fact that we have betrayed ourselves.

To be betrayed is to be crucified by one's trust, says Jean Houston. Yet it is at this precise point that Christians above all are called to reach out to the Vietnam veterans, assuring each of them that they are not alone.

Jesus was a young adult.

Like them, he was caught in cross fires of denial, indifference, and betrayal. He was betrayed by "his own," by those in whom he trusted and of whose love he had been assured. He was spat upon, mocked, humiliated, cursed, and crucified. He was rejected by his community . . . by his disciples, his brothers who proclaimed his teachings and were his public defenders.

One betrayed him for thirty pieces of silver. Another, who protested his love for him over and over, nonetheless denied him three times when to do otherwise would have meant political suicide. And in Gethsemane, when he pleaded for their prayer-presence—"You could not stay awake for even an hour?"—they denied him even this small comfort. They escaped through sleep and thus denied his approaching betrayal. "They could not keep their eyes open, nor did they know what to say to him" (Mk 14:27,40).

Even at the end, when he surrendered his spirit, the cross fire continued. His soul called out, "My God, my God, why have you forsaken me?" (Mk 15:34), while the eyes of his heart wept, "Father, forgive them, they know not what they do" (Lk 23:34).

As the voice of Jesus cries out from Calvary across the battlefields of centuries, perhaps he is saying . . . "You are not alone . . . each time you die, I die too! The wounds I bear, the blood I bleed are from your body and the bodies of all those to whom you made promises that you long to keep. My pulse is your pulse and it will never stop beating. My heartbeat contains the heartbeats of all those who died, pleading, in your arms.

"I have gone before you so that you may know that there is a life beyond heartbreak and shattered faith and trampled dreams. There is a life beyond betrayal and it is called the Resurrection, and it is there that I am waiting for you . . . *now, here, today!* It is taking place in the center of your life at this moment in time!

"My Resurrection is not an event frozen in history. It is a continual cycle of dying and rising, of surprise and surrender. It is my way of healing you as you transcend your memories; it is my way of walking with you toward a new heart, a new hope, a new understanding of my belief in you.

Who will separate us from the love of Christ? Trial, or distress, or persecution, or hunger, or nakedness, or danger, or the sword? . . . I am certain that neither death nor life, neither angels nor principalities, neither the present nor the future, nor power, neither height nor depth nor any other creature, will be able to separate us from the love of God. . . . (Rom 8:35,38-39)

"How can you trust me again? How can you believe me? I can only tell you that I, too, was human and I also believed. I did what I was told to do and believed what I was supposed to do. And I was used and lied to and betrayed. And in the end, filled with despair and loneliness, I closed my eyes on a cross, having completed a mission I did not understand.

"But look around. I have not died, not in 2,000 years, not on any battlefield. You would not let them kill me; each time you suffered and died, you remembered me on your cross and called out my name.

"And I have promised you . . . 'I will not leave you
orphans' " (Jn 10:10).

I know your deeds; that is why I have left an open door
before you which no one can close. I know that your
strength is limited; yet you have held fast to my word
and have not denied my name. (Rv 3:8)

As the People of God, how then can we move from the
Crucifixion to the Resurrection? How many more steep
flights must we climb?

"Not flights . . . steps," says Jack McCloskey. "Even
small steps. Once a year, invite a veteran to give a sermon, or
homily. Or have a parish potluck on Memorial Day, and
invite veterans and their families. Invite a veteran to talk to
your school children about being peace-keepers. Once a year,
take up a collection to aid your local vets' self-help group.
Encourage your diocese to sponsor retreats or days of recol-
lection for veterans."

Dr. Hanna Levenson suggests that churches and parishes
be the sites for reconciliation services for individual families
who have undergone stress or trauma. A mutual reconciliation service for the entire parish family might focus on the
simple theme of acceptance and could incorporate some of
the symbols of baptism (welcome), reconciliation (renewal),
confirmation (strengthening), and anointing (healing). The
eucharistic chalice could be passed from person to person as
the congregation stood around the altar in a circle, symbol-
izing their unity as the Body of Christ.

Dennis Geaney's words bear repeating: "The strength of
the Catholic Church is in the neighborhoods. It wins or loses
in parishes or neighborhoods in proportion to the kind of
leadership it provides for a community." [12]

It is "right and just" that the Vietnam veteran be welcomed and accepted with care and concern and love in the setting of the parish family. Until this happens with both sincerity and sensitivity, the Vietnam veteran will never be able to be "at home."

"I want so much to belong again," says one veteran. "I want so much to believe and feel the incredible peace and energy that I used to experience at Mass. Most of all," he says, "I want to be able to walk into a church and not be embarrassed to cry. I need to make atonement. I am so tired," he says, "of walking on broken glass."

O Jerusalem, Jerusalem, you slay the prophets and stone those who are sent to you! How often I have wanted to gather your children together as a mother bird collects her young under her wings, and you refused me! (Lk 13:34)

They are all around us, in our homes, our lives, our communities—needing us as brothers and sisters, sons and daughters, spouses, lovers, neighbors, friends.

As veterans, they have experienced a profound shattering of images of both self and humanity. They are, says Dr. Arthur Blank, victims of "the broken connection" in whom radical suffering or radical exposure to mutilation, death, and absurd, meaningless misery has caused a basic fault to appear in the individual's link to civilization. How this shows, says Blank, varies widely. But he believes Vietnam veterans have much in common with the survivors of Nazi death and concentration camps because they have lost some of basic faith in the capacity of humanity for goodness. [13]

"That's why the group is so important," says Ras Raswyck. "Each of us is coping in a different way, and we can share that

way with the others. Even if they don't choose it for themselves, they see someone else cope in a way that works for
them."

Peggy Tuxen was never on a search-and-destroy mission or
in a fire-fight, but she, too, felt the need to make atonement.
After Vietnam, she went back for a year and nursed in a
refugee camp on the Cambodian border.

"It wasn't easy to feel so unprotected during the sudden
bombings," she said, "but I felt I wanted to make up in my
own way for the damage we had done to that country and its
people."

Now, as a nurse-practitioner, Peggy's ministry continues.
She works in the area of human sexuality with underserved
populations like the native Americans and with teenage
Southeast Asian refugees in the heart of the city.

"I'll never forget, but I can forgive," says one veteran who
is a carpenter. "I don't think we're anything special; we're just
ordinary human beings. We went and did what we did
because we thought that's what you wanted. We don't really
need a parade anymore; we just want some respect, some
simple acknowledgement. Maybe Jesus died for our sins, but
those boys died for yours, too. People lived a good life in the
sixties, and part of it is because we went over there. Now
everybody's paying the dues . . . economically, spiritually . . . we're all in this together," he says.

"There are vets out there who feel and who are caring,"
says Ras Raswyck. "It's not so much that they want recognition. They just don't want to be ashamed. They just don't
want to have to always not talk about it, to change the
subject. And I think," he says, "we're seeing that happening
more and more. It seems to me, for a long time, nobody
talked about Vietnam except us. Now everybody seems to be
talking about it, and we're the ones who are listening."

While they have their own agenda, Vietnam veterans are, in many ways, a metaphor for all young adults in the Church.

Both feel ignored, angry, alienated, forgotten. As members of the Body of Christ, they are the "walking wounded." Because their questions challenge the Church's conscience, they have become battle casualties, and, on the deepest level, both feel handicapped and paralyzed.

As young adults, they have become disenchanted with institutions. Though their politics may differ, in a sense, they join with all conscientious objectors of their generation in their flight from a church which does not reach out to welcome them and to which they feel they can no longer "come home."

The vitality of the Body of Christ cannot continue without the lifeblood of the young adult population. Their presence and power are critical; without them the eyes of the Body of Christ will dim and cloud over; the ears of the Body of Christ will strain to hear.

But whatever need the Church may have for them is far outweighed by the need young adults have for one another. Only they, as peers, can understand one another's spiritual longings; out of their woundedness, only they can minister to each other in terms of their generation's needs.

We can no longer deny them that opportunity. The legacy of the Church of the eighties should be one of welcome, beginning with ways to welcome all young adults who, perhaps more than any other generation, have fought and paid for private and public wars in the name of peace. Certainly, there is no more exhausted warrior than the Vietnam veteran. They have waited for a long time. What will it take to finally begin?

"Little steps," says Jack McCloskey. "Little steps like those which brought young adult veterans like Margaret Walker to the door of the Haight Vets Counseling Center when she was scared to death and almost turned and ran away."

Little steps, such as those Jack McCloskey took when he walked forward to welcome her . . . little steps such as those which occurred over the weeks when others in the group reached out across the room to Margaret's pain.

There was once another room . . . an upper room where men and women also huddled together in fear and anguish, uncertain, and, in some cases, terrified. They, too, longed to be delivered, to trust again, to have the strength to believe. That time and place has come to be called the Feast of Pentecost.

Though they are separated by centuries, the upper room and the room in the Haight are one and the same. For Pentecost is the Feast of Knowing At Last That You Are Not Alone. . . .

Brothers and sisters, we do not wish to leave you in the dark about the trouble we had in Asia; we were crushed beyond our strength, even to the point of despairing of life. We were left to feel like men and women condemned to death so that we might trust, not in ourselves, but in God who raises the dead. He rescued us from that danger of death and will continue to do so. We have put our hope in him who will never cease to deliver us. *But you must help us with your prayers* so that on our behalf God may be thanked for the gift granted us through the prayers of so many. (Adapted from 2 Cor 1:8-11.)

TOUCH ME

Touch me in secret places no one has reached before,
in silent places where words only interfere,
in sad places where only whispering makes sense.

touch me . . . in the morning when night still clings,
at midday when confusion crowds upon me,
at twilight as I begin to know who I am,
in the evening when I see you and hear you—best of all.

touch me . . . like a child who will never have enough
    love,
for I am an adult who has known enough pain to love,
a child who wants to be lost in your arms,
a parent who sometimes is strong enough to give.

touch me . . . in crowds when a single look tells
    everything,
in solitude when it's too dark to even look,
in absence when I reach for you through time and miles.

touch me . . . when I ask, when I'm afraid to ask.

touch me . . . with your lips, your hands, your words,
your presence in the room.

touch me . . . gently for I am fragile,
firmly for I am strong,
often for I am alone.

Author Unknown

CHAPTER TWELVE

HEALING

Binding the Wounds

"Is there no balm in Gilead, no physician there? Why grows not new flesh over the wound of the daughter of my people?"

Jeremiah 8:22

All over the world, the Body of Christ cries out to heaven for healing. And the cries are heard and the healing happens when the human hands of Christ reach out and touch the wounded and brokenhearted with love.

Those who minister to the sexually wounded are confronted daily with distortions of sexuality and spirituality which these victims have internalized in their bodily self-understanding. For some, these distortions include inappropriate role definitions and expectations especially for women; for others, the acceptance of suffering as powerlessness; for still thers, spiritual despair resulting from sexual self-loathing when one's sex is experienced as a commodity.

The young, as either active or passive participants, carry very deep scars.

At St. Joseph's House in Minneapolis, Sister Charlotte Madigan, CSJ, ministers to women and children, many of whom are victims of violent or sexually abusive husbands, fathers, or pimps. In the five years since the Catholic Worker facility opened, almost 1,000 women and children have sought shelter there.

In another shelter in the St. Cloud, Minnesota, area the

plight of the battered woman in rural areas is evident. Seventy-five percent of the women who seek shelter there are Catholic. Their geographical isolation only compounds their problem. Mary Bader Papa relates the story of one such woman who was brought to the Center by a sheriff.

> The woman, a Catholic, was pregnant with her tenth child. She was not permitted by her husband to leave their farm except to go to church. He would not even permit her to do the shopping. He also beat her regularly, especially in anger about her repeated pregnancies, yet the husband refused to practice any birth control, including abstinence. At the time she came to the shelter, the husband was trying to force the woman to have an abortion, however. [1]

What advice does the Church offer to that part of the Body of Christ which is black and blue with battering? What advice does it give the women who have run screaming into the night, their terrified children running after them? How many phone books in rectories and convents list the telephone numbers of battered women's shelters to which they can refer these women? Who does it send to the rape centers and women's shelters to minister to them?

The statistics are stark. One out of every four women will be sexually assaulted sometime during her life, says Linda Eberth, Program Coordinator for Sexual Trauma Services, sponsored by San Francisco's Department of Public Health. The statistic for men is one out of every ten.

Throughout the world, violence to women's bodies victimizes the entire Body of Christ. The rape of the 30,000 women of Bangladesh continues to haunt the world. Among those victims are children of eight and grandmothers of seventy-five. Rejected thereafter in their villages, thousands of these women saw their only solution in suicide. [2]

A million women in twenty-six African countries have undergone circumcision through the surgical removal of either their vulva or clitoris, often under the most primitive conditions. The major reason given is that by eliminating these points of genital stimuli, the women will not feel sexual desire and will, therefore, not stray. [3]

And yet here in this country, ironically, tragically, down the street, across town, American women pay to participate in their own rape and battering by subscribing to hard-core pornographic movies and videotapes in their own homes. The sale of these porno tapes often outnumbers the sale of Hollywood movie videotapes by three to one.

These same women subscribers watch the six o'clock news and are horrified by the rape of our Maryknoll Sisters in El Salvador. But they do not make the connection. They do not see the human price tag, the linkage between one rape and the other, when they pay their monthly subscription bill. They would be shocked if you suggested that they encourage women's bodies to be used as society's trampoline.

What is tragic is that these are good women, generous women, women who are friends of ours and members of our families. But something has happened to cause them to become disembodied. Something has turned them into disspirited observers, even voyeurs, as they watch other women being brutalized.

What kind of spiritual sterilization has taken place in these women's lives which has caused them to deny their own denigration and brutalization?

Is it because, in their own lifetimes, they have undergone a thousand unwanted abortions . . . the forced abortions of their women's hopes and images? Will they go to their graves grieving over the words and music of their stillborn dreams? And what of their children? What do the women say to them? How does their denial affect their children's dreams?

. . .

Father Bruce Ritter, OFM, describes the Minnesota Strip as the slimy underbelly of Manhattan, a fifteen-block stretch of Eighth Avenue porno parlors, strip joints, pizza places, cheap bars, fleabag hotels, and thousands of drifters, hookers, and their pimps. It parallels Times Square and intersects that block on 42nd Street where a couple dozen third-rate movie houses crowd together in grim brilliance. At night, the crowds of castoffs and nomads and derelicts mingle with the crowds of affluent theatergoers from the high rent districts and suburbs. A lot of kids go there and make their living. One of them sits across the desk from Father Bruce, a fifty-three-year-old Franciscan priest who directs Covenant House, a rescue protection agency on West 41st Street. The kid is one of 12,000 young people under twenty-one Father Bruce will try to help this year.

He is seventeen years old. He has syphilis, ulcers, intestinal parasites, lice. He is an alcoholic. He tells the priest that he has been a male prostitute for three years, that he has survived by hustling on the streets of New York City. He has sold himself in perhaps a thousand beds and a thousand cars. He does not like what he has known of life, and he challenges the priest to tell him why he should not jump off a bridge.

The priest insists that the boy has better choices than the streets or suicide. The boy finally agrees to stay over and talk again in the morning. He gets a shower, a hot meal, and a clean bed. Silently, Father Bruce says a prayer of thanksgiving. Maybe he'll be lucky with this one. [4]

. . .

The Body of Christ weeps for its young adult Body. It is a
Body called to glory, a body designed to dazzle us with the
Creator's imagination . . . the interlocking of limbs, the
multiplication of cells, organs that routinely perform miracles
minute by minute, lifetime by lifetime, a heart that beats, for
some, without ceasing for almost a century. Yet, for many, it
has been a body and soul dwarfed . . . a body stunted and
broken and beaten because it never truly believed it was born
in the image and likeness of God and was, therefore,
beautiful.

. . .

In France, the Little Sisters of Jesus minister to prostitutes:
"Our ministry to *our friends*," they write, "is one of welcome
and hospitality. They seek in us the family they have never
known. Theirs is a constant struggle of dying and rising, of
hopeful 'come-backs' often followed by undertows which
pull them back into 'the life.' "

In 1957, two "Petites Soeurs" (Little Sisters) established a
small "fraternity of contact" in Marseilles in the midst of the
area where prostitution was rampant. They very easily made
contact, and word of their ministry spread rapidly. Very soon,
the Little Sisters perceived the need for another "fraternity"
outside the quarter of prostitution "where we could receive
our friends in a family spirit. The welcome we offer there is
always free of charge. Our friends can stay there for a few
days or a few weeks, according to their needs, alone or with
their children. They share the life of the Little Sisters as a
family. That is why we are only able to have one or two at a
time. Counseling is always done respecting their ideas. They
are gradually directed towards social service which is capable

of helping them legally. Our primary goal is to offer them a respectful friendship, a patient 'listening ear' without judgment and a warm family atmosphere."

"A" is one of the women. She was without a family. She married very young after a miserable childhood. She was unhappy and went to live with a male friend, by whom she had a child. He then left her and she was alone with the baby, without money. She gave up her baby, and a nervous breakdown followed. After hospitalization, she went to Marseilles looking for a job and was picked up at the railroad station by a man who introduced her to prostitution. Over and over she attempted to get out of it and finally was able to find other work. Her second marriage ended in divorce, and she lost her child (with whom she had reconnected) in an accidental death. Despondent, she turned again to prostitution and alcoholism. Finally, after several stays in the hospital and at the home of the Little Sisters, she married again but ran away. Today she spends her life in mental hospitals and then returns to the prostitution quarters. Her alcoholism gets progressively worse, and she cannot gain stability. "But she is a symbol of hope," say the Little Sisters, "because she starts from zero all the time and believes she will make it each time, though she is so deeply ill."

When the Little Sisters care for her, she says to them, "Tell the Judge that I do like Our Lord: I fall under my Cross, then I get up again."

. . .

We offer these women . . . our friends . . . a listening ear. . . .

For I was hungry and you gave me food,
I was thirsty and you gave me drink. . . .

In hospitals where women have undergone surgery
for mastectomies
and hysterectomies.
I was a stranger and you welcomed me,
naked and you clothed me. . . .
When I lost my infants at childbirth,
you wept with me when I was inconsolable.
I was ill and you comforted me,
in prison and you came to visit me. (Mt 25:35-36)
"I was in shock after the rape," said one.
"I kept denying the fact that incest could exist
in our family," said another.
"It has been years, but I am still numb after
the abortion," said still another. . . .

. . .

*Connie had never written anything before that she hadn't felt
ready to write. She'd never put down on paper what she wasn't
ready to say out loud.*

*And she wasn't ready to say this out loud yet because she
wasn't ready to answer the inevitable question that would come
afterward.*

"Why?", they would ask. "Why did you do it?"

*The time would come, she assured herself, when she would be
ready, but that time was not now. Someday it would come.
Someday, she would stand up before God, the world, and herself
and admit the abortion. But that day had not yet come, until
today. . . .*

As I watched the twins, daughters of a close friend,
coming home from school in their "catholicly" creased
uniforms, long blonde hair like dancing sunlight in the

autumn afternoon, I knew the time had come, however unready or uneasy I felt.

I thought of her, the child of mine who would have been ten now. Ten years ago, my husband and I paid to have her taken from my body. We weren't evil; we simply didn't believe in life, not even our own, not individually nor collectively as a couple.

When David said to me in London, "You can either have the abortion and stay with me in England for the rest of the summer, or you can fly back to the States, have the baby, and when I come home, we'll get a divorce," he wasn't being evil; he was simply taking his revenge. It wasn't that he really wanted the abortion; he just didn't want to be a father, not any more than I had wanted to be a wife when he'd been in Vietnam.

Latent hippie that I was in 1969, David and I married, foolishly and flippantly, one week before he left for Vietnam. I don't think I ever comprehended what had happened. We drove to Waukegan, Illinois, were married by a justice of the peace, lived with his mother for one week, and then he was gone.

And while he was gone, I fulfilled every suspicion he ever had about "lonely wives." I projected omniscient powers upon him in his absence, assumed he would accept my unfaithful behavior, and thus had no problem telling him the truth when he came home. His understanding was nil; his hurt complete. And that's why, in 1970, an innocent unborn child died in London.

How is it now, eleven years later? How is it after the abortion, after the divorce? How is it remembering?

My life these days reminds me of a movie, *Journey to the Center of the Earth*, only my movie is entitled

Journey to the Center of My Self. I find the same gargan-
tuan monsters lurking inches beneath the surface; I
climb insurmountable, treacherous peaks, losing my grip
again and again, never reaching the top; I hide in dark,
dank caves wishing to spend the rest of my life
entombed within their walls, however lonely it may be; I
stumble through unbearably hot, endless jungles forever
chopping away at the same underbrush I thought I'd
finally cut through yesterday. There are glorious victo-
ries, although devastating defeats have taken their toll.
But there is humor still, in spite of hunger and hurt, and
above all else, there is an unimaginable respect for life—
all life, no matter how small or insignificant it may
appear.

Ants are forever safe from my footstep unless care-
lessness makes me heedless of their presence. Flies
trapped in my office are maneuvered toward the open
window to stop them from beating themselves to death
against the promising pane of light. I find it impossible
to stop tears from appearing at the sight of a fallen tree.
I scream silently at chainsaws, "Life is precious. It is
sacred. It must be preserved."

Christmas will be with us soon. We will celebrate
life—a life that called forth life, a life that gave life even
in death. I wish I could look into his eyes, into the eyes
of that child born so long ago, into the eyes of that man
who died so long ago, into the eyes of that Jesus I long
to know.

I wish I could stand before him face-to-face and
tell him how sorry I am for messing up so many things
so many times. I wish I could hear him say I am
forgiven.

I need to hear him say, "I love you, Connie. I love
you no less than I love your child. I thought you knew
that. Life doesn't come from your womb. Life comes
from your self, from you. Go now and bring forth that
life from others. Do it with your smile, do it with your
presence, do it with your words. I never had a child
either, Connie, but I have you."

And I would say, "Yes, Lord. . . . Yes, you really
do."

. . .

Reconciliation is the missing piece in the abortion picture,"
says Father Edward Bryce, director of the U.S. Bishops' Office
for Pro-Life Activities. "With the increasing incidence of
abortion . . . the percentage of Catholic women in need of
reconciliation is growing. Pastors must be present in a manner reminiscent of the healing Christ," he writes. "To a
woman who has had an abortion he must bring assurance
• of God's overpowering love for her;
• of Jesus' agony in Gethsemane and his death on Calvary as
including and embracing her;
• of the full forgiveness Jesus offers in the sacrament of
reconciliation;
• of forgiveness as a gift of God to be accepted, not earned;
• of God's love for the child he has called into existence;
• of God's ability to love the child uniquely and in a manner
beyond her comprehension;
• of God's hope for her that is implied in the gift of each new
day."
Father Bryce also offers practical suggestions. He advises
pastors *to talk to the women who have been through the mill and*

who are able to say what it was like and how they put their lives together again. He suggests that pastors "talk to your people in the pulpit, in your witness, in your speeches—as the ambassador of Christ. Petitions at Mass might include those parents who have been involved in an abortion. Retreat houses should be especially aware of the abortion issue and be prepared to provide spiritual guidance. Each parish should have women trained in emergency pregnancy-sevice skills. Every junior and senior high school should have someone alert to the pastoral dimensions of teenage pregnancy. Remember, too, the parents and siblings of the one who has aborted suffer guilt, as well as those who were participants in the abortion. It is critical that seminary professors and future priests be well-prepared to minister to those whose lives were affected by abortion." [5]

. . .

As the Body of Christ, do we ask, "When will violence end? . . . Where does it begin?" As Church, what attitudes do we communicate by our language and our actions? What words do we use to describe women—*useful, partner, nuisanace, doll, workhorse, necessary evil, trouble, joke*? How do the words contribute to the image of woman as object, as someone to be ignored, tolerated, used, or punished? The questions are being asked increasingly by both young adult men and women in the Church today.

"Maybe we need to go back and ask what the 'laying on of hands' has come to mean to us. Has it become an empty symbol for Christians? they ask. "What is it saying about how we should touch each other? Do we touch with tenderness or is our touch that of the man with the 'withered hand'?"

"To touch with love is a miracle," says Nancy Hennessey Cooney. "Touch heals other people of their hungers and gives them a good feeling about being alive. Look at what Jesus' touch did for people—it turned a fisherman into a leader of thousands, a prostitute into a friend, a doubter into a believer. Jesus didn't just touch people's bodies—he touched their hearts. He was unafraid to touch others and be touched. He never forced his touch on anyone, but he always responded to their needs in a positive outgoing way." [6]

All over the world, the Body of Christ cries out for healing. . . . And day after day, the Body of Christ, which is the image of the healing Jesus, opens its arms to touch the members of that broken Body with love and reverence. Father Edward Bryce, Sister Charlotte Madigan, Father Bruce Ritter, and the Little Sisters of Jesus are but a few of the healers in the Body.

And each time healing happens, it is because the healer speaks with the compassionate voice of Jesus and touches the person with Jesus' transforming love.

But if Jesus walked today among us, would he ask us other questions about his Body? Would he ask . . . "Beloved, as my Church, why do you bleed needlessly? My sisters, why do you allow men to use your blood, *my* blood against you as a sign of weakness and ritual impurity?

"My brothers, why are you blind? *Where* are you blind? What is it you cannot or will not allow yourself to look at, to see? Are you deaf and dumb? Why? Is it because there is something you cannot bear to hear or refuse to say? What evil spirits do you long to have cast from your body? What are your vanities, your appetites, your addictions? What are your hidden fears and hungers? Where are you lame? Is it because you are terrified at the thought of taking a step forward? Why are you paralyzed? Is it safer than taking any risks at all?"

Again and again, we need to hear Jesus say "Beloved, if you

truly believe that you are my Body, then 'Fear is useless; what is needed is trust and [your lives] will be spared' " (Lk 8:50).

We need to accept the amazing gift of life which Jesus pours out to us at his Resurrection. We need to believe life is something he wants us to cherish and celebrate.

We have been assured that "*by his wounds [we] were healed*" (1 Pt 2:24). His Body has suffered enough! Thus, do we give scandal when we allow woundedness in ourselves or in others.

Will we continue to distrust him? Will we continue to be blind and deaf and lame and paralyzed as an excuse to camp out on Calvary rather than accept the pilgrim risks for new life which he holds out to us on Easter morning?

Must he say to us, too. . . .

Take your finger and examine my hands.

Put your hand into my side.

Do not persist in your unbelief, but believe! (Jn 20:27)

When will we, as Church, as the Body of Christ, finally respond . . . as Thomas did . . .

"My Lord, and my God!" (Jn 20:28)

THE GOOD
(FOR EAVAN)

The good are vulnerable
As any bird in flight.
They do not think of safety,
Are blind to possible extinction
And when most vulnerable
Are most themselves.
The good are real as the sun,
Are best perceived through clouds
Of casual corruption
That cannot kill the luminous sufficiency
That shines on city, sea and wilderness,
Fastidiously revealing
One man to another,
Who yet will not accept
Responsibilities of light.
The good incline to praise,
To have the knack of seeing that
The best is not destroyed
Although forever threatened.
The good go naked in all weathers,
And by their nakedness rebuke
The small protective sanities
That hide men from themselves.
The good are difficult to see
Though open, rare, destructible.
Always, they retain a kind of youth,
The vulnerable grace
Of any bird in flight,

Content to be itself,
Accomplished master and potential victim,
Accepting what the earth or sky intends.
I think that I know one or two
among my friends.

Brendan Kennelly

CHAPTER THIRTEEN

TRUST THE PEOPLE
Young Adults Reclaim Peer Ministry

"The young should become the first apostles of the young, be in direct contact with them, exercising the apostolate by themselves among themselves, taking account of their social environment." [1]
Decree on Apostolate of Lay People

"Programs and projects for evangelization should be developed in terms of the situation of those to be evangelized, not in terms of what will satisfy the zeal and goodwill of the evangelizers." [2]
Archbishop Francis Hurley

In 1976, fifteen women and men from across the nation gathered and issued the following statement to the Church in the United States. . . .

"In a country which boasts the potential to feed the world, we, as a nation, face a crippling starvation, unprecedented in our 200 years of celebrated history. . . .

"Fed on a daily diet of distrust, cynicism, fear and hopelessness, the American people are crying out, as never before, for meaning in a meaningless world. . . .

"By far the strongest cry for meaning comes from young adults, age eighteen to thirty-five, who, in large numbers, are not only disenfranchised from the traditional structures, standards and messages of society, but, more tragically, from the Church itself. In some cases, that alienation manifests itself in contempt.

"However, the young adults who have left the institution because of what they identify as sexism, racism, cowardice and hypocrisy, continue to hunger for a community of love, hope, and peace, as promised in the message of Jesus.

"As Catholic ministers to the young adult, our commitment is to help build that community. To do so, we must also open ouselves to be ministered to by the disenfranchised . . . in their struggle for liberation from those things which prohibit them from realizing their full potential as human persons loved by God. In that way, we are called to be both advocates and facilitators . . . , to confront both church and secular decision-makers and to enable the disenfranchised to speak for themselves. . . ."

The fifteen voices were those of the first National Young Adult Ministry Board convened by Father Pat O'Neill, OSA, then representative for Young Adult Ministry to the United States Catholic Conference. Because of the first sparks struck by that statement, the fires of Young Adult Ministry in the United States were fanned.

Today, in various dioceses across the country, young adults gather and minister to one another by sharing the Gospel message in terms of their lives and in a language which they can understand.

The models of ministry they employ are striking in their openness to and their honesty about young adults' needs. Sexuality and spirituality rank as issues of critical concern in their daily lives.

In Young Adult Ministry, there are no untouchable issues. Though based in and funded by dioceses, Young Adult Ministry is, by its very nature, a worshipping community without walls. Healing and reconciliation takes place wherever young adults gather, whether it be in the workplace, in the kitchen of an apartment in a singles complex, in a bar, or in a church.

The peer minister, more often than not, is a circuit rider who makes ministerial house calls rather than a priest in residence in a rectory. Working alongside priests and nuns, the young adult minister is, increasingly, a professionally trained layperson, or, in one young adult's words, "one of the folks."

Twenty-nine-year-old Rick Haraway of the Diocese of Raleigh, North Carolina, is one such minister. For five years, he has ministered in a diocese which includes young adults in middle management positions, in rural farming settings, and in an academic community composed of North Carolina's famous university research and industry "triangle" which boasts the highest concentration of Ph.D.'s in the nation. Rick drives nearly 30,000 miles a year in his ministry as one of two staff people in the Raleigh Diocese, one of the first in the country to initiate a full-fledged diocesan program for young adults.

The basis of Rick's ministry to young adults is personal contact and a deep respect for individuals "where they are."

"This involves meeting them, finding out where they live, what they do, what they are interested in, and what their needs are," says Rick. He advises those interested in gathering young adults to "have people over for dinner, one or two at a time, or go visit them for a couple of hours in the evening. *The crucial thing*," he says, "*is simply to listen.*"

"Don't judge people or try to bring them to your point of view. Simply listen and attempt to care for the people you are talking with. This is crucial! This prevents the individual or the team from getting caught up in its own self-interest and lets young adults know that the Church cares about them and is attempting to reach out to them and speak to their life situation," he says.

"Young adults come looking for 'a place to call home,' " says Rick, "a significant sharing community, and, within that context, significant others to whom they can relate. The major questions are not 'religious' but relational. Lots of the young adults are professionally successful, but they don't know what to do with their values. When they speak about careers, the questions often revolve around whether the job is of ultimate value: Simply, does it benefit people? When they speak about morality, they ask questions like, 'Is it more moral to be contraceptively prepared than to get an abortion? Is premarital sex life-giving for me, or is it a using situation out of my own neediness?' What they are really saying," says Rick, "is that they can separate the issues of sexuality and spirituality in their minds but not in their bodies."

Rick sees his job as providing a setting in which to discuss these questions by offering young adults hospitality, by providing community, by welcoming strangers to that community, and by encouraging them to help one another. This is done through peer ministry in a variety of social settings—from ski trips, tennis weekends, white-water rafting trips and beach parties to prayer weekends, workshops, and retreat weekends. A retreat experience called Venture is for eighteen to twenty-two year olds who are in transition from family or school.

"The development of Christian leadership training is seen more in terms of the community than the institution," Rick says. "As a minister, I feel I have a responsibility to listen to the magisterium and then relate what I hear to my own life experience," he continues, "and then relate that life experience back to the magisterium.

"For me, the personal challenge in young adult ministry is to remain a peer and not to become clerical; in other words, I

work as a professional without setting myself apart and setting up walls. Certainly, it's critical to be in touch with my
own feelings in terms of my relationships with women.
Otherwise, my professional position could paralyze me."

Rick, who has worked with approximately 2,000 young
adults in his ministry, sees one of the benefits of his work
occur when his peers move away. "Having had an experience
of young adult ministry with us, they feel more confident in
asking the parishes into which they move to provide the same
opportunity for young adults in their new setting. And
because they have been through leadership-training programs
themselves, they are in a position not only to ask for young
adult programs but to provide them as well. The leadership
training programs we offer are designed not only to surface
leaders and develop leadership but to give young adults the
practical skills and tools to organize.

Another of these programs is a Peer Ministry Formation
Program called Encounter with Christ, which is given by
trained Young Adult Ministers. The weekend experience
combines prayer, study, and action and centers on a personal
relationship with Christ.

"The basic assumption behind an effective young adult
ministry is that it is for, by, and with young adults," says Rick.
"The team should be mostly young adults.

"Perhaps the best thing I bring to my ministry," he continued, "is my own vulnerability. A lot of the time, I don't know
whether a decision is appropriate; as a lay minister, I have no
models. But I've learned that it's not only okay but important
to make mistakes in ministry.

"As a minister, I just have to keep asking the same questions and expressing the same needs we all share in common,"
he says. "I need to be free and human enough to acknowledge that I need someone to just love me and challenge me

and be an equal. The biggest surprise? That I ended up being the type of minister that I am and realizing that it works."

Young Adult Ministers throughout the country report increasing interest in issues of spirituality and sexuality, especially among young adults who have become disenchanted and alienated from the Church. Some attend gatherings around these topics out of curiosity; others have a genuine desire to integrate their sexuality with traditional values; and still others feel a need to challenge the Church on what many young adults think is the Church's "head in the sand" attitude on sexuality.

The program outline for a recent weekend conference on sexuality and spirituality advertised in *The Rainbow Connection*, the provocative publication sponsored by The Young Adult Ministry Office of the Diocese of Milwaukee, is an example of the creative and holistic approach one diocese is taking to address the areas of spirituality and sexuality.

Issues of intimacy, androgyny, loneliness, sexual crisis points, healing through prayer, body movement, sexist language . . . all were addressed by young adults and discussed from a perspective of peer ministry. A values-discernment presentation asked participants—individually in journal writing and then later in discussion with the larger group—to reflect on such relational issues as cohabitation, masturbation, homosexuality, and marriage. In a spirit of reverence, participants were asked to reflect on and share their responses to such questions as "How has the loving concern of God and others broken through the barriers of my isolation to heal the ambivalent, even destructive, tendencies my sexuality also contains? How have I grown in my ability to be intimate with others and thus with the Lord of life?"

"It was," said one participant, "exhausting but joyful because it helped me to grow spiritually. I realized that if I

could not take joy in sex, I could not take joy in God." Still
another noted, "It gave me an opportunity to analyze my
personal values and beliefs in an understanding environment.
I left with a feeling of self-esteem, contentment, and yes—
holiness."

In their liturgies, the participants proclaimed their belief
that

Sexuality is the unfolding of creation . . .
inside the flesh and blood, God made man and
woman,
in the genes and the chromosomes are the inheritance
of sexuality, desire, compassion, hormones, hair on
the chest, soft skin, of passion. . . .
Sexuality is to say yes to creation,
   Yes to life
   Yes to the living
   Yes to the unborn. . . .
Sexuality affirms the creativity of man and woman.
It believes in God the Creator. . . .
Sexuality is when two are one,
Each is whole, when two are side by side.
Sexuality is the life of repentance and forgiveness.
Sexuality affirms the reconciliation of man and
woman.
It believes in God the reconciler. [3]

Young Adult Ministry in the United States is, both by
necessity and evolution, peer ministry. The decline in vocations to religious life is one reason why laypersons are assum-
ing responsibility for young adult ministry. Another is lack of
funding. Both would seem to indicate that if young adult

ministry is going to survive in the Church, it's going to have to find a life of its own.

In the Diocese of Toledo, Ohio, Young Adult Minister Tom Puszczwicz reports that for young adults in his area, that is already happening. The diocese's two main projects, Exercise in Christian Living, a retreat movement for eighteen to thirty year olds, and the Catholic Youth Association are essentially self-supporting and are based on the concept of peer ministry. While some funding for the nineteen counties comes from the diocese and the Community Chest, the bulk of the money is raised by the young adults themselves. Some of it is used for an active advertising campaign to recruit young adults for the Catholic Club, a campaign that asks, simply, "Are you young? . . . Are you Catholic? . . . ," and then goes on to extend an invitation to participate in events and recreation at the sports center, the health clubs, and the Coffeehouse, all of which are part of the Catholic Club's activities.

Tom's calendar includes workshops and retreats on sexuality. In response to one young adult's comment that "I never rejected what the Church taught about sexuality, but I never bought it either," Tom says, "I think that the Church has a stand on sexuality that young adults can live with, but I don't think the young adults are buying it because I don't think the Church has done a very good job of selling it. That is one of the things I think young adults need to discuss."

Thom O'Neill, a California consultant in Young Adult Ministry, agrees. "So often, young adults are rebelling in a vacuum," he says. "They reject the entire institution because of some isolated bad experience or because they think the only thing the Church ever taught about sex was that it was wrong. So often they have no real understanding or knowledge of the underlying theology of marriage or family, and no sense of church history which shows how, over and over, the Church underwent change and reform. The Church is a human institution with a long and rich tradition. I would like to see young adults be made aware of that. I think, for the most part, in this area they've been shortchanged. I tell them they should have the whole picture on the current theology of sexuality before they make a decision to discount the Church," he says.

Father John Cusick, Coordinator of Young Adult Ministry for the Archdiocese of Chicago, agrees, and he challenges young adults first to test their sexual values against church teaching and only then to take a stand. At a conference on sexuality, he asked them to reflect on such questions as: "What is sacred about sexuality? Where is its specialness? How does it promote human dignity?" Then he asked them to answer those questions in terms of their own lives.

"Church happens when people meet and discuss 'meaning questions'—questions about what it is to be human," Cusick states. "And those discussions need to happen in a place where we can go and be ourselves and have a good time and feel that there are others like us around. What we need is a Catholic bar," he continued, "a place where we won't get hustled or hassled, where we don't have to act the part.

"In the past, the Church has offered young adults only two models of sexuality," Cusick continues, "virginity and marriage. Most of today's young adults are not comfortable with the first or ready for the second. They see the Church as a Club, where you either obey all the rules or you break all the rules. But in reality, they are hoping the Church will stand with them and be helpful to them. Down deep, I believe they want it to be credible and significant in their lives."

Cynthia Hicks-Halloran, Director of the Harvard-Radcliffe

Catholic Student Center, which is in contact with about 1,000 undergraduates each year, agrees.

"I think we're seeing a new wave of young adults now, a group which has grown up in the post-Vatican II Church and has had a good experience of community. While their theology may be vague, on certain levels they're aware that because of the Church, they live with a tradition of incredible truth and wisdom. At this point in their journey, they're trying to make sense of that in terms of their own lives.

"They have a hunch that the Church has something to say to them which they haven't yet heard. The best of them," says Cynthia, "are very patient with that. They want to give it an honest try. Their sexual questions revolve around relationships. Some are looking for rules and regulations and permissions. Others are simply listening."

Cynthia notes that while a good many students only go to Mass when their parents visit them it is not unusual for a hundred or more to show up at the Catholic Student Center to participate in the Spaghetti Supper "traveling show," which the Center stages on a regular basis at the various Harvard houses during the year. She notes that the students join enthusiastically in the shopping, cooking, and serving. "It has become," she said, "a wonderful experience of community.

"It's in this kind of context that a lot of them end up testing and discussing their ideas about spirituality and sexuality," says Cynthia. "And they are doing it in the Church's best tradition: by sharing a meal and sharing their stories in the company of their peers. They are, in the best sense, building community.

"What will come from these kinds of experiences of 'church' remains to be seen," says Cynthia. "This is a generation which is marked by its openness as much as by its

questioning. For the most part, these young adults are not
hobbled with 'bad dreams' about a priest or a nun who hurt
their feelings or broke their heart in the third grade.

"It's a golden opportunity for the Church both to reach out
to young adults and to learn from their questions," claims
Cynthia. "It's also a generation that the Church might never
meet in the same way again."

For ten years, sexuality workshops have been an integral
part of the Channel program in the Archdiocese of Seattle,
according to staff person Mike Edwards. Channel provides
professional assistance to young adults as they begin ministry
in the church of the Northwest. To date, the Seattle program
has "channeled" 113 committed and talented men and women
between ages twenty-one and twenty-six into parishes,
schools, and agencies in the diocese. During a three-month
program, Channel participants are trained in theology, ministry, and communication skills, and study such key ministry
issues as social justice, sexuality and adult development, parish ministry and legal services, and prayer and spirituality.
Though it receives about twenty percent of its funding from
the Archdiocese, Channel is a nonprofit orgaization and takes
responsibility for raising the remaining eighty percent of its
funding from the community.

Edwards commented on both the evolution and the
flexibility of the sexuality workhops and retreats Channel has
sponsored in the decade since its founding. "Each year the
agenda has been somewhat different, according to the needs
which surface from the particular group. The participants
enter the program from a variety of backgrounds. Many have
had a wide range of sexual experiences, others have had little
or none. Some years we need to address personal issues in the
sense of simply recognizing that we have problems in the
areas of sexuality and sexism, and we need to deal with it;

other years we need to bring in a theologian to provide
direction, information, or perspective.

"The important thing is to have members of the group
name the issues and take responsibility for discussing them.
Recently, the issue was sexual politics; the women in the
group were able to talk about their confusion, fear, and anger
in terms of role expectations. It's this kind of open dialogue
which is healthy in ministry," Edwards says.

He feels that in the past the Church has not spoken about
sexuality to young adults in "a real way." "They talk a lot
about sexuality, but they don't *say anything* that really relates
to the daily experiences of young adults in terms of their
sexuality. As a consequence, young adults are continuing to
take ownership for such issues as their sexuality. This is part
of the shift in ministry in the Church today."

The challenge to address the everyday issues of sexuality is
one which calls for both patience and creativity. Father Bob
Lotz, Co-Director of Young Adult Ministry for the Diocese of
Milwaukee, spoke of both the challenges and options he
offers young adults who are living together and who approach
him about witnessing their marriages in the Church.

"In most cases I ask them to prepare for the sacrament by
spending some time living apart or in separation from each
other prior to their marriage. In a sense, I guess you call it a
time of prayer or reflection . . . a kind of personal, spiritual
retreat.

"If they choose to continue living together, I invite them to
preach the homily at their wedding to publicly acknowledge
and comment upon how they believe their decision has
helped them to focus on the sacrament. Also, how they
believe it has helped them to move to the next step in their
personal and spiritual growth.

"I see a real value in such a homily," says Bob. "I think it publicly acknowledges the issue, and I think the church has something to learn from this. It's certainly more honest. I believe the whole Christian community can only benefit from this kind of openness, which calls prospective marriage partners to accept responsibility for decisions they make regarding their sexuality.

"I also try to be as open as possible to their suggestions about how the marriage ceremony should unfold," says Bob. "It has been my experience that, in many ways, preparing sexually active couples for marriage is easier in the sense that they have been more free to concern themselves with the sacramental nature and importance of the vows to one another which they are about to make."

In San Francisco, which claims the largest concentration of young adults in the country, a variety of models of young adult ministry operate. The San Francisco Young Adult Network, seen by many to be one of the most creative programs in the country, describes itself as a "constellation of people, places, and plans" which works for the empowerment of young adults. Each night of the week, a program is offered that focuses on personal and intellectual growth, alternate life-styles, spiritual growth, political change, and social action. The programs are designed to provide intense intellectual and emotional stimulation, and participants are invited to engage reality rather than escape it.

Founded by the Reverend Glenda B. Hope, a Presbyterian minister, and Professor Scott Hope of San Francisco State University, the Network sponsors a Coffeehouse and a number of "house churches" throughout San Francisco. One of the tenets of the Network is that "it goes where the people are, not that we invite them to come to us." A glance at any one of the Network's monthly calendars reveals the sensitivity with which young adults' needs are addressed. Power and Loneliness, Creativity as a Biological Need, Sexuality as a Spectator Sport, A Current Perspective on the Draft, and Re-membering Your Body are but a few of the topics discussed at meetings.

Still another creative response to church vocations is provided by Directions, a ministry-discernment program for young adults. Jointly sponsored by the Archdiocese of San Francisco and the Diocese of San Jose, this program is sponsored and supported by lay leaders throughout the Christian community. The diocesan college seminary staff has also committed itself to support the growth and development of Directions.

Participants in the program have gone on to make decisions about ministries. For example, one decided to enter medical school; another, to enter youth ministry. One man entered the seminary while a woman in the same class went on to study theology. Because of the wide range of support the program has received, Directions Coordinator Sister Beverly Dunn, SP, believes it is an important model of ministry discernment and formation for young adults in the future Church.

The groundswell of young adults who are responding to the call to exercise their gifts in peer ministry is seen more and more to be a movement of the Spirit. In some cases, this kind of ministry is light years away from the understanding of "ministry" which the peer ministers' parents grew up with and may even have imparted to them as children. It is a response by young adults to a church which they see as having failed to satisfactorily address such cultural issues as the women's movement, the Pill, equal employment opportunities, the Peace movement, the economic boycott proposed against states which failed to ratify the ERA.

It is a response, but folded within that response in also a call—a call of the Spirit. A call which can hardly be described as a "problem" peculiar to the United States. It is a call reverberating throughout the Church, a call encircling the globe.

An example of this worldwide witness of young adults took place on November 28, 1980, on the occasion of Pope John Paul's visit to West Germany.

Barbara Engl, a twenty-five-year-old single employee of the Archdiocesan Office of Young Adults in Munich, stood before the Pope as the spokesperson of German Cathoic Youth and read an approved text. The text contained what the German publication *Der Spiegel* called "harsh criticism of the Church." It focused on the areas of ecumenism, celibacy, and sexuality.

According to *Der Spiegel*, Barbara's text dealt with the Church's "negative prohibitions to young adults' questions on friendship, sexuality, partnership, and how it clings, in spite of the scarcity of priests, onto celibacy and holds off women from church ministry."

It said further that initially "her words were given a blessing by the Project [planning] Group of the Pope's visit and were accepted by the Cardinal [Ratzinger] without resentment and with his knowledge. Then, the article stated, "the higher-ups got cold feet." Newspapers and agencies were given a manuscript from which, without Barbara's knowledge, all criticism was omitted. Thus, the media were set up to create the impression that this lone church employee had planned the protest and thereby spontaneously challenged the conservative reaction of the Pope. [4]

In a letter, Barbara writes simply, "What I conveyed, I did not write alone. Together with the Chairman of the Munich

Union of German Catholic Youth, we worked with the Planning Committee on the text. . . . ."

Responding to an inquiry about German youth's attitudes toward sexuality, she replies, "In the matter of sexuality, inquiries demonstrate Catholic young people barely hold onto the sexual morality of the Church. In courses and seminary training, this difficulty emerges very frequently. But the subject is pushed aside and covered with prohibitions. Consequently, hope can scarcely be offered to youth. . . .

"As for celibacy, there is a striking shortage of priests and few pastors to care for the souls of youth. Those few who are charged to care for youth are failing, and thus spokespersons for youth are lacking as those youths move into the adult community.

"There are scarcely any intelligent grounds why a priest cannot be married," Barbara continues. "Many good and involved priests must separate from their official duty because they cannot live in celibacy."

Barbara, described by the German press as "not a radical but a girl from the heart of Catholicism," [5] reports that her office received about 700 letters, two-thirds of which were favorable. A good many of the others were "so shameful and insulting, they could hardly be taken seriously." The positive letters came from all age groups, Barbara notes, adding that "many were from older priests who were delegates and therefore drew attention to the fact that they had already, and for a long time, dealt with these questions. . . . We also received criticism from the bishops although our text was submitted beforehand to and approved by our Cardinal Ratzinger."

Noting the urgency of surfacing questions of sexuality and celibacy, Barbara nevertheless stated that "I proceed out of the assumption that these questions and problems are already so pressing that they scarcely startle anyone. . . . The searching for the meaning of sexuality by Catholic young people continues and indicates that young adults are not in agreement with Catholic teaching on sexuality."

Barbara was careful to state, however, that "love and fidelity for young people are conditions or pre-requisites for intimate relations with the opposite sex. I can confirm this attitude from my own professional experiences with young adults. I also hold it necessary and correct to strengthen the individual conscience of young people so they can decide responsibly in these important matters. I lay claim to this for myself also. Unfortunately," she concludes, "discussion on these topics in the Church is the same as before . . . extrememly difficult."

An ocean and a continent away, the questions of love and fidelity are of equal importance in the life of another young adult minister.

Mark Jablonski is a twenty-nine-year-old young adult minister from the Diocese of Denver, Colorado. Like Barbara Engl, Mark finds himself in the midst of a dilemma which calls him to challenge the Church in yet another way. For Mark and his wife Kris, the question is one of economics. His decision to stay in ministry hinges on the question of receiving a just wage. Without this, Mark and Kris, a psychiatric nurse who volunteers her services when she ministers with him, will have to forego the possibility of having a child and raising a family.

"I have seen so many of my peers leave ministry at this point," said Mark sadly. "As single young adults in their early twenties, they are able to minister with total dedication. They can make it financially if they pledge themselves to a simple life-style or have another source of income or choose to live with their parents at home.

"But when they marry and the question arises of having children, couples in the Church just can't make it on a lay minister's salary. I've seen the Church lose some of its most creative lay ministers because they have to make a choice between ministry and family.

"There's such an irony in this," Mark continued. "These ministers love the Church! They believe in and teach the ideals of marriage and family which the Church espouses. Then they're faced with the realization that when it comes down to supporting their teachings in dollars and cents, the Church says family and ministry are 'incompatible.'

"In other words," says Mark, "the message is this: Married or single, if you want to stay in ministry, you're not supposed to procreate."

Who will minister to the People of God in the Church of the future? In what forms and under what circumstances will that ministry reflect a Body of Christ that no longer chooses to deny its sexuality?

If religious vocations decline and lay ministries emerge, what might be the pivotal issues in the areas of sexuality which will emerge in the Church?

In 1976, the fifteen voices of the first National Young Adult Ministry Board called out to the Church to minister to young adults whose lives were marked by spiritual thirst and hunger. Today those fifteen voices have swelled to include the voices of thousands. Those voices are reflected in a document called a Plan of Pastoral Action for Single Young Adult Ministry. It was issued in 1981 by the United States Catholic Conference of Bishops.

Just as he had done in 1976, once again Father Pat O'Neill, OSA, gathered a group of people together to solicit opinion through a nationwide listening and discernment process.

Young adults throughout the country were invited to share
their concerns, their needs, and their dreams.

A seventeen-member national committee headed by
Bishop John S. Cummins of Oakland, California, worked with
young adult leaders throughout the country to produce a
document that contains both a vision and a plan and that
reflects the thousands of young adult voices asking to be
heard.

Asking for a ministry of presence, a ministry of listening, a
ministry of healing, and a ministry of integration, the plan
addresses issues young adults claim are critical in their lives.
Some of the specific issues are work and leisure, relationships,
powerlessness, and human sexuality.

In regard to sexuality, the plan states, "At the very heart of
human sexuality is a quest for wholeness and unity. Although
some single young adults seem to be at ease with the sexual
permissiveness of contemporary society, many are struggling
with questions of personal integrity and commitment. Their
need to love and to be loved in a specifically sexual way is
heightened by the general breakdown of nurturing relationships like the family. . . . In this age, it is difficult for some
young adults to believe that enduring commitments are possible or that they are capable of making them. . . . Mean-
while, their need for affection, support, and gentleness, which
is traditionally fulfilled in marriage and family life, finds out-
lets which, though often expressed physically, frequently
prove to be unfulfilling and disillusioning. Sexual minorities,
because of their sexual orientation, deal with a similar
pain. . . . Most young adults hunger for relationships based
on depth and integrity which nurture and challenge the best in
each person. . . .

"These single young adults need the constant loving support and encouragement of a faith community that accepts their gifts and talents." [6]

Will the Church provide that support by dialoguing with young adults in an attempt to realistically address their questions, questions which, increasingly, seek to integrate spirituality and sexuality?

"It will take imagination, courage, and determination to allow the word of Jesus Christ to be heard and to bear the fruit of salvation among these young men and women who are unchurched or on the fringe of the Church," Archbishop Jean Jadot, then apostolic delegate in the United States, told a meeting of the National Conference of Catholic Bishops in 1979. [7]

In many segments of the young adult population, the question young adults ask has moved from "Why won't the Church deal with human sexuality openly?" to "What are the real reasons why it cannot?"

The answers to those questions might well determine which young adults will leave the Church and which will stay.

Like the sound of a ticking clock, the question is insistent.

As the Body of Christ, we may block our ears and bury our heads, but the question will not go away.

FROM *MENSCH*

I am getting stronger and healthier.
A process of rejuvenation is taking place in me . . .
I am coming to have more and more freedom . . .
I am becoming harmonious and whole
I experience a great zest for life . . .
I'll be able to enjoy all kinds of relationships,
    even those that may be difficult and challenging
I'll be able to take interest in and make something creative
    out of any kind of challenge
My senses are becoming more acute
My brain—my good friend—is functioning better
My memory is functioning better, and I am able
    to harvest the seeds of my life
The rhythms of life flow through me
    making me more creative
    imaginative, wiser,
    more caring and compassionate
    and increasingly present both in what I do and what I
    feel . . .
Beauty shines through me
I am becoming more and more able to heal myself and
    others
Life flows through me . . .
Loving, Healing, Wholing, Growing, I am moving more
    and more
    to that natural and extraordinary way of life
    that is my own higher self

I am the microcosm of the universal love, creativity and
   mindfulness that is.
I am mensch.

Jean Houston

CHAPTER FOURTEEN

YOUNG ADULTS PLACE
A CONFERENCE CALL
TO THE CHURCH

*"The focus of one's life is not the church as a womb but a posture of
one searching for the sacred in the unexpected."*[1]

Dennis Geaney, OSA

"If anyone had told me ten years ago that I'd be here in Los
Angeles attending this kind of a conference, I would have
told them they were crazy," said the middle-aged priest in the
Hawaiian sport shirt.

He looked around the room, shaking his head at the sight
of the 200 people chatting and laughing. Then, folding his
arms across his chest, he smiled and said to no one in particular, "But then, by now I should know that in this job, you
never get what you expect and you always get more than you
bargained for."

The priest was entitled to his surprise.

The conference was titled *This Is My Body.*

The subject: spirituality and sexuality.

The focus: the life and faith journeys of young adults
between the ages of eighteen and thirty-five.

The task: to "do theology" and, in the process, experience
"peer ministry."

The participants: men and women, single and married,
divorced and separated, parents, priests, nuns, brothers
(including some who had moved on from those life-styles).
They were straight, gay, sexually active, and celibate.

Among them were teachers, students, psychologists, ministers, health professionals, writers. Also, a former male model, a nurse, a drug addict, a gardener, a book salesman, a professional storyteller, an actress, a union organizer, a dancer, and a garbage man. There was also a religious brother in his early thirties who had a wallet full of pictures of his nieces and nephews, which he showed off proudly. "What gnaws at me is the idea that I'll never have a child of my own," he confided to one friend quietly. "I wouldn't be surprised if that's the question I'm supposed to deal with here."

And folded into the event were still more "firsts" . . . more surprises. . . .

This conference was one of the first attempts of the Church in the United States to respond to the needs of a bilingual, bicultural community. The conference was given in both English and Spanish in recognition of the fact that Hispanics already comprise majority Catholic populations in many areas. Thus, this event acknowledged what was already a Catholic Young Adult reality.

The conference was designed to provide these young adults with an experience of theologizing, an awareness of their ability to write "theological textbooks" with pages from their own lives. In the process of sharing their stories, their lives and faith journeys, they would become reflecting mirrors for one another, each of them a unique expression of how God is acting within the faith community.

This, they would learn, is what it means to "do theology." It is simply to reflect on one's own life experience—in this case, in the areas of sexuality and spirituality—by speaking one's own words, out of one's own needs and dreams.

In recognizing the authenticity of their own faith experiences, they would be taking part in one of the best traditions of their Church—*sensus fidelium*—the sense of the faithful. As a result, they would no longer have to approach theology as some mysterious, impenetrable smokescreen behind which only designated authorities dared to go. Rather, they would begin to see theologizing as a part of their responsibility as Christians, a responsibility to listen, to share, to respond, to reach out, to heal.

In short, to become an evangelizer: to upset the environment and transform it in the direction of the Kingdom. (*Evangelii Nuntiandi*) [2]

"Theology," said St. Anselm, "is simply faith seeking understanding." [3] Isn't that, after all, why they were here?

Ten years previous, neither the subjects nor the objects of such a conference could have been imagined. The country had turned the last pages of the sixties, but the sexual uproar that decade had spawned continued to affect people's lives. Even before the sixties had ended, there were prophets-at-large, already hoarse with pleading for the spiritual needs of the so-called flower children of that generation.

These prophets kept raising the question of what these young adults' coping patterns implied for the future. Countless numbers in this age group were no longer aligned to their families, their roots, their communities, their religious heritages. Fewer and fewer of them were to be found in the churches.

In rectories, they called them a vanishing breed. Their baptismal records remained on file. Their addresses were unknown. Where were they? And were they aware that they were missed and that people cared very much that they were gone?

One of the people asking that question was Father Pat O'Neill, an Augustinian priest who first worked with young adults as director of Campus Ministry in the Diocese of Orlando, Florida. He knew the territory. He saw the signs of the times in the eyes and the empty lives of the young adults he encountered. He saw religion become a revolving door for students who came in with questions which did not have the kind of answers that could keep pace with their life experience. Time and again he saw them walk away in loneliness.

Now, as Representative of Young Adult Ministry for the United States Catholic Conference of Bishops, Father Pat was still asking the question. Only now he was asking it in the name of a national network of young adults, grassroots folks who, through his love and energy, were convinced that the prime ministers to young adults were the young adults themselves.

"It is the task of young adult ministers to reach out to their peers and minister to them in terms of their mutual search and struggle," Father Pat stated. In the process it becomes the responsibility of young adults to seek out leadership within their communities. In this way, young adult ministers act as both models and catalysts as they convene their peers around the country.

In welcoming young adults to the conference, Father Pat said simply, "I look at each of you and tell you, from my heart, that you are gifts to the Church, We thank God for you!

"The basic gift for evangelization is a human life. We have here in this room several thousand years of experience of living that Christian life, and the time has come for us to draw on the wealth of that experience.

"In the past, it never occurred to us to use our own lives for reflection. We always looked to the saints, to the Church to interpret our experience for us," he said. Young adults must minister to one another because only they can name their needs.

"But if I 'address you' in your need, I leave you in that need.

The hungry, the poor, the powerless are still with us after 2,000 years. The poor of the Gospel are the people of the Gospel who are without power, without resources. The poor of today are the young adults of the Church.

"As Christians," Father Pat continued, "our job is to make the life of Christ visible. It is not to 'bring Christ' to young adults. Christ is here! Christ, in creation, is all-pervasive! It is our task to help them to see their connectedness to God's creation and their value as part of it. And to do it with a sense of perspective. We need to match the Church's ideal with an awareness of the reality of those whom we welcome with the Chruch's promise of God's love.

"It is one thing to welcome," Father Pat noted. "But it is another thing to extend hospitality. Welcoming in the Lord's name doesn't always have to be formal, sensible, or even logical. Sometimes, all we have to do is listen.

"I believe that Young Adult Ministry has ushered in a new catechetical moment. It is a moment which calls us to take ourselves seriously as Christians. In this light, we must continue to ask the question which urges us on in our ministry. . . . Where are the tens of millions of young adults whom we long to welcome home again? Without them, we are a bankrupt church," he said.

For many young adults sitting in that room it was the first time they heard the Church's loneliness for their missing brothers and sisters spoken publicly. Later, they commented on how moved they were to hear those words expressed as a longing rather than as a reprimand.

The choice of sexuality and spirituality as a conference theme was explained by Cynthia Hicks, a full-time diocesan young adult minister from Paterson, New Jersey, who, with Sister Yolanda Tarrango of the Diocese of El Paso, Texas, had designed and coordinated the conference.

"Young adults have a great need to understand sexuality as more than a moral code," Cynthia explained. "Young adults are looking for a way to integrate sexuality into the wholeness of their lives. The cutting edge of sexuality is experienced in relationships . . . but the search for meaning to interpret and nurture those relationships becomes a search for God.

"Intuitively," she continued, "young adults have come to recognize the necessary connection between spirituality and sexuality, and what they are asking for is a theology that mediates both God and relationship.

"We believe that that theology is already part of our Catholic tradition," she said, "and our purpose this weekend is to help recover the best of that tradition, and in doing so, *reclaim the teaching that sexuality and spirituality are gifts and essentially good.*"

This was the heartbeat of the conference. . . . This is what they had come to hear. Spirituality and sexuality . . .

On each person's lap was an empty notebook, a journal waiting to be filled. By the time the participants were ready to leave, each of them would have recorded a part of history . . . *their personal history* as Christians. Together, in this time and place, they would become part of the unfolding revelation which is the Church's journey through history.

And each of them, in the search for the meaning of sexuality in their lives, would be responding with integrity to the Church's recent plea for evangelization, for helping to move the world closer to the Kingdom of God. Pope Paul had said simply, "This century thirsts for authenticity" (*Evangelii Nuntiandi*). [4]

. . .

The keynote speech set the tone for the conference by

focusing on the question: "How do you define your sexuality?"

Speaking alternately in Spanish and English, Father Frank Ponce of the Secretariat for Spanish-Speaking at the United States Catholic Conference of Bishops explained the process in which they would be involved.

"This weekend, we will not be talking about sexuality and spirituality from a schizoid mentality," he said. "We will not separate these two realities in our lives as human beings. Instead, we are going to deal with our sexuality as a religious question rather than a moral question: *sexuality as who we are striving to become* rather than how we behave in a specific act.

"We are going to ask *how our sexuality binds us as persons to ourselves, to others, to God.* Knowing how to *express* our sexuality depends on knowing what role we believe our sexuality was meant to have in the building of the Kingdom. Therefore, each of us must ask: As a body-person, how am I building that Kingdom? As a flesh-and-blood-Christian, how am I witnessing to that Kingdom with my life every day?" he asked. Do I really believe I am loved by God, created in God's image? That I am called to be an expression of God in the world today?

"These are deeply religious questions which I can only deal with through my sexuality," Father Frank continued. "Sex may be something we 'do' but sexuality is who we 'are': the whole person taken all together with his or her history, be that history stunted, glorious, tragic, healthy, or unclear.

"If we believe that sexuality is indeed an expression of the total person, then we have to find out what it means to be a person. We have to do this through a process of introspection, of looking into ourselves and finding out what's there, deep down where we really live. And, in the process," he stated, "getting away from our fixation of looking at our sexuality primarily in physical terms.

"That is why it is critical for me as an individual to examine my life history, to reflect on how I relate to others through my sexuality, whether male or female. It's important to ask, What are the motivations and values which determine my choices? I need to hold the tapestry of my life up to the light and see what patterns are part of that tapestry and to reflect on how they got there and why they were woven into my life when they were.

"Only by examining these patterns in my own life can I hope to address them in the lives of those to whom I relate as friend and minister," he said. "Only by acknowledging my weaknesses and shaking hands with my strengths can I call others to the health and wholeness which are meant to be hallmarks of Christian sexuality.

"What makes this conference different from others you may have attended," Father Frank explained, "is that you will also be sharing in the collective truth that arises from your individual answers. You will be doing this in small groups with one another by saying, together, 'These were the messages I received . . . from my family, my church, my teachers. This is what I accepted, this is what I rejected. Today, these are the questions I need answered and the answers I need tested; both of them brought me here.'

"In this process of reflecting on your life and faith journeys as Christians, *you will be theologizing*," he explained. "And by listening to, sharing with, and healing one another, *you will be ministering to one another as peers*. You will be bound to one another in a special way which says, 'You are not alone.' In the deepest sense, you will be building community.

"Whatever this conference calls forth from us, we must trust it; we must believe that we are worth it," he said. "We must see this dialogue as an exciting opportunity to discover an adequate vocabulary to express who we are in the sense of our sensuality and sexuality. It's exciting also because we're looking for new categories, we're cutting new ground! We're going where perhaps no one else has dared tread before. And it's exciting because we're not doing it in isolation, without support, but we're doing it together as a community. We're doing it as a group of people who believe and trust in one another."

The welcome had been given, the tasks had been outlined, the issues had been named. And then they prayed. . . .

. . .

Over the next three days, the questions kept beckoning . . .

• *What do you hope to receive from this conference?*

"I want to put out the brush fires that always seem to surround my feelings about sexuality."

"I want to weed out the jungle of fears that linked sex and sin in my life . . . stuff that I grew up with."

"I want to find a way to ask God to give my emotions back to me."

• *How did you learn that you were male or female?*
• *What messages did you receive from family and friends?*

"Physical changes were important . . . the first bra, the first period."

"Sex was mysterious . . . dirty . . . only the 'bad kids' knew about it."

"Sex is for men."

"Men can't control themselves."

"Sex equals babies: my mother had ten."

• *Imagine you are at the dinner table and you ask a question about sex. Imagine how your family would react. . . .*

"My father would be silent.
My mother would be horrified.
My sister would laugh and embarrass me.
My brothers would snicker."
"In my culture, we don't talk about sex at the dinner table. My parents would either ignore you, get angry at you, or give you a lecture."

• *At the time you were sitting at that dinner table, what was your relationship with God?*

"My family was a strong, strict Catholic one. I didn't know you could get to know God. I felt he was inaccessible!"
"God knew everything. It gave me a fearful feeling. I thought if I memorized my catechism and was tops in my class, that 'by being my best,' I would be close to God."
"My family was Mexican Catholic. The saints were very important in our lives. In my community there was a strong element of witchcraft. I had a fear of the end of the world coming and that I would burn in hell. . . . I wasn't interested in anything in the church except the music. I went to church when I had to. When I drifted away, it was the music which brought me back."
"I was on a real guilt trip. I wasn't good enough. I was out to earn my way to heaven. I used to apologize to God whenever I asked for anything."

• *Can you recall taking a definite stand about some important sexual value, religious or not?*

> "I can't remember *not* taking a stand!"
>
> "I decided to remain a virgin til I got married. As a result, I don't date much anymore because I won't put out."
>
> "I never single-dated, I always double-dated for protection."
>
> "Because I was taught that sex outside marriage was wrong, I grew up avoiding friendships with women to whom I was attracted. I still have trouble taking risks with the 'right' women."
>
> "Nobody ever explained to me whether exploring my sexuality meant that I could masturbate."
>
> "I remember playing strip poker when I was in my early teens. I remember praying desperately to the Holy Spirit for the strength to resist, but I never was successful. When I was fourteen, however, I did take a firm stand against French kissing. I was sure it would lead me to doom. I guess I was more uncomfortable with genital contact than with nudity."
>
> "I said 'no' because I was thinking of entering the convent." (Question from another participant: "When were you really sure *you* had made the right choice, Sister?" Answer: "About twenty-five years after I entered the order.")

• *In looking over your past, what symbol would you use for yourself as a sexual person?*

> "A ballet dancer. I can express the fullness of my

femininity without words, without fear of interruption or contradiction. My family is very wordy."

"I'm like a tightly-corked bottle of champagne. I'm very uneasy because the cork's not out yet. I'm not sure what's going to happen."

"The sky would be my symbol. Spacious . . . cloudy . . . smoggy. . . ."

"I'm like a colorful and delicate Spanish guitar, full of music. . . ."

"A playful spirit! But only in my attitudes about sex, not about God."

"A tree! Rooted in faith, knowing God loves me, and that as my branches reach out I will be fulfilled as others come into my life to be with me."

The questions rose and fell like waves in a restless ocean. And the answers gave the participants both the courage and support to continue exploring uncharted seas.

And guiding them on their journeys were friends and fellow travelers, people like theology graduate Tom Halloran, who spoke to them about sexuality and the Scriptures.

"Although Scripture has no single word that is used for sexuality, either in Hebrew or in Greek, the authors of Scripture do use sexual imagery in describing other concepts. By studying that imagery in the Old Testament we can learn how the Hebrews viewed their sexuality. One of the ways they talk about it is as a gift from their Creator, a gift that enabled a person to escape loneliness and isolation. They said that 'it is not good for man to be alone' (Gn 2:18).

"It was through their growing religious awareness that a loving God had drawn them, as a people, out of abandonment that helped them gain a new awareness of their sexuality. They saw sexuality as a God-given gift, inviting the individual

out of loneliness into relationship with others, just as each of
us is called out of our loneliness into a relationship with
God."

Tom cited Abraham's story as one which gives us further
insights into the Hebrews' ideas about sexuality. "Abraham
understood the promise of God in terms of posterity. For
Abraham, that was the common myth, the common success
story of his day. If you had a lot of children, you had found
favor with God. The power to procreate was seen as a gift
from God. You could see that powerful reality at work in
birth, in family, in the number of generations.

"But sexuality was also seen in the Hebrew scriptures as
something to be regulated. The demands of cultic purity
bagan to surround worship and, in the process, sexuality
became unclean, separated, taboo.

"In the Christian scriptures Paul's early writings viewed
sexuality from the perspective of the death and resurrection of
Christ and of a community which waited anxiously for
Christ's second coming. The new Christians were so preoccu-
pied with being ready for that great event that everything,
including sexuality, had to be regulated in terms of its importance. Nothing," Tom noted, "could stand in the way.

"In both Hebrew and Christian scriptures, the basic goodness of sexuality is affirmed throughout, but the goodness
comes from and is always viewed from the perspective of how
the community saw its relationship to God," he explained.

"Although it is important to have this understanding in
terms of our tradition, perhaps the important thing to realize is
that the history that's important to us today is the history that
we will make our own.

"And thus," Tom concluded, "because we belong to a
community we call Church, we belong to a specific time and
age. We need to take responsibility for this 'moment.' We

need to come to an awareness that we are blessed with both the skills and the opportunity to theologize about our experience of this time and place, here and now, as we gather here today."

. . .

The questions moved from the past to the present. Participants were asked, How have your attitudes changed?

• *What is your image of what the Church now says about sex and sexuality?*

"A neon sign: ABSTAIN."

"The symbol is the confessional; the dominant figure, male."

"Sex is a no-no unless you're married; after that, I guess they figure it's something you're supposed to enjoy."

"The symbol for me is the statues covered in purple. They do this during Lent, but as far as I can see, shrouding the body is the Church's state of mind all year."

"Past is prologue. The image is hypocrisy. In the past, there were popes who were libertines. In the present, they use women's brains along with their bodies."

"Power. As in a woman confessing to a man who sees her not as a person but as an occasion of sin."

• *What is your image of what the culture says about sex and sexuality?*

"Sensations!"

"Bumper stickers which proclaim how various persons and professions 'do it.' "

"Everybody's doing it. Not why, but why not?"

"Symbol: hot tub; dominant figure, female."

"Our culture doesn't distinguish between sex and
   sexuality."

"I can't climb out of the guilt I was taught. And I'm full
   of self-hatred for still feeling guilty."

"Our whole economy is based on sex as a commodity.
   If you took sex out of mass media, we'd have a
   national nervous breakdown in forty-eight hours."

• *Name three things you learned about sex that are worth
keeping.*

"Sex is fun. It's the most fun two people can have
   together."

"Sex can create a climate for tenderness. It can heal
   damaged psyches."

"Women have the right to have multiple orgasms."

"God didn't make a mistake on the drawing board."

• *And three things you learned you'd like to forget.*

"Sex is a battle; the marriage bed is a battleground."

"All women secretly want to be raped."

"Religious persons are asexual."

"Sex is a nighttime activity with the lights out."

"Sex is babies . . . birth contol . . . dirty."

"Paul's message that the flesh *wars* against the spirit. It's
   just another image that links sexuality with violence."

• *Who in the "Church" helped you grow in your understanding
of sex and sexuality?*

"My lover's belief in me. I am a priest, and she is a

divorced woman. I owe my continuing vocation to her."

"The people in our congregation who have loved me along with their warmth and understanding."

"Interestingly enough, the priests and nuns. I saw that the struggle with sexuality was a universal human problem."

"My family—especially my three sisters. We all went to Catholic school and used to share everything. We still share, but none of us go to church anymore."

"Directed retreats and sex education in Catholic schools and Marriage Encounters."

"A combination of faith and common sense. It's nothing anyone 'taught' me; it grew out of my life and love experience gradually."

• *Who in the Church hurt you by their teachings or attitudes?*

"The mind games the Church played on us. They paralyzed us with fear so we would be ripe to accept sacrifice."

"My mother and father. They have a 'button-up' attitude toward sexuality. They laid a negative trip on me, even about modesty."

"The Church's mechanical approach to birth control. It's dehumanizing. They expect you to flip a switch about sex. It's hard to be relaxed and playful without spontaneity. You have sex by the calendar. It's like a dentist appointment."

"The monsignor who spent our whole graduation breakfast talking about the sexual sins that would be committed that night at graduation parties."

- *Name the words you commonly use in prayer.*
  "Thank you."
  "Please, show me!"
  "Lord, why?"
  "I don't need this, God, but I accept it."
  "Give me that peace which the world cannot give."

- *When did you take a stand for or against church teaching?*

  "When I was fourteen, I just couldn't hack going to
      Mass anymore. I told my parents, and they looked
      sad, but they didn't hassle me."
  "I believe in sex within marriage. But I also think the pill
      changed everything."
  "You can't send nineteen year olds off to war and then
      tell them when they come home that they can't live
      with a girl. What does that say about taking
      responsibility?"
  "With the patience of one of the brothers who taught
      me in high school, I began to face my fears about
      sexuality. What he asked me was not whether I was
      gay or not, but rather, what my alternatives were for
      being a loving person."

- *In view of the Church and the cultural setting, how would you
  symbolize your sense of belonging to each?*

  "Hang on, baby."
  "I see myself running back and forth between each."
  "I feel like an old stagecoach, with uneven wheels and
      rickety. I expect a bumpy ride through life."
  "Overlapping circles: Church, culture, me."
  "A round peg in a square hole."

"I'm like a door, sometimes closed, sometimes open."

"A trust walk."

"I'm a window pane; part of me is outside in the cold, looking in at the party."

"I'm at the outermost tip of a branch of the tree called church; I can be cut off without being noticed, but somehow, even then, I'll feel connected."

"I feel like an outlaw; I'd like to believe I can move to a place where I'm challenged to be a prophet."

. . .

The conference, which began with strangers, was forty-eight hours old now. A glance around the room showed small groups of people sitting together as old friends. Their body language said that they were relaxed, comfortable, absorbed in one another's sharings. Together, they had walked with one another through the past, each one spreading out his or her memories on the table in a way which said, "Let me show you what I have in my pocket so you will have the courage to show me what you have in yours."

After all this sharing, it was time for another question. Sister Rosa Marta Zárate asked it.

"Well, now, what are you going to do with everything you've learned about yourselves . . . about the positive and negative feelings you have discovered about your sexuality? If you're angry, do you intend to stay with that anger and wrap it around yourself like a blanket? Or are you going to give it up and let it go?

"In the deepest sense, why are you here, and what did you hope would happen? What is there about your sexuality that is in need of healing? What can you build on? What is missing? How can we put the words and feelings together in order to pray?"

. . .

The liturgy centered on the theme of living water.

"Long ago, in the days when Jesus' feet still touched the earth, he stopped at a well to refresh himself, for he was exhausted and sorely in need of rest after traveling so many miles. . . ."

And participants listened to the story of the Samaritan woman at the well whose encounter there with Jesus was a source of astonishing revelations . . . revelations which rippled out like the living water he promised to those who thirsted for eternal life.

Jesus said . . .

Everyone who drinks this water will be thirsty again.
    But whoever drinks the water I give him will never be thirsty;
    no, the water I give shall become a fountain within him,
    leaping up to provide eternal life.
    (Jn 4:13-14)

And they talked about how that living water has flowed down through the centuries, struggling, always, to find a way around the stones which piled up in places, blocking the water's passage, preventing people from finding ways to quench their thirst . . . stones of doubt and fear and discouragement which were piled high. . . .

And from the group, people came forward . . . risk-takers who were willing to not only name the stones but ask for the community's help in removing them. . . .

And one by one a symbolic stone was removed . . .

- one was for the lack of respect shown to women
- another for the lack of birth control
- one for the lack of sex education and touch for the young child
- another, for the lack of trust in young couples to take pre-marital responsibility for their sexuality

Participants spoke of their pain. . . .

We are celibate . . . and we are hurting.

You have called us to an intimate relationship with Christ, yet tell us we must be wary of intimate relationships with other people. You have told us much about our spiritual journey but little about our sexual journey toward God our Father and Mother. You have told us to love but warned us too often of the dangers of getting close to others.

You have sometimes separated our spirits from our bodies and made us fear the very impulses of creative power within us. You have hidden the value of our choice in life behind the masks of fear and frustration.

Teach us how to love, fully, richly, unafraid, yet maintaining the value of our celibate commitment. Help us be creative and life-giving, a positive sign of God's loving kingdom yet to come.

. . .

We are engaged . . . and we are hurting. . . .

God has given us love, but you have warned us not to love too much, too soon. God has asked us to abandon each of us ourselves to the other's care, but you have told us to be on guard.

Your moral code speaks more of actions and individual events than of relationship and celebration. Your guidance has been more restrictive than directive.

Help us understand our longing to be together, our longing to be one, as an invitation God gives us to covenant ourselves with him as well as to each other. Teach us not to be afraid but trusting of the call to commitment.

· · ·

The group no longer saw each problem as "someone else's problem" but as the collective responsibility of the community. And at the end, when they prayed aloud, they thanked God for new awarenesses, for . . .

• the chance to listen to others without judgment, in a way causing me to listen to myself without judging

• the gift of naming the things that have never been named before

• sharing in a way that took the sting out of painful memories

• the sheer relief in watching the masks dissolve.

· · ·

Dr. Dan DiDomizio spoke to them, touching upon many of the issues they had been discussing, helping the group see the connection between sexuality and spirituality.

"Is the sexual revolution fact or fantasy?" he asked them, as a way of beginning.

"I would like to begin by saying that I not only believe that sexuality is integral to our life process, but I also believe that sexuality is a pivotal factor in the process of authentic spiritual development. There is no relationship to God which is not sexual. We are called to celebrate our humanness rather than subjugate it.

"Overall in our Christian past we have viewed sexuality as genital and generative"; Dan noted, "in a phrase, sexuality deals with what happens in and around bed. Marital sexual activity was tolerated both as a concession to human weakness and as a necessity for continuing the species. Sexuality was an entirely private matter, so private that discussion of sex even between spouses was ideally minimal and only functional. It was an area of marital life that one normally took for granted. For example, the drama of cultural sexism was acted out largely in the sexual arena—the double standard for men and women; the myth of the dutiful, pleasureless woman.

"In religious circles," he stated, "sexuality fit snugly into a narrow moral sphere, the zone of dos and don'ts. In the mind of the average religious person sexuality was viewed as a basic human need that somehow had to be dealt with, largely in the moral realm.

"But," Dan noted, "while documents on sexual norms from bishops' conferences or from theologians retain an importance, the life experiences of countless believers has already propelled them to a different level of discourse.

"Lived experience is always the rockbed of theology; indeed, the testimony of life normally precedes and catalyzes the movement towards new theological directions.

"In regard to sexuality, the traditional moral approach seems to have locked us into a view of sexuality which is predominantly biological, even though we give a nod to psychological data. The birth control debate was an obvious case in point. The controversy around the homosexual expression of sexuality rarely rises above the level of biological concerns.

"Moreover," he continued, "traditional sexual morality tends to be individualistic in its orientation; it demands that moral discernment be focused almost exclusively within myself and stresses my rightness or wrongness vis-a-vis a God out there. The broader implications of one's sexuality for the life of the community are rarely addressed.

"The past limitations on the area of sexuality cannot be underestimated," Dan stated. "The traditional discourse about sexuality situates the sexual experience in the realm of marriage and family; in this context the discussion of sexuality becomes at times an alienating discourse for the single, including divorced and widowed, as well as for celibates. These groups are implicitly seen as asexual at best and sexually immoral at worst. The bottom line for most discussions of sexuality for the unmarried inevitably reads 'do not.'

"This sexual dualism is not an entirely past experience," he stated. "It finds expression today in cultural attitudes, in legislation, indeed in our very socio-political structures and decisions. Witness the suspicion directed towards single people, the so-called 'swingers' in our society; our attitudes and legislation regarding homosexuality. What clearer symbol of our flight from a healthy sensuality than the neutron bomb, a weapon which preserves material objects as it disintegrates human flesh and bones! The fallout from this distorted view of human sexuality is all around us as well as within each of us.

"And then came the sexual revolution," said Dan. "Or was it a real revolution? Sex is fun. A generation of younger people, or part of one, threw our fears and inhibitions in our face; you are afraid of your bodies, they cried; you hide behind your hang-ups and gross inconsistencies. Physical touch and the expression of intimacy are profoundly important in human life; playfulness is a central ingredient in sexuality. And in this, they were right, painfully so.

"But," he said, "their subsequent conclusions were neither logical nor healthy: Sex is a purely natural function, having no relationship with the meaning of life and of one's existence. Furthermore, we *need* genital expression to be 'normal.' Celibacy became an expression of perversion. Sexuality again became identified almost exclusively with genital behavior. Freedom of expression replaced restraint and discipline as the basic norm of sexual activity.

"The results," he noted, "soon followed: a manipulative hedonism which proved as destructive of real love as the former rigidity; a spiritual wasteland characterized by a return of the old dualism, namely the separation of the spiritual from the physical and biological, this time under the guise of freedom, freedom from restraint, from responsibility, freedom from the demands of love.

"And what about freedom *to*? What am I now free to do or to become?" Dan asked. "Many people today, out of their experience of various sexual attitudes, have begun to articulate a new set of questions and values.

"For these people, *sexuality is viewed as our total thrust towards life, a way of being and relating to the world as male and female persons.* Sexuality is seen predominantly as relational, rather than only genital; it's the mode by which we touch others, care, love, and share with them. The distinctions between marriage, single life and celibacy, between homosexuality and heterosexuality recede into the background.

"Thus sexuality is oriented towards the entire process of human integration; it finds its most authentic expression in the meaning we give to life," he explained.

"As both Christian spirituality and the Christian viewpoint on sexuality have evolved, we detect a clear convergence of the two movements. On the one hand, Christian spirituality, seen as the total style of human life, must focus on the healthy integration of sexuality into every facet of our human-religious experience; and on the other hand, the healthy integration of human sexuality cannot take place outside the orbit of the spiritual dimension of life. There is an integrity to life which must be recognized, embraced, and celebrated."

Focusing on the areas of spirituality and theology, Dan pointed out that "it is precisely out of the experience of an integrated spirituality that the Christian community develops the language and symbols, the theology and liturgical expression, to assist individual Christians in understanding and interpreting their life experience.

"Again we can look to the Hebrew scriptures for a model of this process: the Song of Songs, a popular wedding song, supplied the basic language to proclaim the Jewish experience of God; later this nuptial imagery enriched Paul's and the patristic vision of the Church," he said.

"The issue of articulated experience is a crucial one for the Church. Every individual, especially the young, depends upon the community's interpretive ability to grasp the full impact of their own life experience and to integrate it into the community. This is, in fact, the very heart of the meaning of tradition."

He noted, however, that "during the past couple of centuries the Church's official interpretation of the experience of sexuality left us with a set of ambivalent categories to work with; consequently sexuality has been relegated to the exclusive domain of moral theology, and thus it has remained only on the periphery of the dialogue concerning spirituality and systematic theology.

"What we must now do," Dan said, "is to look again to other, more ancient elements of our tradition, especially our Jewish roots, so the sexuality can begin to assume a more formative role in our Christian experience. We would do well today to pursue this direction, to probe the richness that such an integrated sexuality can contribute to our continuing quest for holiness.

"In the past we have tended to impose rather abstract theological categories on our experience of sexuality. We have seen the results," he said. *"Today it is time to look to our sexuality, to allow our experience as sexual persons to be a resource for our theological reflection.* What, for example, does the struggle for intimacy say to the possibility of reconciliation and of real community in the Church? What would our theology of the sacraments look like if we were to really acknowledge the sacramentality of lived sexual experience? Whose task is this sort of reflection? Professional theologians have an important role, to be sure. But," he stated, "the primary challenge is to every Christian, married, single or celibate, who has recognized his or her sexuality for what it really is, the graced event of Emmanuel, of God bursting forth into our lives. It is time," he said, "that we get on with this task."

. . .

The risk of reconciliation. . . .
The pulse of the conference was clearly centered here.
Do we have the courage to embrace our potential for goodness by being a welcoming person? Do we see our bodies and souls as God's way of loving us into existence for the ultimate good of the community? Do we view our sexuality as a sign of God's confidence in our ability to love creatively?

A new way of seeing, a new way of looking, a new way of loving. . . . As one man said, "This is a thousand light years away from Playboy centerfolds and hot and cool sex."

"I am larger, better than I thought. I did not know I held so much goodness!" [5]

And, as they shared now in their small groups, one thought surfaced over and over: the realization of the meaning of community. . . .

"It's so good to know that I am not alone!"

Their sharing moved now, in trust, to even deeper levels. . . .

"I have always dreaded the pain of being close, of somehow being 'found out.' The feeling I have with this sometimes approaches terror."

"I never thought of touch as affirmation. It was always an invitation to something sexual, something more."

"You should know that I came here hoping to find the words, the courage to take back home to help me tell my folks I'm gay."

"In our group, all four of us women were able to share that we had had intimate relationships with priests . . . and we shared that with the two men who completed our group . . . men who were priests themselves! What strange power drew us together? What did God hope we would understand? What did he want us to see?"

"A man in the group shared the fact that he often had a 'wish,' a fantasy about being female; a woman in the group responded by saying that she understood because she felt the same fantasy in reverse."

"I think about sex twenty-four hours a day. I go around thinking, 'Where is it? *I want it!*' It's worth everything just knowing others feel that way!"

"It's such a relief to know I am not alone!"

When Rosemary Haughton spoke to the group, she took that awareness and held it up to light.

"Not only are we not alone," she said, "there is no way we can exist if we are separated from each other. Each of us is an indispensable link in the intricate pattern of creation.

"Begin," she said, "by imagining that you are sitting at the seashore. Perhaps it is a stormy day in the rocky part of the coast and you watch the waves coming in, one after another. They beat on the rocks and the shore, shooting up into a spray and coming back down again. And then, the waves come in again and crash once more onto the shore.

"You watch that happening for a while and think about what's happening each time the waves come in, each time a tiny little amount of the rock is being worn away, each time particles of the rock are being carried out in that water by the receding waves and deposited somewhere.

"What's happening is 'timing,' " she said. "And though you can't measure it, you know it is happening. You know that the shape of the coast is being changed by the water and the chemical composition of the water is being changed by certain kinds of minerals.

"In thousands of years, if nothing interferes, that part of the coastline will look different, because two kinds of beings exchanged with each other. And they changed each other by exchanging parts of themselves. In a sense, they are becoming each other, and also changing their being in relation to one another. A constant state of exchange is taking place. A constant giving and receiving of life."

She continued, "The same is true of plant life and its relationship and exchange with the soil. You pick a flower and hold it in your hands. And yet, when you look at it, you are looking at just one moment of a being who is giving and receiving life, a being who is part of a whole complex system of exchanges with other forms of being.

"No being exists by itself," she stated. "No being can claim that and cut itself off. If it does so, it ceases to have real existence. There is a giving and receiving of life in every being all the time; there's no point at which it reaches a kind of stopping point.

"And if you reach out your imagination far enough, you're going to find that *every living being is living in exchange with every other living being.* And yet, every being has its own unique existence at that particular point of exchange where all those different things are coming together.

"Further," she noted, "it is that uniqueness which is shared and exchanged with other life.

"When two people fall in love something strange happens to their awareness of reality. It happens, first of all, when they come to an extraordinary sense of knowing each other. A kind of knowledge, and awareness of relationship has been established, and yet there is a feeling that something has been *discovered*, not created. There is a curious sense of recognition about being in love. A sort of 'oh, yes!' feeling that you know something has been there all the time . . . waiting in you and in life . . . that you hadn't learned 'til now. So it's not that two separate beings got through to each other, but rather that they discovered that they're not separate, that they share, instead, something about what it means to be a human being. And they come to see that human discovery occurred at the point at which they encountered each other.

"When you fall in love, everything, everyone looks different," she noted. "Suddenly the world seems a whole lot nicer, more interesting. It's as though you've discovered a kind of key to the nature of reality that you didn't have before.

"Then you can turn around and ask, Why was it so difficult to trust? So difficult to overcome our reluctance, to articulate our feelings? Why were we so afraid of each other?

"We begin to realize that our assumption about relationships is based on the fact that we assume we are cut off from each other and so we have to work at getting through to each other. We have to work at breaking down barriers. But why?" she asked. "If all we had to do was to exchange, why was it so hard?

"The same things happen when groups try to work together. They come together, initially, because they want to do something together, something about which they care deeply. They discover an identity, a sense of being in the group, almost as if that group were a person. When you've worked with a group like that for some time, you know exactly where you are. When you get together, you have a sense of coming home.

"That's the way it was with the apostles and Jesus," Rosemary explained. "In their relationship with him and in their sharing, they were constantly aware of their being in exchange with him. And in the process, they came to a new sense of wonder.

"But it became very hard to find language to express the absoluteness of that oneness, especially when he reached the point at which he had to tell them that he had to die. At that time he expressed that oneness—and gave it a deeper and more vibrant dimension of reality—by taking bread and wine and saying to them, in effect, 'This is our sharedness, this is our exchange. This is my body and my blood that is given for you.' And they received it and it became part of them. They didn't understand then what was going on. They didn't need to. A way had been found to establish a level of exchange far beyond anything which had been conceivable in the whole of creation.

"That's why," Rosemary continued, "when St. Paul talks about life and the body of Christ as being *with* the Lord or *in* the Lord or *from* the Lord, he's struggling to explain a reality so deep and so exact that there's no way he can actually say it clearly enough. It's a depth and precision of exchange which goes through every level of reality from the most physical to the most spiritual.

"Since that time, we have tried, endlessly, to describe that exchange. . . .

"We talk of God pouring out his life in Jesus . . . Jesus pouring out his life in us . . . we pour out our life to him in response to that . . . and that life is given to the Father . . . and we receive the life of the Father in Jesus . . . on and on. . . .

"And then it clicks. We suddenly realize why we are in the image of God and why creation is in the image of God.

"*God is exchange* . . . God isn't a thing or even three things," she said. 'God is the outpouring of life from Father to Son through the Spirit . . . no moment of stillness, no moment of fullness, but a constant outpouring . . . a giving and receiving which is endless and is constant and total.

"And in that giving and receiving, one discovers one's own uniqueness and irreplaceability. We know that we are now in Jesus; we know that we are in exchange with him. Where does that recognition happen? For us, in the place we call church. In that place, we discover an awareness of that exchange and of who we are and what we want to do.

"On the day of Pentecost, a little group of people came to that awareness. It was a tremendous explosion. They had to go do something once they were aware of who they were and the exchange in which they were involved. 'Be baptized, repent!' they said. Be baptized, change!'

"Baptism, in this context, is like the kinds of things people say to each other when they're in love, when they try to describe what's happened to them, to understand just where they are together. And what to do about it now that they know.

"That's what the Christian community has to do," she

continued. "And when people come together as you have these few days, it's out of an awareness of what is . . . or perhaps isn't . . . going on. And when that happens, the whole situation opens up and all kinds of things can begin to happen. And that's the beginning of church as such.

"God is always at work bringing people together. But until they begin to articulate what kind of exchange is going on, then they aren't church. When this happens, however, all kinds of new things suddenly become possible. It occurs at that moment when people say, 'This thing that's happening to us in the group is Christ happening, the body of Christ, the Church.'

"Each time I interact with another," she said, "I am interacting with Christ. My body *is* the Body of Christ. My relationship, my love for a person, whether I'm married to them or not . . . the way I use my sexuality . . . is also an exchange with the Body of Christ. It's one of the countless exchanges we have been talking about.

"It's as if each couple coming together to make love was, as it were, recapitulating the meaning of creation. The physical and spiritual exchange which they have together depends on, grows out of, all those other exchanges which have made them what they are. Explicitly and lovingly, they bring together all that has made each of them and they give this to each other. They are at a point of exchange in a very precise and rich way.

"And when it is a Christian marriage," Rosemary said, "a sexual encounter really means that at this point, Christ is present and exchanging his life in the Church, in the human race.

"The making of the Church, the coming of the Church is in particular groups, in unique kinds of exchanges; no two are alike. And we need people to create that sense of exchange in a very much wider area, in the sense of the tremendous overarching reality of the larger church in the world.

"But," she noted, "the exchange begins here in this room and in the places to which you'll be going back. And it begins in the context of sexuality, in your own personal relationship which you come to discover as your love exchange with the Body of Christ.

. . .

They had come to the conference expecting to find concrete answers. All their lives, this is what they had been taught to expect from the Church.

Instead, they were challenged to begin finding different approaches to use in addressing their new questions which flowed out of the experience of their own lives. They were asked to do this by reflecting with others in the faith community, with confidence that this is how the Holy Spirit works in the Church.

In this process, they were accepting an invitation which went back to the beginnings of the infant church community. To be invited to participate in this process signaled a whole new respect for them and for the Church at this time in history.

Further, it was a continuing response to the challenges of the Second Vatican Council.

"The Church always has the duty of scrutinizing the *signs of the times* and of interpreting them in the light of the gospel. Thus, in *language intelligible to each generation*, she can respond to the perennial questions men ask . . . about the relationship of the one to the other." (Italics mine.) [6]

This Is My Body was the name which had been chosen for the conference. In so many ways, the events which had occurred in the past few days were a microcosm of what was happening to the Church in the world today.

Cultural attitudes towards sexuality were tested and found wanting. The challenge for young adults at this conference had been to discern the effects of "sexual freedom" in their lives.

"Morality" took on newer and deeper meanings. Sexuality moved away from a moral question—"How much can I 'do' and even get away with, without feeling guilty?"—and became a religious question—"How can I use my sexuality to enrich my life, my relationships, and my community?"

And most important of all, "In order for me to use my sexuality for such enrichment, in what ways do I need to be reconciled with my own sexuality?"

The conference's inclusive approach to sexuality was evident on many levels, from workshops conducted in both Spanish and English and dealing with sexuality in single, gay, and married life-styles to recreation sessions. (Notices for a *"Body Shop*: Requirement: Do Something Good for Your Body!" Options included swimming, tennis, hiking, yoga, and dance.)

The bicultural environment provided consciousness-raising and challenges. The alternate use of Spanish and English provided the group with a concrete example of the difficulties of communication within a church which is multicultural and multilingual. It also illustrated the need for values clarification and patience on both sides.

"Funny, I had some idea that the Anglo attitude toward sexuality was different than the attitudes of us Hispanics. Now I realize we are the same."

"I was expecting that your Anglo parents were so open
about sex . . . not like my own. Now I find out
that that isn't true at all."

And the conference had taught them the wonder contained
in the gift of symbols and images and how those symbols and
images had been a gentle invitation to reflect on their
sexuality.

The participants shared observations and insights about the
conference. . . .

"All our symbols about our feelings in regard to sexuality were ones of contrast . . . a turtle: open but
guarded . . . the sun: bright, but behind
clouds . . . waves: coming in, pulling back. . . ."

"My image is that of a person being broadcast in living
color but of being received on a black-and-white TV
set by the Church."

"I can't believe that only three days ago, I defined sexuality as 'twice a week!' "

"I don't have to confuse love with sex anymore to know
that I'm lovable."

"It was good to be reminded that there is a common
experience of Church as people rather than institution. And that the frailty and vulnerability I so often
see there is so much like my own."

"Just to know that as a lesbian Hispanic woman it is
possible for me to be a Christian and to find Christ
through that. It's so tremendous to know I can still
be a church member, that it's possible for me to
belong!"

"To rage against past history is to be involved in a
theological tantrum which is not life-giving. What

good does it do? It's a waste of energy!"
"Through listening and being listened to, I feel I have a
new sense of hearing . . . like a gift of ears."

As the conference drew to a close, the participants
exchanged the scraps of paper containing their names and
addresses and extracted promises to "call when you pass
through my town."

And then, one by one, in the small groups, they commissioned one another by the laying on of hands on each other's
shoulders . . . each one naming his or her wish for that
person, a wish that person had earlier expressed in the group
sharing.

And the wishes were spoken in the language of the liturgy
of reconciliation they had celebrated together; wishes for
"wellsprings," and the "gift of bodies," and "living water
which refreshes."

And in their eyes and smiles, there was a kind of reluctance
to leave this place where they had shared so much of themselves with people who, only a few days ago, had been strangers . . . strangers to each other as well as to themselves.

In time, the words they had spoken and the words they had
written in their journals might be forgotten. But the sharing
of their stories of sexuality and spirituality signaled a
profound change for the Church they were creating and
which they were destined to help transform.

For the Holy Spirit embraces each generation with the kind
of Pentecost experience that generation cries out for. . . .

"Ah, Lord, God!" I said,
    "I know not how to speak; I am too young."
But the Lord answered me,
Say not, "I am too young."

> To whomever I send you, you shall go;
> whatever I command you, you shall speak.
> Have no fear before them,
> because I am with you to deliver you,
> says the Lord.
> Then the Lord extended his hand and touched my
> mouth, saying,
> See, I place my words in your mouth!

(Jer 1:6-9)

The tongues of fire which would hover over this Body Generation would empower it to lay its hands on the Body of Christ with the courage and tenderness born of a new kind of reverence and give it the confidence to speak of spirituality and sexuality as synonyms.

. . .

Note: See Appendix, page 344, for a review of the guidelines used at the workshop on spirituality and sexuality that was part of this conference.

YES

I am rooted with the generations of children I have
brought into the world like new ideas. Full of grace.
Yes, I will leave my people and go with you. Stand with
you, remember with you. Back to the night you first
came to me. I was a girl then. It was early. A light
surprised me, and told me that a new light would be
born through me. And it was. Full of grace. And my
life changed.
Yes, I said. I will have you in my house. I will feed you.
I will teach you to sing. To play. I will teach you the
word yes. I will take you to the temple. And you will
amaze me there.
Yes, I will walk the road with you. All the way to the
top of the hill. I will weep with you there. I will hold
your broken body in my arms and weep, as if it were
my own.

And yes, I will be there when boulders that enclose tombs
are broken into pebbles. I will be there when illusions
are shattered and hope is restored.
I will be there when you and I become pure light
together. In myself I will always put you together. I
will always remember you. Your flowering days. Our
long talks. Full of grace. Full of love. All yes. To
life.
I will be lonely with you. I will rejoice with you, light
from light. You came through me. You come through
me. As you will.

I am your mother, your sister, your daughter, your friend. You are within me. I am within you. We share one body.

Carole Coleman Michelson

CHAPTER FIFTEEN

PROMISED LAND

The Cosmos Within

*"Kindness and truth shall meet; justice and peace shall kiss.
Truth shall spring out of the earth. . . ."*

Psalm 85:11-12

"I dwell in possibility." [1]

Emily Dickinson

In Pope Paul VI's encyclical *Humanae Vitae*, the central phrase on which the world focused was contained in the eleventh paragraph of that document and dealt with the regulation of births.

"The Church, calling men back to the observance of the norms of the natural law, as interpreted by constant doctrine, teaches that each and every marriage act *must remain open to the transmission of life.*" [2]

The principle of openness to life means that no artificial means or chemical contraceptives may be used to interrupt or block the possibility of new life.

While the reference in the encyclical is to the act of sexual intercourse, young adults are challenging the Church to expand the theory of openness to life to include questions that embrace both spirituality and sexuality. The link between the two is creativity. They are asking, simply, "In what ways is the connecting flow of creative energy which links spirituality and sexuality being blocked and thwarted in the Church?"

"Ethics and the process of moral judgment is not just a matter of sitting in state and passing judgment on the passing goods and bads," writes moral theologian Dr. Daniel Maguire. "Moral thinking at its best perceives goods that have not as yet existed and brings them into the creative act. Creative imagination, obviously, will be most concerned with the *reality-revealing* question about alternatives and with the *enlargement of reality* and advancement of moral evolution that new alternatives may provide." [3] (Italics mine.)

For today's young adults, the division between body and spirit is being rejected. The dualism is seen not only as a contradiction but an impossibility. Increasingly, this generation speaks of their bodies and spirits as inseparable. Their journeys to the heart of love validate this. Sexuality without the spiritual values of love and care and trust makes it just another bodily function. Spirituality that does not risk vulnerability or mutuality or surrender makes it another "head trip" which never "touches" them and which never succeeds in enfleshing whatever dazzling rhetoric they may display.

But the integration of one's sexuality and spirituality provides the climate for transcendence and ecstasy. It is through the senses that one comes to know God's wonder. It is through the touch of love that one can begin to believe that each of us began as an act of love in the mind of God.

Young adults believe this act of love repeats itself each time they experience themselves as body-persons, involved in ever-richer and more fertile forms of creativity. Through their senses, they are able to experience the constellation of wonders that surround them in their world and nourish the wellsprings of their imagination. This creativity often includes an approach to prayer as an experience in creative dreaming, which they describe as an act of the spiritual imagination.

Young adults have grown up in an era exploding with creativity: the space program, cloning, computerized technology, test-tube babies.

In their parents' day, comparable scientific advancements took a lifetime to unravel. For this generation, such advancements have telescoped into a decade of time. For them, openness to life means to ask not "Why?" but "Why not?"

They have come to expect that the same impossible dream that put a man on the moon yesterday will put them in a space shuttle tomorrow. This is a generation for whom heart transplants and eye banks are exciting but not extraordinary. These are future parents who have the opportunity, through amniocentisis, to learn the sex of an unborn fetus as well as to discover certain abnormalities while the fetus is still *in utero*.

An increasing number of today's young adults are beginning to look at the human body with a new kind of reverence, and at the same time they are taking a second look at the environment. "What is happening to my lungs in a polluted environment?" "What kind of stress can I expect in the choice of this profession?" "What will be the effects on my infant if I am drugged during labor?" "Where does our water supply come from, and what kinds of chemicals does it contain?"

And, most important of all, they are asking questions at every turn in their journey: Is this how I want to spend my life? Is a career that involves constant stress worth it? What are my alternatives? For some they are questions that are often a far cry from the premium their parents might have put on pensions and security and "settling down."

"There is more to life than paying off a mortgage," says one twenty-six-year-old carpenter at a construction site, "I work hard and put in all the overtime I can get for six months straight," he says, "and then I take off and travel for the other six months. There's no better time in my life to travel through South America on my motorcycle or stand before the Taj Mahal or ski in Switzerland. The wonder of such experiences," he says, "feeds my soul."

A twenty-four-year-old woman who was valedictorian of her graduation class at a large Jesuit university says simply, "It is not only our responsibility but our mandate to question the set boundaries which limit us from exploring and expanding our potential in every area of our lives. I am never more aware of this than when I am dancing," she continues. "Over and over, I have stretched my mind and body, realizing new creative boundaries which I have been challenged to explore. Through long hours of practice and discipline, I have attempted to leap higher and stretch farther . . . learning that each new leap is worth the risk I take that I might fall.

"I continue to take that risk," she says.

"The alternative is not to dance."

. . .

For one young adult, openness to life means working on issues of human liberation as an act of love for the Body of Christ. For community psychologist Michael Myszka it is a peace and justice ministry dedicated to issues of sexism in the church. The focus is on the area of power.

"Ministry is about turning power over," says Michael, a thirty-year-old doctoral student in North Carolina. "It is a process which is both revolutionary and ongoing. Such ministry defines rape as a justice issue, as a metaphor for the stereotypical need for male power and domination of the world.

"It is critical for the Church to address this issue to men, who are taught in the marketplace that competition is sacred. Unless they can begin to see power as creative, they go through life with a clenched fist instead of an open hand. They are free to give but not to receive. To be a man and to be needy is inappropriate in our society. To some, it signifies that he is out of control and failing in important ways. As a result," he says, "it's hard for men to admit their needs, even in a church setting. Spirituality does not come easily to men in the Church," he says.

"The damage that results from this denial of needs wounds everyone," Michael continues. "It heaps inordinate demands on women to be ever-available nurturers and rescuers. And it offers men few opportunities to have nurturing experiences in healthy and life-giving ways."

Michael says that for him building a grassroots young adult ministry provided that opportunity. "It allows me to participate in a deeply-satisfying ministry of hospitality." For three years, Michael joined with others in actively searching out young adults who were in need of church support groups. "As a community psychologist, I have learned that there is an assumption that community exists automatically," he says. "Not true. Communities must be built and nourished and supported," he says. "Those of us in young adult ministry have learned how important it is to just listen and not assume anything. Sometimes I think the Church doesn't trust the Spirit enough. Creative power is enabling, not controlling. For Christians, the only valid power is that which empowers others."

. . .

For some young adults, openness to life means taking radical risks and exchanging security for alternate life-styles. For two young adults from very different backgrounds, such an experience has taught them a new meaning of community and a new appreciation of God.

Mitch Kincannon ran away to join the circus at twenty. He is nearly thirty now but is still on the road. Catholic born and raised, Mitch was surprised to find within the circus "a church without a label." He says, "Wherever I look, I find a metaphor for the Christian faith journey: risk, trust, balance, magic, mystery. There are even time-honored rituals complete with glittering costumes and flowing robes. It elicits the same kind of awe and rapt attention one can experience in church.

"Every time I watch a trapeze artist let go of the handlebars and fly through the air to the waiting arms of a partner, I think of the phrase 'leap of faith,' and I feel I'm seeing it happen before my eyes. When I see men and women work with the tigers or bears, I realize that the animals are still unpredictable, and the danger is always there.

"When I watch these artists take these risks, I always ask myself, 'Are we worth it? Are we worth their risking their lives for our sake?' And then I ask myself if God mustn't wonder sometimes whether, for all he went through, we're worth it, too.

"But when I see people laughing and having fun and being mystified, I know we're in the right place at the right time. It's great to see people relax and forget their troubles for an hour or two. Laughter is the best gift we can give to people in terms of their minds and their bodies," says Mitch. "And because they're in touch with their sense of wonder, it's a transcendent experience, too.

"The capacity for peer ministry and community building in the circus is something really beautiful. In a sense, traveling as we do, we're 'all we have,' so it's easy to be aware of and sensitive to people's needs. We're pilgrims—in the Gospel sense, marginal people. We're always on the edge of town, always among strangers, always on the road. Circus folk don't say 'The show must go on.' They simply say 'The show goes on.' It doesn't have to; it could fold tomorrow; but it doesn't and I don't think it ever will. Everyone knows that if that happened, something in our spirit would die, too.

"In the circus, there is a very deep sense of camaraderie. It takes absolutely everyone to make it work; it's very balanced that way. It's a case of both shared dependence and shared responsibility.

"I've worked on a large commercial show, Circus Vargas, and with the smallest show on earth, The Royal Lichtenstein ¾ Ring circus headed by Father Nick Weber, SJ. If we ever have any doubts about the value of our 'ministry' and the need for the circus, we have only to read the love notes we receive in the hat at the end of the show. No matter what words they use, one note always says, 'The circus saved my life today!' "

The experience of "church" described by Mitch is one described over and over by men and women who grew up during the sixties. Part of it is due to their mobility. Numbers of that generation left home early and started traveling. "Church" became a place where two or three or more literally gathered and broke bread together. They came together out of a common need to replace or find a "family." The religious values they had received during their early years came to the fore in those informal gatherings.

"Whether or not young adults can articulate their beliefs in theological form, *I see them living their faith*, responding to the deep call within to build a new order of love and peace and justice," says Father Angelo Fazio, CP, Director of the National Center of Young Adult Ministry at Merrimack College in Massachusetts.

"For the past fifteen years, I have watched young adults feed the poor in the name of Jesus, some never recognizing that it was Jesus with whom they actually were breaking bread."

For the second young adult, Toni Tomacci, openness to life was a decision to risk financial and professional security for ten years in order to respond to the next step in her spiritual growth. At twenty-nine, her decision to leave a secure and highly successful career as a Montessori teacher was based on a decision to enter medical school.

"As a specialist in early childhood education, I had been thinking for some time about developing a consultancy to pediatricians," Toni says. "As a teacher, I saw a real need for a service to families to help bolster their self-confidence in ways which would enrich family life."

This decision was confirmed following publication of a book which she coauthored on creative learning experiences for children in school and at home. In it, she provides a wholistic approach to learning designed to encourage children's creativity. [4]

"One day, I realized that my lifelong fascination with medicine was my real motivation for the consultancy," says Toni. "I found myself thinking, 'Wouldn't it be marvelous to bring all my gifts as an educator to the field of family medicine?' At that moment, I decided to leave everything and begin to prepare for medical school.

"It was the element of 'going for the highest first,' " says Toni. "All I knew was that it was the next step, and I had to respond to it. On one level, I never consciously thought it through. I simply saw it as a call to love more, grow more, give more. I trusted the conviction and moved on it," says Toni. "In the deepest sense, I felt it was the place to which God was calling me.

"If I had thought it through for any length of time, I probably never would have done it," Toni admits. "I would have had to face the fact that as a full-time pre-med student, I would have to find some way to support myself. I would also have had to face the fact that I was scared to death of chemistry, that I had a math disability, and, though I loved biology, I never did well at it because I didn't have sufficient discipline. All I had to go on was the fact that I had tremendous spiritual energy around my decision. So many times since then, that energy has helped me laugh and push on through.

"Suddenly I found the ability to study ten hours a day; I discovered skills I didn't know I had. I found myself surrounded by people who helped me and encouraged me in every way. There were some grim times," she admits, "like when chemistry didn't start clicking until three weeks before the final! But I kept on trusting and reminding God that I was doing my part and that *She* had better do hers.

"All I can say is that despite the dire warnings and predictions, I somehow seem to be making A's in my studies. And most importantly, my faith has grown more than in the twenty-nine years preceding my decision. Faith has become a lifeline of trust and belief that God is walking with me. I can only describe my journey as a call to *More*."

. . .

In the document *Evangelization in the Modern World* (*Evangelii Nuntiandi*), Pope Paul VI writes, "*The Church is an evangelizer, but She begins by being evangelized Herself by* . . . *constant conversion and renewal* . . . *in order to evangelize the world with credibility*." [5]

That process begins by listening in new ways.

One can listen as an observer: an authority figure, an expert, one who expects to admonish, instruct, critique, but emerge undisputed. Or one can listen as a learner: one who is willing to receive the speaker with respect and sensitivity, recognizing that each of us has, in some way, a part of the truth to share with the People of God.

The listener as learner is one who cannot afford the luxury of false pride. The truth is too important to forfeit; the seeker never knows how or where God will speak to each of us. Like the Good Shepherd, he or she must find the patience and make the time.

The listener as learner is not afraid to say "*I need you*! I need you to tell me what is in your mind, what is in your heart. I need you to tell me what it is like for you to have grown up in a world which I must admit is foreign to me, a world in which I am uncomfortable. I need you to tell me, because unless you do *I will never know*!"

For the institutional Church to say "I need you" calls for a profound act of humility on its part. Perhaps even more humility is required for it to say "I don't know."

But in doing so, the Church, much like parents everywhere, can experience the surrender that eventually must occur when children come of age. To admit that one does have needs and that one is not always omniscient is only to acknowledge one's humanity. Such an admission on the Church's part would not threaten centuries of tradition, compassion, and hard-won wisdom. That would be like saying parents cease to have any meaning or importance in a child's life when they admit to not having all the answers.

Children grow up and change. They cannot remain children in order to reinforce their parents' need to be "in control." As one young adult asked his parents: "What's the real problem here? My image or your pride?"

To be able to say the words "I don't know" (when appropriate) about some things is only to admit "I don't know *everything*." As a human institution, does the Church think such an admission would surprise anyone? To admit that it is *open to new life*, to learning, to discovery, to creativity, is not to admit weakness but to express the trust and strength that is at the heart of humility.

In so many ways, the Church has as much to learn from the People of God as it has to give to them. If church attendance is dwindling, does the Church ask itself if this might be one of the reasons why?

Michael Valente reminds us that authority dies when it becomes irrelevant. [6]

"As Christians, we are called to live passionately, to live with compassion," says Sister Marjorie Tuite, OP. "There is a groaning in the universe which calls us to be free. We can no longer allow ourselves the illusion of believing that by 'fitting in' we will see harmony as holiness. As the People of God, we must challenge a church which sidesteps our questions and dismisses our dreams."

. . .

For a young adult nurse in an intensive care unit, openness to life is an act of love, which often means assuring a dying person that he or she is filled with eternal light.

"My assignment that day included a thirty-year-old oncology patient," says twenty-four-year-old Beth, who works in a large metropolitan teaching hospital.

"When I walked into the room, I was momentarily stunned to see him lying there. He was handsome, with sensitive, well-defined features. I fould myself catching my breath, not wanting to believe that someone so beautiful and young was going to die. If I had met him in a cafe, I would love to have sat and talked with him over a cup of cappuccino. Instead, I met him here, weak and helpless, as a dying man.

"I introduced myself," said Beth, "but at first he was not responsive. When he did finally open his eyes, he tried to smile. He looked at me with what I can only describe as infinite vulnerability. In that instant, there was an immediate sexual attraction. I fought back the tears as I began to care for him.

"Throughout the day, he moved in and out of consciousness," said Beth. "But when we did have eye contact, there was a recognition of mutual sexual attraction. I had to feed him. He had very little control and was embarrassed. Because we were peers it made it harder to hide behind the nurse role. When I gave him a bath, his eyes searched out my face endlessly. I touched him gently in every way to let him know how beautiful and special I found him. I tried to relate to him as someone I knew and cared for deeply.

"His eyes kept looking at mine as if they were saying, 'I can't believe this is happening . . . thank you! . . . you're really pretty . . . thank you!' As I bathed him, all this nonverbal communication was coming back to me. I felt a total blending of my spirituality and sexuality in that experience. I knew that I was facilitating the spiritual expression of myself, my soul. I prayed that my gift to him would be my tenderness.

"When I came to work the next day, his bed was empty. He had died in the night."

· · ·

I give thanks to my God every time I think of you—which is constantly, in every prayer I utter—rejoicing . . . at the way you have all continually helped promote the gospel from the very first day.

I am sure of this much: that he who has begun the good work in you will carry it through to completion. . . . God himself can testify how much I long for each of you with the affection of Christ Jesus! My prayer is that your love may more and more abound. . . . (Phil 1:3-6, 8-9)

. . .

For another young adult, openness to life means challenging the Church to keep pace with science as it delves deeper and deeper into the patterns of creation.

For twenty-seven-year-old geneticist Dr. Jim Baum, a fascination with life and of "why things are the way they are and how they fit together" continues to enrich his conviction that there is a God.

"The longer I'm in the field, the more amazed I am at the awesome order one finds in nature," says Jim. "Everything one encounters is a miracle within a miracle."

Jim's work is in molecular genetics involving recombinant DNA technology. It is a field of research which has already revolutionized our understanding of life and its complexities. "The deeper and more closely one delves into an understanding of life's possibilities," he says, "the more beautiful and open life becomes."

For Jim, there is a parallel in his scientific and spiritual journeys. He does not see those journeys as contradictory or competitive. "The questions asked by each discipline are intimately related: 'Why am I here? How have I come to be here and for what reason? What am I called to do with the gifts which have been given me?'

"My scientific background has helped me to keep on asking questions," says Jim. "Science must ask questions or it stagnates. But the institutional Church stops asking questions at a certain point and proceeds as if it has all the answers. It behaves as though truth ends, somehow, at a certain point in time. As a result, the gap between science and religion grows greater and greater. We must dialogue with ethics systems," he says.

"The Church should be a leaven in society, not a reflection of it," Jim continued. "As a geneticist, I challenge my colleagues to see themselves involved in a process of spiritual discernment as well as scientific research.

"My God is a God who understands what it means to be both human and creative. I believe the Spirit hibernates in our hearts as well as our minds," he says. "That helps me to trust that no matter how deeply I'm drawn into life's mysteries, the Spirit will be there to welcome me."

. . .

"The designer of DNA went on to challenge the human race to a new and higher purpose: membership in His own Body," writes surgeon Dr. Paul Brand. "The community called Christ's Body differs from every other human group. Unlike a social or political body, membership in it entails something as radical as a new coded imprint inside each cell. In reality, I become genetically like Christ himself because I belong to his Body. 'Do you not realize that Christ is in you? . . . I am in my Father and you are in me and I am in you?" [7]

. . .

Storyteller Kathy Szaj believes that the process of empowerment begins by actively encouraging the artist in every minister.

"Only then can I, as minister, call people to dream impossible dreams," she says. "Only by illumining my imagination can the dreamer be called forth in me.

"Every great moment in human history began as a spark in someone's imagination," says Kathy. "Imagination is not just idle daydreaming but a way of *creating possibilities from which people can choose.*"

You can't make decisions unless you see alternatives, and

you can't see alternatives unless you use your imagination. Kathy believes this process provides power to enrich and expand pastoral ministry.

"If people can imagine what they have never done and then choose wisely from these imaginings," she suggested, "we will have people making better and more thoughtful decisions for themselves and the community."

At thirty, Kathy is one of a small but highly successful band of religious troubadours for whom storytelling has become a way of helping people to connect with God in human history. Her love affair with storytelling began with a fascination with Old Testament concerns about human experience and "meaningful existence," the very same issues which consumed her as a religious studies student in the sixties.

It was then that Kathy explored a theology of fantasy and celebration and drew up a curriculum of nurturing skills that allowed for storytelling.

But it was in the religion classroom that Kathy introduced storytelling methods and realized their immediate power. Adolescents who ordinarily turned off traditional Scripture lessons would unfailingly stop what they were doing and listen when she used storytelling techniques.

As an artist, writer, teacher, and workshop designer in Milwaukee's Office of Young Adult Ministry, Kathy has discovered more and more innovative ways of using storytelling to help Christians to appreciate scriptural rhythms as these rhythms unfold in parables and people in the Bible. Most importantly, Kathy feels, she helps people to become their own storytellers and add their unique richness to a continuing tradition that incorporates the faith journeys of the People of God.

"The purpose of the story is to give an answer that presents an bigger reality than a simple fact," Kathy explains. "Stories are always needed as long as we do some truth-seeking on a deeper level. I believe people have a deep need to share their stories and listen to the stories of others. In our human struggle" she says, "it is a way of knowing we are not alone."

Kathy believes that impromptu storytelling allows the teller to "break away from a script" and be surprised and delighted by his own creativity. It also allows the teller the immediate satisfaction of knowing—by the hushed, attentive silence—that her creativity is valued. This supportive energy surrounding the storyteller allows him or her to draw even more deeply from wellsprings of myth and wisdom and symbol.

"In this context, one has a sense of the sacred that is inherent in spontaneity," says Kathy. "One senses the freedom with which each person shares his or her faith and humanity. Once released, the words and feelings become part of the rich tapestry of Christian experience. It is, in the truest sense, holy ground."

One of Kathy's favorite stories illustrates her belief in the creative power and spiritual importance of imagination. It is drawn from the folklore about St. Joan of Arc.

When St. Joan told her accusers that she had received her instructions to lead the French army because of "voices" she heard, she was laughed at and told "How foolish. It's all in your imagination."

"But of course," she replied. "Of course it's imagination. That's always the way God speaks to his children."

. . .

Among young adults, the new spiritual consciousness, the new appreciation of creativity as the unfolding of wonders, is growing. "Sin," they say, "is anything which alienates us from

our sense of wonder, anything which blocks us from exploring new ways of thinking or being that can help us to know
God in ever more exquisite detail."

Our bodies, they believe, are our bridge to wonder. Within
each person's body there is a creative seedbed much like a
quasar, a cyclone of stars. Each of those seeds has the
possibility of bringing infinite light to our understanding of
our human potential. And creativity, they believe, links their
spirituality and sexuality.

Dr. Jean Houston, Director of the Foundation for Mind
Research, is one of the world's leading researchers into the
nature and applications of human capacities. She sees the
challenge of the future in the examination of the patterns of
creation that provide the context and substance necessary to
form, sustain, and encourage the growth of the psyche. Dr.
Houston sees human transformation as a creative and spiritual
process. It is at the juncture of personal history and "sacred
process" that insight can be gained, meaning exists, and healing and transformation occur, she believes.

Describing herself as "a mid-wife, an evocateur of people
in terms of what they are and what they can be," Dr. Houston
believes that "we are more capable of using a great deal more
of our potential. . . . The task of educator is in the old
Socratic sense of *educare, a leading out of what is already
there* . . . training people how to use their brains and their
neurophysiological systems much more efficiently, teaching
them how to extend their whole sensory systems, teaching
them to think in images as well as words.

"For the first time in human history," she says, "we have
enough complexity, crisis, challenge, absolute necessity and
global sensibility that demands, quite literally, *that we become
what we are, that we grow or die.*" [8]

For young adults in the Church, the challenge to risk new

growth and to birth new life presents exciting possibilities. "Pastoral ministry, indeed the life of the Christian, is and must increasingly be seen to be a work of art," says pastoral theologian Reverend Philip Murnion. "It may be time for a new spirituality of action and relationships and renewed emphasis on a spirituality that accents creativity rather than redemption." [9]

Increasingly, young adults are taking up the challenge. For them, ministry is becoming more and more of a "trust walk," a surrender to their spiritual imagination, a belief in the creative capacities to call the Body of Christ to a deeper understanding of its own power and dignity.

"If Christmas, the feast of Christ's Incarnation, is to be for us more than just a memory of something that happened long ago," says Father Bob Lotz, "then we must take the time to withdraw and realize that his Incarnation is all around us and, yes, even within us. We are to be Glad Tidings, too!

"As the Body of Christ, we must take responsibility for that Incarnation by realizing how much real power we have within us to change the face of the earth on which we live," he says. Father Bob writes,

And we, the memory of Jesus in our time,
the continuance of Incarnation,
create with Him the Climax of the Dance
draw to completion the last movement of the music
If we but trust the Promise:
our differences are now Harmony's many voices
adding Beauty
to Unity's single Note.

. . .

Openness to life as an act of love means being open to the kind of creativity which "upsets the timid little order we have

achieved and makes the uncourageous cringe." [10]   Increasingly, young adults want to know and share the Jesus to
whom they have pledged their life as someone who, while he
was on earth, was at home in his humanity.

Ken Guentert, editor of the "New Age" publication *Body
& Soul* is one of them. An issue of the publication titled *The
Sensual Jesus* explored dimensions of Jesus' sensual healing
power as teacher, healer, miracle-worker, and a man who
wanted to be sure no one went hungry. "The parables are full
of food stories," Ken notes.

"Jesus is the last guy you'd expect to be God," he says.
"You don't expect God to hang around with bums and
sinners. You don't expect God to die like a derelict, abandoned by his closest friends. You expect his friends to
recognize his face, for Pete's sake, on the road to Emmaus. A
God should get more respect.

"But this is the Incarnation. What makes Jesus God is not
his great teaching (give him an A for storytelling and a D— for
plagiarizing) nor his wonderworking (a B+), but his passionate identification with the lost sheep of his day, the *am ha
aretz* (the irreligious)." Guentert writes that the belief of the
modern *am ha aretzs* in the sexuality of Jesus runs deep in the
popular imagination. For these modern irreligious, he says, it
is a matter of faith.

"Of course Jesus was compassionate, but his compassion
was laced with sensuality and the joy of living, not asceticism.
His symbol was the wedding feast, not the soup line. Where
is the risk in doling out food to a bum? Eating with him,
pledging your life to him over a bit of bread and wine, is
something else. And for Jesus, the pledge finally came due.
He died like one of them."

Guentert cites writer Peter Marin, who sees a connection
between moral power and the feel of the elements against the

skin—what you might feel while climbing a mountain, skydiving, or galloping a horse across a plain:

> The thirst for the world, when powered by love—to enter it and be entered—is almost always a moral impulse. . . . There is a kind of penetration, a connection between the self and the world, out of which arises, beyond all questioning, a sense of wedding. . . .

Ken concludes, "Whatever Jesus may have done or not done with Mary Magdalene, surely he felt, in Peter Marin's words, the 'world against his skin.' " [11]

. . .

Openness to life is happening naturally in church environments. . . .

At a Confirmation Retreat, a group of teenagers lies on the floor in a large conference room. They are praying. Their bodies do not touch each other. They are relaxed, they breathe deeply, their eyes are closed.

At each step of the prayer, they are invited to reflect on how God speaks to them and to each part of their body. Initially, they concentrate on the sensation of breathing. They are aware of whether or not they breathe easily . . . nothing more. At first, there are many sighs.

Slowly, they are asked to become aware of their hearts . . . to be aware of the wonder of that heart which pumps blood through their bodies throughout their lifetimes without a day off or a lunch break, without bursting or disconnecting . . . "God's love never quits either," a voice says, spontaneously. "It's like he never gives up on us," says another, "even when we get wasted."

They are asked to be aware of their eyes . . . to think of

the wonders those eyes allow them to celebrate . . . the
people they love, their favorite colors, their favorite places in
nature.

They are asked to celebrate their noses . . . to remember
the smell of their favorite foods cooking, the fragrance of
flowers, the memories of a certain perfume, the ocean. . . .

Now, their ears . . . the sound of someone telling them
they're loved, the sound of praise, the sound of someone
calling their name, or telling them not to worry, the sound of
music that they never want to stop. . . .

Taste . . . cool water on a hot day . . . ice cream, slip-
pery on the tongue, chocolate chip cookies, hot soup, salty
potato chips. . . .

Touch . . . touching, being touched . . . clean sheets
touching their bodies, their hands holding the wheel of a
car. . . .

Their genitals . . . a source of pleasure, a source of
power . . . the awesome possibility of bringing new life into
the world . . . the generosity of God who provides a man
with 500 million sperm each day . . . and a woman with tens
of thousands of cells in each ovary out of which four or five
hundred will ripen in her life ahead.

How do they pray with their bodies? they are asked. Where
do they begin to give thanks? What parts of their bodies give
them pleasure? Which parts make them anxious or afraid?
How do these feelings affect their relationship with God?

. . .

Openness to life. . . . In another place a group of young
adults mostly in their mid-twenties begin and end a workshop
on sexuality with prayer, passing around a Bible from which
each reads a few lines of Scripture. The passage they read is
from the Song of Songs. . . .

Let him kiss me with kisses of his mouth! More delight-
ful is your love than wine! Your name spoken is a
spreading perfume. . . . (Sg 1:2,3)

As an apple tree among the trees of the woods,
    so is my lover among men.
I delight to rest in his shadow,
    and his fruit is sweet to my mouth. . . .
(Sg 2:3)

Each time the group ends with the appropriate clo-
sure. . . . *This is the word of the Lord.*
And one woman among them remembers a letter written to
her by her mother . . . a legacy of love the woman has held
in her heart over the years. . . .

I gave you a Bible but I never told you that the Good
News begins in your body . . . it *is* your body! I never
told you your baptism included your body, with all its
contours and folds and hidden wonders. Your body was
given as gift, not punishment. Learn to know it and love
it, to touch it with joy and reverence as you would a holy
thing. Praise God for the curve of your mouth, the span
of your hips, the arch of your feet, the symmetry of your
separate toes.

Everything about your body *belongs to you* and should
be *cherished.* There are no secret places to be avoided, to
be ashamed of, to avoid looking at. To believe that is to
say that God made some kind of terrible mistake in your
design.

It was God who fashioned your body with all the
miracles contained within it: the sound of laughter that

wells up from your throat, spontaneously; the tears that baptize your joy and pain.

It was he who decided there should be, within your body, the gift of orgasm . . . that sweet, sudden shuddering rising from your vagina, filling your whole being with intense delight.

> My lover put his hand through the opening;
> my heart trembled within me. . . .
> I rose to open to my lover,
> with my hands dripping myrrh. (Sg 5:4,5)

We are his *creation*. He designed us *to be* (feel, respond) the way *He* wanted us to be! He sees our bodies as beautiful! Why can't we? [12]

. . .

He illuminates his own Incarnation when he tells us . . . "I have come that they may have life, life to the fullness."

Openness to life . . . each generation presents a different set of calling cards. . . .

"The New Breed of the 1980's is more likely to think of God as mother and lover," reports Father Andrew Greeley, "and of heaven as a life of action and pleasure." Commenting on the study on Catholic contemporary teenagers, Greeley also reported that "its story of its love affair with God, and thus the meaning of life, represents a dramatic change in Catholic religious sensibility, a change apparently caused by Vatican II and transmitted by devout mothers, sympathetic parish priests and passionately loving spouses." [13]

How will this reality affect the future of a patriarchal church on issues like sexism, celibacy, indeed, all attitudes on human sexuality? How will it also enrich and empower the Body of Christ?

The religious imagination of today's young adults signifies the dawning of a New Age in the Church's life-line. This imagination calls the Body of Christ to stand naked before the mirror of its assumptions and securities and confront its own image. As it looks inward, is its heart weak? Is its womb empty? Are its lungs clear so that it can breathe? As it sees its reflection, are its eyes alert and searching, its ears unblocked so it can hear? Does it listen for its children's footsteps? Are its arms open, waiting to embrace its young?

"From a multi-cultural perspective, Young Adult Ministry represents the most critical challenge to the Catholic Church in the United States," says Father Joseph J. Kenna, Representative for Campus and Young Adult Ministry to the United States Catholic Conference of Bishops. "The Young Adult crisis demands immediate action. The sheer number of young adults needing pastoral attention in the Church continues to grow."

How can the Body of Christ reclaim and redefine the gift of its human sexuality in order to address the critical issues in the lives of young adults today? How can it transform the power of its sexual energy from life-threatening to life-giving forms of creativity?

Certainly it could begin by dignifying human sexuality in its sacramental life. From birth to death, Christians should be inspired by continuing reminders of the revitalizing spiritual powers contained in their sexuality.

In the welcoming rite of baptism, the creative potential of the human body could be celebrated. The senses—the eyes, ears, nose, tongue and hands—in addition to the genitals, should be acknowledged or blessed as life-enriching gifts of the Creator.

In the sacraments of reconciliation and anointing of the sick, those specific areas in the body which are *weak* as well as wounded could be singled out and prayed over as places in need of healing. These sacraments could also emphasize the body's powers of self-healing as a reflection of their faith in God and God's divine life within.

The sacrament of confirmation administered in puberty could acknowledge that the body is undergoing both spiritual and sexual rites of passage *both of which* call for strengthening. The rite could also include a blessing of the body in its spiritual and sexual maturity as it takes its place in the adult Christian community.

The sacrament of holy orders, which includes a vow of celibacy, could be explicit about asking for a special blessing of the body that it may honor the vow which includes a gift of one's body to God in its totality.

Both the sacraments of holy orders and matrimony could *both* include a consecration of the hands: the priest because his hands consecrate the Eucharist; the marriage partners because their hands consecrate each other's bodies in love and fidelity.

The eucharistic prayer could include a special prayer which blesses the human body as the temple of the Holy Spirit. That blessing could also occur at the reception of the Eucharist, when members of the Body of Christ are nourished by Christ's body and blood.

We might learn to place our hand over our heart when we pray so that our spiritual prayer may be connected to our body. The feel of our heartbeat would remind us that the source of our life is in our body, and that that same heartbeat is also a symbol of God's love for us which never stops throughout our lives.

Openness to life means that, from the beginning, we teach our children that their bodies are gifts from God and that they are beautiful and full of amazing possibilities. We should teach them that it is a blessing to receive pleasure from one's senses and that each time we do, we are celebrating God's generosity and creativity. We must teach them that their genitals are as sacred as their lungs which help them breathe, that their menstrual blood and their semen flow naturally to signify that their body rhythms are in balance. We must teach them that nothing that is a natural part of the body or contributes to the good health of the body is shameful or should be denigrated in any way.

We must be alert to imposing negative moral judgments on bodily functions that are beyond the control of the ego or the conscious mind, says psychiatrist Alexander Lowen. "To feel guilty about sexual desires, for example, makes no biological sense. Sexual desire is a natural body response to a state of excitation and develops independently of one's will. It has its origins in the pleasure functions of the body. If this desire is judged morally wrong, it means the conscious mind has turned against the body. When this happens, the unity of the personality is split.

"The acceptance of one's feelings does not imply that one has the right to act upon them in any situation," Dr. Lowen continues. "A healthy ego has the power to control behavior so that it is appropriate to the situation." [14]

To Christians, the challenge is to truly believe that our human bodies are gifts of God and signs of God's love for us. Cell by cell, each of us is a multiplication of miracles. And at the still point of our beings, our souls illumine and magnify the wonder of our bodies. They call us to take delight in our senses and celebrate them throughout our lives.

The challenge is to also believe that each of us, *just as we are*, is a unique creation of perfect, centered symmetry . . . a spiraling translucent seashell glistening with wisdom from the depths of that sea which is the womb of God.

Each of us carries in that perfectly centered body the song

of our specialness, the song of our sexuality, designed to resonate in harmony with all of creation . . . a seashell, unique and beautiful, singing forever in the ear of God. That song calls us to believe that God's caress created our bodies. . . .

Truly you have formed my inmost being; you knit me in my mother's womb. I give you thanks that I am fearfully, wonderfully made. (Ps 139:13-14)

To be open to life is to be open to God. It is to embrace Jesus in his human body. It is to see his human body as the form through which he lived and loved when he walked and wept and healed among us.

It was through Jesus' human body that he gave love and received love, that "he cured the people of every disease and illness" (Mt 4:23). . . . It was to his human body that they carried "all those afflicted with various diseases and racked with pain: the possessed, the lunatics, the paralyzed. He cured them all." (Mt 4:24)

He heals us even now, that same power and love going forth from his body, the light of that love touching us still.

He is in every heartbeat, every tear, every kiss, every breath of life and act of love in every human body until the end of time.

The Jesus of the Gospels was not an aged, white-haired prophet. The Jesus we came to know and trust and dedicate our lives to was thirty years old. In this full bloom of his life, he was called savior, Messiah, miracle-worker. Today, if he walked among us, how could we explain to him that young adults no longer feel welcome in the Church which bears his name? Surely he would ask us "Why? If they are wounded in their bodies and souls, why aren't you healing them? If they weep, why aren't you stopping to question their tears? They, too, are my beloved! Are you making them beg for what is theirs?"

Would he remind us . . . "I gave up my body so that they might have their bodies given back to them."

The Body of the Risen Christ is a transparent body. But it is a luminous body shimmering with the light of continual re-birthing. It beckons us to claim that creativity which calls us to be free.

Openness to life is the ultimate act of trust, a channel of never-ending freedom that allows us to risk the impossible, dream the unimaginable, dare the unthinkable. It allows us to stand on each other's shoulders and reach for the stars.

We cannot do it if a whole generation of the Body of Christ is missing. It is time to acknowledge how much we need and long for our young. We need their creativity . . . their "leaps into unsuspected light . . . their explosions of joy . . . their fiery roots." [15]

God whispers in our lives in many ways. To pray is to listen for the sound of those whispers.

But if we listen carefully, we will hear another sound within those whispers. It is the echo of Christ's footsteps as he walks through his Church searching for his beloved, seeking out his young . . .

He is calling them to a new wedding feast, a wedding of their souls and their bodies. He is calling them to be an act of love in the Church a sign which calls the Body of Christ to a new awareness, a new understanding of the great hope to which they have been called.

He is telling them, too, that he is with them; they are not alone. He is wedded to them forever in love and longing . . .

For Christ plays in ten thousand places,

Lovely in limbs, lovely in eyes not his. . . . [16]

. . .

For I know well the plans I have in mind for you, says the Lord, plans for your welfare, not your woe! Plans to give you a future full of hope. When you call me, when you go to pray to me, I will listen to you. When you look for me, you will find me. Yes, when you seek me with all your heart, you will find me with you, says the Lord, and I will change your lot; I will gather you together from all the . . . places I have banished you, says the Lord, and bring you back to the place from which I have exiled you. (Jer 29:11-14)

NOTES

Frontispiece

1   Rosemary Haughton, *The Mystery of Sexuality* (New York: Paulist Press, 1972), p. 32.

Chapter One   Wasteland

1   George Bernard Shaw, *The Devil's Disciple* (Act II) (New York: Franklin Watts, 1967), p. 41.
2   Patrick O'Neill, OSA, "Ministry with Single Young Adults," *New Catholic World*, Sept./Oct. 1979, pp. 202-203.
3   Dolores Leckey, "New Resources for Ministry," *New Catholic World*, Sept./Oct. 1979, pp. 224-227.
4   Michael Warren, "Evangelization of Young Adults," *New Catholic World*, Sept./Oct. 1979, pp. 215-217.

Chapter Two   The Church as Body Language

1   Walt Whitman, "Song of Myself," *Leaves of Grass* (New York: Modern Library, 1891).
2   Donald Attwater, *A Catholic Dictionary* (New York: Macmillan Co., 1961), p. 165.
3   Ibid., p. 36.
4   Marina Warner, *Alone of All Her Sex: The Myth and the Cult of the Virgin Mary* (New York: Alfred Knopf, 1976), p. 200.
5   Ibid., pp. 221-222.

Chapter Three   Legacy: A Body and Soul in Search of a Heart

1   Pierre Teilhard de Chardin, *The Future of Man* (New York: Harper & Row, 1966), p. 12.
2   Richard McBrien, *Catholicism*, Vol. II (Minneapolis: Winston Press, 1980), p. 790.
3   William Phipps, *The Sexuality of Jesus* (New York: Harper & Row, 1973), p. 77.
4   Richard McBrien, *Catholicism*, Vol. I (Minneapolis: Winston Press, 1980), p. 534.
5   Leonard Swidler, *Biblical Affirmations of Women* (Philadelphia: The Westminister Press, 1979), p. 342.
6   Ibid., pp. 345-6.
7   Ibid., p. 343.
8   Ibid.
9   Dennis Doherty, ed., *Dimensions of Human Sexuality* (New York: Doubleday & Co., 1979), #17, p. 70.

10 Swidler, op. cit., p. 347.
11 William Phipps, *Influential Theologians of Wo/Man* (Washington, D.C.: University Press of America, 1981), p. 52.
12 Phipps, *The Sexuality of Jesus*, p. 87. Also see Doherty, op. cit., p. 45.
13 Swidler, op.cit., p. 347.
14 Ibid., pp. 348-9.
15 Phipps, *Influential Theologians on Wo/Man*, p. 70.
16 Doherty, op. cit., p. 47.
17 Michael Valente, *Sex: The Radical View of a Catholic Theologian* (New York: Bruce Publishing Co., 1970), p. 48.
18 Doherty, op. cit., p. 47.
19 Sr. Albertus Magnus McGrath, OP, *What A Modern Catholic Believes about Women* (New York: Thomas More Press, 1972), p. 68.
20 Phipps, *Influential Theologians on Wo/Man*, p. 72.
21 Valente, op. cit., pp. 32-34.
22 Anthony Kosnik, et al, *Human Sexuality: New Directions in American Catholic Thought* (New York: Paulist Press, 1977), pp. 48-51.
23 Dylan Thomas, "Do Not Go Gentle into That Good Night," *Dylan Thomas: Collected Poems* (New York: New Directions, 1957), p. 128.

Chapter Four   Hall of Mirrors: The Media Generation
1   Suzanne Gordon, *Lonely in America* (New York: Simon & Schuster, 1976), p. 241.
2   Sr. M. Timothy Prokes, SSND, *Women's Challenge: Ministry in the Flesh* (New Jersey: Dimension Books, 1977), p. 50.
3   Dr. Neil Postman, "TV's 'Disastrous' Impact on Children," *U.S. News and World Report*, Jan. 19, 1981.
4   Doherty, op. cit., p. 67.
5   O'Neill, op. cit.
6   Dennis Geaney, OSA, *Full Church, Empty Rectory: Training Lay Ministers for Parishes Without Priests* (Notre Dame: Fides/Claretian, 1980), pp. 66-67.

Chapter Five   Where Are the Lovers?
1   McBrien, op. cit., Vol. I, p. 536.

2 William Phipps, *Was Jesus Married? The Distortion of Sexuality in the Christian Tradition* (New York: Harper & Row, 1970), p. 36.

3 Phipps, *The Sexuality of Jesus*, p. 39.

4 Ibid., p. 45.

5 Ibid., p. 44.

6 Phipps, *Was Jesus Married?*, pp. 25, 33.

7 James B. Nelson, *Embodiment* (Minneapolis: Augsburg Publishing, 1978), p. 75.

8 Ibid.

9 Ibid

10 McBrien, op. cit., Vol. I, p. 537.

11 J.M. Hervé, *Manual of Dogmatic Theology*, Vol. II (Paris: Berche et Pagis, 1935), p. 439. See also Philip Schaff and Henry Wace (eds.), *A Select Library of Nicene and Post Nicene Fathers of the Christian Church* (New York: The Christian Literature Co., 1894), Vol. VII, p. 440, Col. B, Letter #101 - Gregory Nazianzen to Cledonius.

12 Phipps, *Was Jesus Married?*, p. 189.

13 Nelson, op. cit., p. 76.

14 *St. Joseph Daily Missal* (New York: Catholic Book Publishing Co., 1966), pp. 1195, 1208.

15 Marjorie P.K. Weiser and Jean S. Arbeiter, *Womanlist* (New York: Atheneum, 1981), p. 381.

16 Donald Attwater, *A Dictionary of Saints* (Harmondsworth, England: Penguin Books, 1965), pp. 259-60.

17 Swidler, op. cit., pp. 343-344.

18 Ibid.

19 Attwater, op cit., p. 183.

20 Wilhelm Schamoni, *The Face of the Saints* (New York: Pantheon Books, 1947), p. 206.

21 Michelle Bernstein, *The Nuns* (New York: Lippincott, 1976), p. 117.

22 Edmund Colledge, OSA, and James Walsh, SJ, *Following the Saints* (Gastonia, N.C.: Goodwill Publishers, 1970), p. 593.

23 D.W. Robertson, Jr., *Abelard and Heloise* (New York: Dial Press, 1972), p. 49.

24 Ibid., p. 55.

25 Phipps, *The Sexuality of Jesus*, p. 131.
26 Nelson, op. cit., p. 95.

Chapter Six Buried Treasure
1   Gerard Manley Hopkins, "Thou Art Indeed Just, Lord," in Helen Gardner, ed., *Oxford Book of English Verse* (New York: Oxford University Press, 1972), p. 790.

Chapter Seven Celibacy: A Clash of Symbols
1   Pierre Teilhard de Chardin, SJ, *Toward the Future*, tr. Rene Hauge (New York: Harcourt, Brace, Jovanovich, 1975), p. 187.
2   Pope John Paul II, "The Apostolic Exhortation on the Family," *Origins*, Dec. 24, 1981, p. 443.
3   Samuel Laeuchli, *Power and Sexuality: The Emergency of Canon Law at the Synod of Elvira* (Philadelphia: Temple University, 1972), p. 95. See also Rt. Rev. Joseph Hefele, DD, *History of Church Councils to A.D. 325*, Vol. I, tr. William R. Clark (Edinburgh, Scotland: T&T Clark, 1922), pp. 148, 150.
4   Edward Schillebeeckx, *Ministry: Leadership in the Community of Jesus Christ* (New York: Crossroad Publishing, 1981), p. 85.
5   Ibid., p. 86.
6   Ibid., p. 89.
7   Hans Küng, "Hans Küng Writes to the Pope About Celibacy," *National Catholic Reporter*, May 16, 1980, pp. 15-16.
8   Philip S. Kaufman, OSB, "An Immoral Morality?" *Commonweal*, Sept. 12, 1980, p. 496.
9   McBrien, op. cit., Vol. II, p. 613.
10 Ibid., p. 621.
11 Schillebeeckx, op. cit., p. 89.
12 Kosnik et al., op. cit., p. 26.
13 Gary Wills, "Rome's Obsession with Sex," *Chicago Sun-Times*, August 28, 1980, p. 68.
14 Ibid.
15 Martin Pable, "Psychology and Asceticism of Celibacy," *Review for Religious*, 1975, Vol. XXXIV, p. 273.
16 Donald Goergen, *The Sexual Celibate* (New York: The Seabury Press, 1974), p. 152.
17 James J. Gill, SJ, *MD*, and Linda Amadeo, RN, MS, "Celibate Anxiety," *Human Development*, Winter 1980, pp. 16-17.

18 Philip S. Keane, SS, "The Meaning and Functioning of Sexuality in the Lives of Celibates and Virgins," *Review for Religious*, 1975, Vol. XXXIV, p. 313.

19 Ibid., pp. 286-7.

20 *Fifty Facts and Insights About Priests Who Marry*, Nos. 11, 6, 10, 12, 14 (*Corpus*, P.O. Box 1649, Chicago, Illinois 60690).

21 Joseph A. Tetlow, SJ, "The Second Half-Generation," *New Catholic World*, Sept./Oct. 1980, p. 196.

22 Pope John Paul II, "Homily to Priests, Deacons, Seminarians," *Addresses and Homilies Given in West Germany*, tr. N.C. News Service (Fulda, West Germany, Nov. 17, 1980), p. 56.

23 "Encyclical Letter of His Holiness Pius XII on Holy Virginity," *Selected Documents of His Holiness, Pope Pius XII* (Washington, D.C.: National Catholic Welfare Conference, 1954), p. 8.

24 Ibid., p. 9.

25 Ibid., p. 10.

26 Ibid., p. 24.

27 Pope Paul VI, *Encyclical Letter on Priestly Celibacy (Sacerdotalis Caelibatus)*, June 24, 1967 (Washington, D.C.: United States Catholic Conference), p. 1.

28 Ibid., p. 22.

29 "Letter of the Supreme Pontiff John Paul II to all the Priests of the Church on the Occasion of Holy Thursday 1979," (Reprint of the official text), *National Catholic Reporter*, April 20, 1979, p. 13.

30 Ibid.

31 John Paul II, *Addresses and Homilies Given in West Germany*, p. 52.

32 Ibid., p. 53.

Chapter Eight   Sexuality as Prophecy

1 Haughton, op. cit., p. 37.

2 Rev. Patrick H. O'Neill, OSA, *The Single Adult* (New York: Paulist Press, 1980), p. 48.

Chapter Nine   Gay, by God!

1 Dr. Daniel Maguire, "Of Sex and Ethical Methodology," *Dimensions of Human Sexuality*, ed. Dennis Doherty, p. 133.

2   Archbishop Rembert Weakland of Milwaukee, Wisconsin, "Who
    Is Our Neighbor?" *Catholic Herald Citizen*, July 19, 1980.
3   Rev. Paul R. Shanley, "Changing Norms of Sexuality" (AMPRO
    Audio Cassettes, 101 Tremont St., Boston, Massachusetts
    02108).
4   Ibid.
5   Robert Nugent, SDS, "Homosexuality and the Hurting Family,"
    America, Feb. 28, 1981, p. 156.
6   "The Declaration on Sexual Ethics - Sacred Congregation for the
    Doctrine of the Faith - December 29, 1975," *L'Osservatore
    Romano*, January 22, 1976. See also Kosnik et al., op. cit.,
    p. 305.
7   "To Live in Christ Jesus," *A Pastoral Letter on Moral Values*,
    National Conference of Catholic Bishops, Nov. 11, 1976.
8   "Principles to Guide Confessors in Questions of Homosexuality,"
    National Conference of Catholic Bishops: Committee on
    Pastoral Research and Practices, 1973.
9   Nelson, op. cit., p. 210.
10 Shanley, op. cit.
11 Lockwood Hoehl, " 'We're in the Lull Between Two Storms': An
    Interview with Robert Bellah," *Witness*, May, 1979, pp. 9 and
    13.
12 Dr. Georgia Fuller, "Human Sexuality," *Probe* (Chicago, Ill.:
    National Assembly of Women Religious, Jan. 1980), pp. 3, 4.
13 Robert Nugent, SDS, Jeannine Grammick, SSND, and Thomas
    Oddo, CSC, *Homosexual Catholics: A New Primer for Discussion*
    (Dignity, Inc., 1500 Massachusetts Ave., NW, Washington D.C.
    20005, in cooperation with New Ways Ministry, 4012 29th St.,
    Mt. Rainier, Maryland 20822).
14 Steve Askin, "Gays in Religious Life Discussed at Meeting,"
    National Catholic Reporter, Dec. 4, 1981.
15 Philip S. Keane, SS, *Sexual Morality: A Catholic Perspective* (New
    York: Paulist Press, 1977), p. 168.
16 James J. Gill, SJ, MD, "Homosexuality Today," *Human
    Development*, Fall 1980, pp. 24-25.
17 Shanley, op. cit.
18 Robert Nugent, SDS, "Homosexuality and the Hurting Family,"
    America, February 28, 1981, p. 157.

19 Charles E. Curran, "Dialogue with the Homophile Movement:
    The Morality of Homosexuality," *Catholic Moral Theology in
    Dialogue* (Notre Dame: Fides Publishers, 1972), p. 217.
20 Kosnik et al., op. cit., p. 215.
21 Paula Ripple, FSPA, *Called to Be Friends* (Notre Dame: Ave Maria
    Press, 1980), p. 24.
22 "Team Works to Reconcile Church, Gays," Richard Hewitt, *The
    Times-Herald* (Tarrytown, New York), April 21, 1980.
23 Sr. Jeannine Grammick, SSND, "Human Sexuality," *Probe*
    (Chicago, Ill.: National Assembly of Women Religious, Jan.
    1980).
24 Shanley, op. cit.
25 "Threats Force Cancellation of Gay Support Gathering," *The
    Catholic Virginian*, Jan. 19, 1981.
26 Sharon Hatfield, "Gay Meeting Stirs Opposition on Sandy
    Ridge," *Coalfield Progress* (Norton, Virginia), Jan. 6, 1981.
27 Most Rev. Francis J. Mugavero, *Sexuality: God's Gift* (Brooklyn,
    N.Y.: The Chancery Office, 1976).
28 Brian McNaught, "Is Our Church Big Enough for Gay
    Catholics?" *U.S. Catholic*, June 1980, pp. 9, 11.

Chapter Ten   The Body Politic
1   Elizabeth Janeway, *Man's World, Woman's Place: A Study in Social
    Mythology* (New York: Dell Publishing, 1971), p. 287.
2   Dr. Phyllis Chesler, "Patriarchs, Warriors and Lovers: A
    Psychologist Takes on Male Mythology," *Ms.*, April 1978,
    p. 80. See also *About Men: A Psycho-Sexual Meditation* (New
    York: Simon & Schuster, 1978).
3   Nancy Van Vuuren, *The Subversion of Women as Practiced by
    Churches, Witch Hunters and Other Sexists* (Philadelphia:
    Westminister Press, 1973), pp. 55-56.
4   Ed Fronske, OFM, "Honoring the Gifts of Mary," *Way of St.
    Francis* (San Francisco), July-August 1981, pp. 15-17.
5   Haughton, op. cit.
6   Ken Dychtwald, *Body-Mind* (New York: Jove Publications, 1977),
    p. 19.
7   Ibid., p. 22.
8   Ibid., pp. 187-188.

9   Ibid., p. 145.
10 Ibid., pp. 138-139.
11 Ibid., pp. 40-41.
12 Janeway, op. cit., pp. 296-297.

Chapter Eleven   Cross Fire: The Vietnam Veteran and the American Conscience

1   William P. Mahedy, "Veterans' Ills Are Rooted in Moral and Religious Malaise" (VietNam: Will There Be a Collective Healing?), *The Center Magazine*, July/August 1981, p. 16.
2   Arthur S. Blank, Jr., MD, "Psychological Aspects of Experiences in the Viet Nam War," *Stresses of War: The Example of Viet Nam*, Symposium 0852, American Psychological Association, 4 September 1980, Montreal, Quebec, Canada, VI. A.
3   Robert J. Lifton, "Advocacy and Corruption in the Healing Profession," *Stress Disorders Among Vietnam Veterans*, ed. Charles R. Figley, (New York: Brunner/Mazel, 1978).
4   Mahedy, op. cit., p. 16.
5   Ibid., pp. 16-17.
6   James Jones, *The Thin Red Line* (New York: Scribner's and Sons, 1962), p. 277.
7   Philip Caputo, *A Rumor of War* (New York: Ballantine Books, 1977), p. 278.
8   Rollo May, "Ecstasy and Violence," *Peacemaking*, ed. Barbara Stanford (New York: Bantam Books, 1976), p. 156. See also Rollo May, "Ecstasy and Violence," *Power and Innocence, A Search for the Sources of Violence* (New York: W.W. Norton & Company, 1972).
9   Lewis Mumford, *The City in History* (New York: Harcourt Brace, 1961), p. 42.
10 Caputo, op. cit., p. xvii.
11 Peter Marin, "Living in Moral Pain," *Psychology Today*, November 1981, p. 74.
12 Dennis Geaney, OSA, op. cit., pp. 66-67.
13 Blank, op. cit., D.

Chapter Twelve   Healing: Binding the Wounds

1   Mary Bader Papa, "Abused Women: 'Clergy, Church Cannot Cope,'" *National Catholic Reporter*, June 6, 1980.

2 Susan Brownmiller, *Against Our Will: Men, Women and Rape* (New York: Bantam Books, 1975), pp. 80-81, 84.

3 Robin Morgan and Gloria Steinem, "The International Crime of Genital Mutilation," *Ms.*, March 1980, pp. 65-70, 98-100. See also Mary Daly, *Gyn/ecology* (Boston: Beacon Press, 1978), pp. 154-168.

4 John G. Hubbell, "Father Ritter's Covenant," *Reader's Digest*, October 1980. p. 116.

5 Rev. Edward Bryce (Director of U.S. Bishops Office for Pro-Life Activities), "Reconciliation: Missing Piece in Abortion Picture," *Origins*, Sept. 2, 1981, pp. 181-184.

6 Nancy Hennessey Cooney with Anne Bingham, *Sex, Sexuality and You, A Handbook for Growing Christians* (Dubuque, Iowa: Wm. C. Brown Company, Publishers, Religious Education Division, 1980), p. 47.

Chapter Thirteen   Trust the People: Young Adults Reclaim Peer Ministry

1 "Decree on the Apostolate of the Laity," *The Documents of Vatican II*, Chap. III, Sec. 12 (Walter M. Abbott, SJ, America Press, 1966), p. 504.

2 Archbishop Francis Hurley (Anchorage, Alaska), "Reaching Out to the Unchurched," (1978 Report Presented to U.S. Bishops), *Origins*, June 1, 1978.

3 "Valuing Your Sexuality," *Creed* (Milwaukee: Archdiocese of Milwaukee Office of Religious Education, 1980).

4 "Ein Schauspieler auf dem Stuhl Petri," *Der Spiegel*, Nov. 20, 1980. Also, *Frankfurter Allgemeine Zeitung*, Nov. 20, 1980.

5 Ibid.

6 *Planning for Single Young Adult Ministry: Directions for Ministerial Outreach* (United States Catholic Conference, Department of Education, Washington, D.C. 20005), pp. 13-14. (Other members of the committee also included Bishop Lawrence McNamara of Grand Island, Nebraska; Bishop Manuel D. Moreno, Auxiliary Bishop of Los Angeles, California; and Bishop Phillip F. Straling, Bishop of San Bernardino, California.)

Chapter Fourteen   Young Adults Place a Conference Call to the Church

1 Geaney, op. cit., p. 41.

2   Pope Paul VI, *On Evangelization in the Modern World* (*Evangelii
     Nuntiandi*) (Washington, D.C.: U.S. Catholic Conference, 1976),
     p. 16.
3   *Saint Anselm, Proslogium, Monologium,* tr. Sidney Norton Dean
     (Chicago: Open Court Publishing, 1903).
4   Pope Paul VI, *On Evangelization,* op. cit., p. 57.
5   Walt Whitman, "Song of the Open Road," *Leaves of Grass,* ed.
     Emory Holloway (Garden City, N.Y.: Doubleday, 1926), p. 125.
6   *Documents of Vatican II,* "The Church in the Modern World," #4,
     pp. 201-202.

Chapter Fifteen   Promised Land: The Cosmos Within

1   Emily Dickinson, "I Dwell in Possibility," *Oxford Book of
     American Verse,* ed. F.O. Mathiesson (New York: Oxford
     University Press, 1950), p. 413.
2   Pope Paul VI, *Humanae Vitae* (Rome, July 25, 1968), No. 11.
3   Daniel Maguire, *The Moral Choice* (Minneapolis: Winston Press,
     1979), pp. 189-190.
4   Barbara Bailey Kelley and Toni Tomacci, *The Vacations and
     Weekends Learning Guide: Ideas and Activities to Help Children
     Learn Throughout the Year* (New York: Prentice-Hall, 1982).
5   Pope Paul VI, *On Evangelization,* pp. 13-14.
6   Valenti, op. cit., p. 28.
7   Philip Yancey and Dr. Paul Brand, *Fearfully and Wonderfully
     Made* (Grand Rapids, Michigan: Zondervan Publishing House,
     1980), p. 46.
8   Allan Newman, "A Short Talk with Jean Houston," *Return to the
     Earth,* October 1981, #2.
9   Rev. Philip Murnion, "The Unmet Challenges of Vatican II,"
     Origins, Aug. 13, 1981, p. 153.
10   McGuire, op. cit., p. 190.
11   Ken Guentert, *Body & Soul,* January 1981, #21. (P.O. Box 257,
     Oregon, Illinois 61061).
12   Joan Ohanneson, *Woman: Survivor in the Church* (Minneapolis:
     Winston Press, 1980), p. 31.
13   Andrew Greeley, "A Post-Vatican II New Breed: A Report on
     Contemporary Catholic Teen Agers," *America,* June 28, 1980,
     p. 537.

14 Alexander Lowen, M.D., *Pleasure: A Creative Approach to Life* (New York: Penguin Books, 1970), p. 188.
15 McGuire, op. cit., p. 190, 197, 199.
16 Gerard Manley Hopkins, *The Poems of Gerard Manley Hopkins*, ed. W.H. Gardner and N.H. MacKenzie, *Inversnaid* (London: Oxford University Press, 1967), p. 90.

APPENDIX

"Sexuality—God's Gift," A Pastoral Letter, by Bishop Francis J. Mugavero

On February 11, 1976, Bishop Francis J. Mugavero of the Brooklyn, N.Y., diocese issued the following pastoral letter. The document from the Sacred Congregation for the Doctrine of the Faith, entitled, "Declaration on Certain Questions Concerning Sexual Ethics," to which Bishop Mugavero refers, was reprinted in the April, 1976 issue of *Catholic Mind*, pp. 52-64.

Dearly Beloved in Christ:

Sexuality is one of God's greatest gifts to man and woman. We can say this not only because sexuality "largely conditions his or her progress towards maturity and insertion into society," [1] but also because it is that aspect of personhood which makes us capable of entering into loving relationships with others. Theology teaches that relationship—the gift of oneself to another—is at the very heart of God. The Father and Son give themselves totally to one another and the mutuality of their response in love is the Holy Spirit, binding them together. We honor God and become more like Him when we create in our lives the loving, other-centered relationships which at the same time give us such human satisfaction and personal fulfillment.

. . .

Recently the Congregation for the Doctrine of the Faith issued a "Declaration on Certain Questions Concerning Sexual Ethics" to emphasize the importance of sexuality in our lives as followers of Christ. [2] Bishops are urged to share the moral wisdom of the church in a way "capable of properly enlightening the consciences of those confronted with new situations" related to the meaning and value of human sexuality.[3] It is with this hope that we share these thoughts with you, our brothers and sisters in the Lord.

Let us say clearly and without apology that chastity is a virtue which liberates the human person. Chastity means simply that sexuality and its physical, genital expressions are seen as good for man and woman—good in so far as we make them serve life and love. Any of our powers can be turned to destructive purposes due to lack of concern, weakness, or even a well-intentioned error. The excitement and adventure of human living is to take our God-given powers and talents and become someone worthwhile—lovable and loving. It should not be surprising that the power and pleasure which are part of sexuality will demand of us the intelligence, honesty and sacrifice that might test our maturity to the utmost degree. But we do not fear sexuality, we embrace it. What we fear at times is our own inability to think as highly of the gift as does the God who made us sexual beings.

Sexuality Serving Love

Sexuality is so much more than genital activity. It is an aspect of personality which lets us enter other persons' lives as friends and encourages them to enter our lives. The dimension of sexuality must be developed by all men and women not only because it is, as we have just seen, a gift making us more like God, but is also so very necessary if we are to follow Jesus' command to become "lovers."[4] It is a relational power which includes the qualities of sensitivity, understanding, warmth, openness to persons, compassion and mutual support. Who could imagine a loving person without those qualities?

Our Lord Jesus Christ was fully a man—with the sexuality of a man.[5] Some men and women choose to conform closely to His life of celibate love in service of fellow man and God's Kingdom; most people will express their love of God and neighbor through "the intimate partnership of married life and love."[6]

Does it appear unusual that as members of the same Church some can embrace married love and others celibate love as expressions of personal sexuality? It did not seem contradictory to Christ, who respected and blessed matrimony as a sacrament of His church yet chose to fulfill His own mission as an unmarried man. Far from condemning sexuality, He knew man and woman were created thus by God as "very good" and may "become as one flesh"[7] in the permanently faithful union of married love. Neither did He discourage those who would sacrifice the genital expression of their sexuality out of love for serving fellow man and God's Kingdom as priests, religious and dedicated laity.[8]

But if we are as honest with ourselves as were the Christians who have lived before us, each of us will recognize that it is not easy to integrate sexuality into our lives. [9] We all want to be loved and accepted. We want to draw close to other people, and many of us will seek fulfillment in that special closeness which married life should be. Helping our sexuality develop in a constructive way—in a way which will help us gain and give the love and affection that brings tremendous joy and peace of mind—demands that we consciously live our lives, that we don't just "let things happen." The relationships with other people which can make our lives full and enjoyable don't just "happen."

We are members of a church whose people have been part of the successes and failures of almost 2,000 years of human living. We are continually being brought out of slavery by the loving Spirit of God. One form of the slavery is the ignorance of how to love—how to use our sexuality for giving life, for truly loving, for deep and lasting relationships.

There may be no convincing way to say this to someone who does not want to listen. We know, however, that the experience of countless human beings and sound psychology support the wisdom of the church teaching regarding both the goodness of sexuality and the unfortunate ambiguity related to its genital expression. Although each of us is called to live our sexuality in the sense of the human qualities and relationships seen above, genital expression (physical sexual contact, arousal, orgasm) needs a special context before it can serve human love and live generously and without deception.

Pre-Marital Relations

Human beings can use minerals for health and strength or turn them into bombs to kill and destroy. The pleasant smile can find its true meaning as a sign of friendship or be used to deceive. Sexuality can find its genital expression serving mutual love and new life in the total commitment of marriage, or it can easily become self-serving and stripped of its true meaning. What is meant to be the expression of the deep love of a man and woman joined forever through marriage in the service of life can be trivialized as merely a way of enjoying this person I am with. [10]

In pre-marital intercourse, the full genital expression of

sexual love is robbed of its proper context of exclusive commitment, the genuine and permanent gift of oneself to one's
beloved, and the possibility of the couple's love showing itself
in a stable enough environment to develop new life. [11]

In truthful human communication, we must accept the
meaning which is present in certain actions. A warm smile
and a tender embrace are universal signs of friendship; to
communicate in a human way is to be true to the meaning of a
sign when I use it in my life. As much as they might like to do
so, no couple can rewrite the meaning of sexual intercourse.
It is tied to committed love; it is tied to life-giving. When a
person engages in sexual intercourse it is a sign of giving one's
very self, whether one intends to or not. To let my actions be a
sign of self-gift, if my heart knows the truth to be different, is
to lie.

We must pledge ourselves to be true to what is really
happening. Is our love so real that it is truly permanent,
exclusively centered on this one person with whom I wish to
link my life forever, the kind of love which could some day
bring forth children as its sign? Then we are ready not for
"second best" but for the joy of marriage in Christ—not in
any sense "a piece of paper from the church," but a chance to
stand at the altar before God and fellow man and say: "We
love one another and want our love to last forever. We ask
you to respect this, to rejoice with us, to help us keep it so."
This is marriage in the church.

How inadequate it would be to propose Christian marriage
merely as a solution to sexual problems or needs! Those who
have grown to a point where they can make that permanent,
exclusive pledge of themselves one to the other in Christ are
people who are alive with hope, signs of the wonderful "fool-
ishness" of a love deep enough to face together an unknown
future. They remind us that life is neither stagnant nor

finished, and their total commitment to one another in Christ is broad enough to share someday with their own children. In light of this beautiful reality, don't the tentative and shallow aspects of "sleeping together" of "living together" without the maturity of a marriage commitment become painfully clear?

We know the pressures society and peers place on unmarried people. The young are made to feel "out of step" or unpopular if they avoid genital sexuality. Loneliness and searching for something or someone can lead the unmarried or unloved of any age to seek an answer to their pressing need in some passing intimacy. But this is a "solution" which is short-lived. The genital expression of sexuality is too much "myself" to let it become something commonplace or shallow, to reduce its significance to a "handshake," to lose the meaning and mystery. I am worth more than that.

Multiple Motivations

We recognize how sexual behavior is often intertwined with many other needs, often unconscious ones. Sexual behavior can be used to express nonsexual feelings and relationships such as the need to prove one's identity or self-worth, to escape from loneliness or to express strong aggressive feelings. To deny these multiple levels of motivation in the human personality would isolate the problems of sexuality from the whole reality of the person.

Certain inadequacies of sexual integration must be worked on from within the person and need pastoral guidance, professional counseling and therapy. Let us not forget, however, that religious commitment has a tremendous influence on the development of our sexual perception and behavior. It is this meaning in one's life that will enable a person to discipline himself and renounce certain destructive types of activity.

We must not, therefore, presume on grace alone to heal what truly requires psychological counseling, nor feel that habit or emotional problems totally excuse one from long-proven means of asceticism and spiritual growth. Here the generosity of our response to God's love can open us to beneficial scientific and spiritual means to achieve greater personal integration.

The Practice of Masturbation

The practice of masturbation is a prime example of the complex nature of sexual behavior. It may begin in adolescence as an immature expression of "self-discovery" or enter a person's life at any time and for any number of reasons.

We wish to encourage people to go continually beyond themselves in order to achieve greater sexual maturity and urge them to find peace and strength in a full sacramental life with the Christ who loves them.

"Modern psychology provides much valid and useful information for formulating a more equitable judgment or moral responsibility and for orienting pastoral action. . . . In the pastoral ministry, in order to form an adequate judgment in concrete cases the habitual behavior of people will be considered in its totality." [12]

Homosexual Orientation

The complexus of anthropological, psychological and theological reasoning in regard to human sexuality has contributed to the church's teaching that heterosexuality is normative. All should strive for a sexual integration which respects that norm since any other orientation respects less adequately the full spectrum of human relationships.[13]

Whatever the causes of the homosexual orientation, both to those who share that orientation and to society in general there are certain cautions we wish to put forward.

We urge homosexual men and women to avoid identifying their personhood with their sexual orientation. They are so much more as persons than this single aspect of their personality. That richness must not be lost.

Being subject to misunderstanding and at times unjust discrimination has resulted in an overreaction on the part of some persons of homosexual orientation. It is not homosexuality which should be one's claim to acceptance or human rights or to being loved by us all; it is the fact we are all brothers and sisters under the Fatherhood of God. Our community must explore ways to secure the legitimate rights of all our citizens, regardless of sexual orientation, while being sensitive to the understanding and hopes of all involved.

On a more personal level, we wish to express our concern and compassion for those men and women who experience pain and confusion due to a true homosexual orientation. We pray that through all the spiritual and pastoral means available they will recognize Christ's and the church's love for them and our hope that they will come to live in His peace.

A Call to Healing

A most important way to aid the human person achieve sexual integration and live the virtue of chastity is to provide from life's earliest years a loving and secure climate. We urge parents and teachers to examine their own attitudes toward sexuality and to set the pace for young people's pride in developing as loving and mature men or women.

We restate the Declaration's plea that responsible sex education be provided for all our people including children who should receive "information suited to their age."[14] Knowing the beauty of sexuality and the wisdom of chastity facilitates the young person's moral growth, as encouraged by the Second Vatican Council: "This Holy Synod likewise affirms that children and young people have a right to be encouraged to weigh moral values with an upright conscience, and to embrace them by personal choice and to know and love God more adequately. Hence, it earnestly entreats all who exercise government over peoples or preside over the work of education to see that youth is never deprived of this sacred right."[15]

We call on all men and women of good will to help create a more wholesome climate in society. There are still so many imprisoned either psychically or physically in the destuctive activity of prostitution. The social problems of pornography must be challenged by community concern. Advertising and media too often miss vitally important opportunities to free the human spirit and instead contribute to a sex-saturated atmosphere that confuses rather than heals.

To those engaged in the ministry of healing—religious people, doctors, psychiatrists, teachers and so many others—

we encourage interdisciplinary work to improve the quality of pastoral care and to help Christians in the delicate task of forming their own conscience. We hope that parish communities will cooperate in studying sexuality and chastity so these important gifts of God can enrich each of us in the way He intends

Together

We are very conscious of the fact that all of us touch one another with our lives. What gratitude we should all have for those who have struggled with the difficulties of sexual integration and chastity in their lives and are now witnesses to us that it can indeed be done—that fidelity, commitment, self-sacrifice and compassion are realities in the lives of so many. We rejoice in you and thank you.

Yet we recognize that maturity in these areas comes only through what for many people will be a long and demanding process of growth. To our brothers and sisters of all ages who are experiencing difficulties—to those who cannot yet see that the personal and public commitment of marriage should be the context for the gift of oneself in sexual relations; to those whose homosexual orientation is causing them pain and confusion; to the widowed and to the adolescent encountering sexual needs; to those separated from their spouses by circumstances or by divorce—to all of you we pledge our willingness to help you bear your burdens, to try to find new ways to communicate the truth of Christ because we believe it will make you free. We respect you in your struggle.

Grace and peace to you from God our Father and from the Lord Jesus Christ.

Faithfully yours in Christ,

+Francis J. Mugavero
Bishop of Brooklyn

Notes

1 Sacred Congregation for the Doctrine of the Faith, *Declaration on Certain Questions Concerning Sexual Ethics*, n. 1.

2 *Ibid.*, n.1.

3 *Ibid.*, n. 13.

4 Mt. 22:36-40.

5 Heb. 2:14-18; 4:15.

6 Vatican II, *Pastoral Constitution on the Church in the World Today* (*Gaudium et Spes*), n. 48.

7 Gen. 1:2.

8 Mt. 19:12.

9 Evident themes in Sacred Scripture, the Fathers and the constant teaching of the living church. See also *Declaration, op. cit.*, nn. 5,12.

10 *Declaration, op. cit.*, n. 7.

11 Vatican II, *Pastoral Constitution on the Church in the World Today, op. cit.*, nn. 49,50.

12 *Declaration, op. cit.*, n. 9.

13 *Ibid.*, n. 8.

14 *Ibid.*, n. 13.

15 Vatican II, *Declaration on Christian Education*, n. 1. See also *Declaration, op. cit.*, n. 13.

Creed: "Valuing Your Sexuality"

I believe in God, as Father and Mother,
Creator of Heaven and Earth:
   Sexuality is the unfolding of creation.
   Inside the flesh and the blood God made
       man and woman,
   in the genes and chromosomes are the
       inheritance
           of sexuality
           of desire, compassion,
           hormones, hair on the chest,
           soft skin,
           of passion.
   Sexuality is the act of creation:
   It is to be male and female, and to say,
       yes, Lord.
   Sexuality is to say yes to creation,
       yes to life,
       yes to the living,
       yes to the unborn.
   Sexuality affirms the creativity of man and woman.
   It believes in God the Creator.

I believe in Jesus Christ,
his only son, our Lord: who was conceived
by the Holy Spirit, born of the Virgin Mary,

   Sexuality is the sign of Incarnation,
   of Christ in the midst of his people,
   of the love of Christ.

Sexuality is
    the evidence of Christ and his church,
    as more dear than the bridegroom,
    more faithful than Hosea,
    more intimate than the vine to the branch.

Sexuality affirms man and woman as the Body of
    Christ.
It believes in the love of God.

I believe in the Holy Spirit, the Holy Catholic Church,
the Communion of Saints, the Forgiveness of Sins, the
Resurrection of the Body, and Life Everlasting.

Sexuality is the cycle of the seasons,
    the seedtime and the harvest
    the spring and the autumn
    for the young and the old.

Sexuality is when two are one,
    each is whole,
    when two are side by side.

Sexuality is the life of repentance and
    forgiveness.

Sexuality affirms the reconciliation of man and
    woman,
it believes in God the Reconciler.

"GUIDELINES FOR WORKSHOP ON SPIRITUALITY AND SEXUALITY"*

Content/Talk	Body Imagery	Messages Received	Significant Relationships
Modeling the Story Process Focus: past	How did you learn that you were male or female? What later contributed to that awareness?	Name six proverbs that you learned from parents and friends about what it is to be male or female, about sex and sexuality.	Imagine you are at your family dinner table. You ask a question about sex. Imagine how your mother would react, your father, your siblings. How did you feel at the time?
Spirituality and Sexuality in the Church Tradition Focus: present	What is your image of what Church says about sex and sexuality? What is your image of what the culture says about sex and sexuality?	Name three things you learned about sex and sexuality that are worth keeping, three things that you would prefer to forget.	Who in the "Church" helped you grow in your understanding of sex and sexuality? Who in the Church hurt you by their teachings or attitudes?
RECONCILIATION: If you believe that your sexuality is sacramental, then . . .			
Theological Categories for Considering Spirituality and Sexuality Focus: a new way of looking at self and the question	Intimacy/Hospitality Name three occasions when your body expresses who you are? who you want to be?	Relations/Prophecy If your sexuality is sacramental, how will you be with others? How will you respond when the culture negates wholeness?	Intimacy/Relations/Prophecy/Hospitality If your sexuality is sacramental, who becomes significant in your life?
Sexuality and the Community Focus: the community dimension of personal relationships			

*By National Office of Young Adult Ministry, presented at the fourth annual Young Adult Ministry Conference, Los Angeles, California, 1979

"GUIDELINES FOR WORKSHOP ON SPIRITUALITY AND SEXUALITY"

Closeness to God	*Taking a Stand*	*Your Image*
What was your relationship with God?	When did you take a stand for some important sexual value?	In looking over your past, how would you symbolize yourself as a sexual person?
Name five words you commonly use in prayer. Are any of them body-words? Where did you learn these words?	When did you take a stand for or against church teaching?	In view of the church and cultural setting, how would you symbolize your sense of belonging to each?

RECONCILIATION: If you believe that your sexuality is sacramental, then . . .

Intimacy/Relations/ Prophecy/Reconciliation	Intimacy/Relations/ Prophecy/Hospitality/ Reconciliation	

"Education in Human Sexuality for Christians"

From text prepared by National Committee on Human Sexuality, Department of Education, United States Catholic Conference, 1981

Principles and Goals

Seven theologically based principles form the foundation for a Christian description of human sexuality:

1. Each person is created unique in the image of God.
2. Despite original sin, all human life in its physical, psychological, and spiritual dimensions is fundamentally good. [1]
3. Each person is created to be loved and to love, as Christ, loved by the Father, loves us.
4. Human relationships are expressed in a way that is enfleshed and sexed.
5. Human sexuality carries the responsibility to work toward Christian sexual maturity.
6. Mature Christian sexuality, in whatever state of life, demands a life-enriching commitment to other persons and the community.
7. Conjugal sexuality is an expression of the faithful, life-enriching love of husband and wife and is ordained toward the loving procreation of new life.

By their very nature, these formulations are somewhat abstract to make them adaptable to diverse situations. Specificity is achieved when these principles are reformulated into goal statements. If we were using the language of curriculum design, this would be the process of translating generic concepts into generic goals. In this process of reformulation, the principles are also specified in more detail. Corresponding to the seven principles are seven goals:

1. The person will develop a deep appreciation that he or she is a unique reflection of God, and, therefore, possesses inestimable worth.

2. The person will acknowledge and understand the physical, psychological and spiritual aspects of his or her nature as fundamentally good.

3. The person will be open to receive love and will love others in accord with his or her level of maturation.

4. The person will be open to the growth which takes place within interpersonal life and will participate in relationships as a sexual person in accord with his or her own state of life.

5. The person will appreciate the responsibility demanded in the transition from immature self-centeredness to mature Christian altruism and generosity.

6. The person will appreciate the role played by sexuality in establishing relationships of commitment and fidelity.

7. The person will appreciate the fundamental purposes of Christian marriage by affirming the mutually related unitive and procreative ends of this sacramental relationship.

A shorthand summary of the seven principles may be useful in providing an overall sense of their dynamism and comprehensiveness. It may be stated that the goal of Christian catechesis in sexuality is to communicate effectively that the person is *unique, good, loved and loving, sexual, responsible, committed,* and if married, exclusively *faithful* and *procreative.*

General Principle	Goal	Summary
1. Each person is created unique in the image of God.	The person will develop a deep appreciation that he or she is a unique reflection of God, and, therefore, possesses inestimable worth.	unique
2. Even though original sin has weakened our human nature, making us imperfect and susceptible to temptation and personal sin, all human life in its physical, psychological and spiritual dimensions is fundamentally good.	The person will acknowledge and understand the physical, psychological and spiritual aspects of his or her nature and appreciate them as fundamentally good, though imperfect.	good, though imperfect
3. Each person is created to be loved and to love, as Christ, loved by the Father, loves us.	The person will be open to receive love and will love others in accord with his or her level of maturation.	loved and loving
4. Human relationships are expressed in a way that is enfleshed and sexed.	The person will be open to the growth which takes place within interpersonal life, and will participate in relationships as a sexual person in accord with his or her own state of life.	sexual

General Principle	Goal	Summary
Human sexuality carries the responsibility to work toward Christian sexual maturity.	The person will appreciate the responsibility demanded in the transition from immature self-centeredness to mature Christian altruism and generosity.	responsible
Mature Christian sexuality, in whatever state of life, demands a life-enriching commitment to other persons and the community.	The person will appreciate the role played by sexuality in establishing relationships of commitment and fidelity.	committed
Conjugal sexuality is an expression of the faithful, life-enriching love of husband and wife and is ordained toward the loving procreation of new life.	The person will appreciate the fundamental purposes of Christian marriage by affirming the mutually related unitive and procreative ends of this sacramental relationship.	faithful and procreative

Mandates for Education in Human Sexuality

" . . . children and young people must be helped, with the
aid of the latest advances in psychology and the arts and the
science of teaching to develop harmoniously their physical,
moral and intellectual endowments so that they may gradually
acquire a mature sense of responsibility . . . Let them be
given also, as they advance in years, a positive and prudent
sexual education."
Vatican II, *Declaration on Christian Education*, no. 1 (1965)

In accord with the Decree of Christian Education of Vatican
Council II we affirm the value and necessity of wisely planned
education of children in human sexuality, adapted to the
maturity and background of our young people.
U.S. Bishops, *Human Life in Our Day*, pp. 20-21. (1968)

We are under a grave obligation, in part arising from the new
circumstances of modern culture and communications, to
assist the family in its effort to provide such training. This
obligation can be met either by systematic provision of such
education in the diocesan school curriculum or by the inaugu-
ration of acceptable education programs under other diocesan
auspices, including the Confraternity of Christian Doctrine.
U.S.Bishops, *Human Life in Our Day*, pp. 20-21. (1968)

We continue to regard this education in human sexuality as an
important priority in Christian education, met in part through
diocesan-approved family life education in Catholic schools
and other instructional programs.
U.S. Bishops, *To Teach As Jesus Did*, no. 56 (1972)

These efforts presuppose parental understanding and approval

and require parents' cooperation with classroom teachers. The aim is not to supplant parents but to help them fulfill their obligation. They have a right to be informed about the content of such programs and to be assured that diocesan-approved textbooks and other instructional materials meet the requirements of propriety. But when these reasonable conditions have been met, parents should not allow continuing anxiety to be translated into indiscriminate opposition to all forms of classroom education in sexuality. Such opposition should be contrary to the teaching of Vatican Council II and the pastoral policy of the American bishops. Also, to the extent that it might disrupt responsible efforts to provide formal education in sexuality for the young it would violate the rights of other, no less conscientious, parents who ask for such instruction for their own children.
U.S. Bishops, *To Teach As Jesus Did*, no. 57 (1972)

Implementation of Resolutions 25,36,39,40 of the Call to Action Conference, Detroit, 1976.

Implementation of the various relevant principles taught by the U.S. Bishops in *To Live in Christ Jesus*, 1976.

It is proposed that there be formulated by an appropriate agency of the USCC/NCCB a catechesis for human sexuality and family life which corresponds to the various developmental phases of life. Also, that there be formulated a specific plan to educate all those who will be primarily responsible for the communication of this catechetical material. Specifically, this includes programs for the continuing education and ministerial development of priests and religious, seminary and deacon formation programs and programs for religious educators and family life ministers. The ultimate direction of this catechesis is its realization in the life of the Christian family. *Commission on Marriage and Family Life*, Proposal no. 1 (1977)

It is proposed that specific plans and programs be mandated within the USCC Department of Education to come up with guidelines and courses of education in the pastoral theology of marriage, sexuality, and family and that frequently updated bibliographies of resource materials be drawn up by the USCC Department of Education and distributed through the diocesan offices of Family Life and other appropriate agencies.
Commission on Marriage and Family Life, Proposal no. 17 (1977)

That present human sexuality and family living education programs be reviewed, tested, and revised when necessary. That a comprehensive curriculum guideline be developed. That a program of training and education be developed for teachers and parents. That recommended guidelines be prepared for diocesan policy statements. That a catechesis for responsible decision making be formulated in regard to human sexuality and family life.
Commission on Marriage and Family Life, Proposal no. 24 (1977)

Implementation of Section II, no. 190 of the *National Catechetical Directory* mandating "positive and prudent sexual education." (1977)